COLUMBIA COLLEGE CHICAGO

3 2711 00175 4526

D1787474

DISCARD

DATE DUE

ENTERED JUN 0 8 2010

LITERACY DEVELOPMENT WITH ENGLISH LEARNERS

SOLVING PROBLEMS IN THE TEACHING OF LITERACY
Cathy Collins Block, Series Editor

Recent Volumes

Comprehension Instruction, Second Edition: Research-Based Best Practices
Edited by Cathy Collins Block and Sheri R. Parris

The Literacy Coaching Challenge: Models and Methods for Grades K–8
Michael C. McKenna and Sharon Walpole

Creating Robust Vocabulary:
Frequently Asked Questions and Extended Examples
Isabel L. Beck, Margaret G. McKeown, and Linda Kucan

Mindful of Words: Spelling and Vocabulary Explorations 4–8
Kathy Ganske

Finding the Right Texts: What Works for Beginning and Struggling Readers
Edited by Elfrieda H. Hiebert and Misty Sailors

Fostering Comprehension in English Classes: Beyond the Basics
Raymond Philippot and Michael F. Graves

Language and Literacy Development: What Educators Need to Know
James P. Byrnes and Barbara A. Wasik

Independent Reading: Practical Strategies for Grades K–3
Denise N. Morgan, Maryann Mraz, Nancy D. Padak, and Timothy Rasinski

Assessment for Reading Instruction, Second Edition
Michael C. McKenna and Katherine A. Dougherty Stahl

Literacy Growth for Every Child: Differentiated Small-Group Instruction K–6
Diane Lapp, Douglas Fisher, and Thomas DeVere Wolsey

Explaining Reading, Second Edition:
A Resource for Teaching Concepts, Skills, and Strategies
Gerald G. Duffy

Learning to Write with Purpose: Effective Instruction in Grades 4–8
Karen Kuelthau Allan, Mary C. McMackin, Erika Thulin Dawes, and Stephanie A. Spadorcia

Exemplary Literacy Teachers, Second Edition:
What Schools Can Do to Promote Success for All Students
Cathy Collins Block and John N. Mangieri

Literacy Development with English Learners:
Research-Based Instruction in Grades K–6
Edited by Lori Helman

How to Plan Differentiated Reading Instruction: Resources for Grades K–3
Sharon Walpole and Michael C. McKenna

Reading More, Reading Better
Edited by Elfrieda H. Hiebert

Literacy Development with English Learners

Research-Based Instruction in Grades K–6

Edited by
LORI HELMAN

THE GUILFORD PRESS
New York   London

© 2009 The Guilford Press
A Division of Guilford Publications, Inc.
72 Spring Street, New York, NY 10012
www.guilford.com

All rights reserved

No part of this book may be reproduced, translated, stored in
a retrieval system, or transmitted, in any form or by any means,
electronic, mechanical, photocopying, microfilming, recording,
or otherwise, without written permission from the Publisher.

Printed in the United States of America

This book is printed on acid-free paper.

Last digit is print number: 9 8 7 6 5 4 3 2 1

Library of Congress Cataloging-in-Publication Data available from the Publisher.

ISBN 978-1-60623-242-2 (pbk. : alk. paper)
ISBN 978-1-60623-243-9 (hardcover : alk. paper)

About the Editor

Lori Helman, PhD, is a faculty member in literacy education in the Department of Curriculum and Instruction, University of Minnesota, Minneapolis. Her research investigates literacy development and effective teaching practices for English learners at the elementary school level. She teaches classes in literacy learning in diverse contexts, literacy instruction with English learners, reading assessment and reading difficulty, and literacy leadership for reading specialists as they develop expertise across their professional careers. Dr. Helman works collaboratively with a number of practicing teachers to investigate the literacy teaching methods that are most successful with English learners. Her three decades in education have included teaching bilingual elementary school for 16 years, leading new teacher support programs, and serving as a district literacy coordinator. She brings this solid teaching background into her university research agenda and professional writing. In addition to numerous published research articles, Dr. Helman has written chapters, articles, and curriculum support materials that guide teachers to apply second-language literacy research in their classrooms. She is the lead author (along with Donald R. Bear) of *Words Their Way with English Learners: Word Study for Spelling, Phonics, and Vocabulary Instruction.*

Contributors

Kathryn H. Au, PhD, SchoolRise, LLC, Honolulu, Hawaii

Donald R. Bear, PhD, Department of Educational Specialties, University of Nevada, Reno, Reno, Nevada

Cynthia Brock, PhD, Department of Educational Specialties, University of Nevada, Reno, Reno, Nevada

Christina P. DeNicolo, PhD, Department of Curriculum and Instruction, University of Illinois at Urbana–Champaign, Champaign, Illinois

Susana Dutro, MA, EL Achieve, Aptos, California

Georgia Earnest García, PhD, Department of Curriculum and Instruction, University of Illinois at Urbana–Champaign, Champaign, Illinois

Lori Helman, PhD, Department of Curriculum and Instruction, University of Minnesota, Minneapolis, Minnesota

Melanie R. Kuhn, PhD, School of Education, Boston University, Boston, Massachusetts

Diane Lapp, EdD, School of Teacher Education, San Diego State University, San Diego, California

M. Kristiina Montero, PhD, Reading and Language Arts Center, Syracuse University, Syracuse, New York

Eleni Oikonomidoy, PhD, Department of Educational Specialties, University of Nevada, Reno, Reno, Nevada

Julie L. Pennington, PhD, Department of Educational Specialties, University of Nevada, Reno, Reno, Nevada

Rachel G. Salas, PhD, Department of Teacher Education, College of Education, California State University, Sacramento, Sacramento, California

Regina E. Smith, MEd, Department of Educational Specialties, University of Nevada, Reno, Reno, Nevada

Shane Templeton, PhD, Department of Educational Specialties, University of Nevada, Reno, Reno, Nevada

Suzette Youngs, MEd, Department of Educational Specialties, University of Nevada, Reno, Reno, Nevada

Preface

Walk into elementary classrooms almost anywhere in the United States these days, and you will see students from diverse ethnic, linguistic, cultural, and economic backgrounds. Many of these students are likely to be learning to speak English as a new language at the same time they are learning to read and write with their peers who are native English speakers. In these classrooms of elementary students, you will find immigrant students from every corner of the globe, bringing a diverse range of languages into the mainstream classroom setting. For example, in the Twin Cities of Minnesota, where I live, you will find many elementary students who speak Spanish, Somali, Hmong, Vietnamese, Arabic, Russian, Oromo, and Karen. Each student brings a unique profile of oral English proficiency, background literacy experiences, and personal expectations to the literacy learning process.

For the majority of English learners in elementary school classrooms, instruction comes from mainstream teachers who speak only English. In most cases, these teachers have had relatively few opportunities in their teacher preparation programs or professional development classes to learn about the most effective teaching practices for students who do not come from Anglo-American, English-speaking backgrounds (de Jong & Harper, 2005). This discrepancy between *whom* teachers are prepared to teach and the actual needs of students in classrooms sets up a mismatch for instruction, making it hard for teachers to feel successful with all of their students. In turn, students may not receive the tailored and appropriate instruction that they deserve and that will help them to learn best.

This book is geared toward monolingual English-speaking teachers who work in mainstream classrooms that include English learners.

It grew out of the need for a cohesive text to use in graduate, undergraduate, or inservice courses that focus on literacy instruction that is specifically designed to meet the needs of students learning English as a new language. The idea for the book came from my own experience teaching just such a course at the university level. In general, current and future teachers receive coursework that teaches them to work with students who already speak English. The time was right for a course that specifically presents foundational knowledge in second-language literacy development, as well as the types of literacy instruction that hold promise for English learners' success.

The goal of *Literacy Development with English Learners: Research-Based Instruction in Grades K–6* is to summarize in a teacher-friendly manner the current research relating to literacy development for English learners. Each of the key components addressed in the National Reading Panel Report (National Institute of Child Health and Human Development, 2000)—phonemic awareness, phonics, fluency, vocabulary, and comprehension—is specifically addressed in individual chapters. In addition, the book provides a broad overview of the many sociocultural, linguistic, and educational practices that play a role in literacy development, and it sketches a road map for implementing effective instruction in the elementary classroom. Simply stated, this book seeks to enlarge the reader's conceptual understanding of literacy learning in a second language and to connect this knowledge to helpful instructional practices.

The book is organized in much the same way in which I teach my class for graduate students, and the list of chapters looks something like a weekly list of class discussion topics. The book may be read from the first chapter through the last for an in-depth exploration of this topic, or individual chapters may be used as resources for particular aspects of second-language literacy instruction, depending on teachers' needs. Each chapter is a cohesive presentation of a particular area within the field of second-language literacy instruction, whether it be phonological skills with emergent learners, assessment with English learners, culturally responsive instruction, or fluency development, just to name a few.

Several foundational chapters set the stage for the rest of the book. In Chapter 1, I provide a conceptual framework for the topic of literacy development in a second language, describing the many linguistic, sociocultural, psychological, and educational factors that influence the literacy development of English learners in mainstream classrooms. The framework is broad, and the chapter asks teachers to conceptualize literacy instruction as a complex terrain in which teachers often have to hold multiple lenses to understand factors as diverse as the cultural values, the cognitive strengths, the previous educational experiences, and the writing systems of the languages students bring with them to the classroom. Periodic reflection questions are embedded throughout the chapter to help readers connect the content to their background teaching experiences.

In Chapter 2, Kathryn H. Au discusses culturally responsive instruction in multiethnic and multilingual classrooms. She outlines the characteristics of this kind of instruction and guides teachers to design a variety of structures that will promote student interaction in literacy activities. Au stresses the importance of using participation structures that are already familiar to students as they learn literacy tasks at school, while they are simultaneously being taught previously unfamiliar structures. In Chapter 3, Susana Dutro and I outline the importance of English learners' deep understanding of vocabulary and language structures for their success in literacy learning. We present an *instructional blueprint for English learners* that ensures that students are taught both the language of the content areas they are studying in class and also the more general English language development they will need to become proficient speakers, readers, and writers in English. We also model several examples of teaching practices that are helpful for teaching students increasingly difficult language structures in English.

Chapter 4, by Georgia Earnest García and Christina P. DeNicolo, focuses on critical issues in assessment with English learners. The authors describe common language and literacy assessments used in elementary schools, their purposes, their limitations, and how their results are used in the current era of high-stakes accountability. García and DeNicolo then present several authentic assessments that directly inform the instruction of multilingual students.

The next series of chapters looks at literacy learning from a developmental perspective, with a focus on key elements of reading instruction such as phonemic awareness, alphabet and phonics knowledge, fluency, comprehension, and vocabulary. In Chapter 5, Donald R. Bear and Regina E. Smith set the stage by providing an overview of the stages of development that can be observed through students' unedited spelling. Bear and Smith show how reading and spelling have synchrony, and they describe the instruction and materials that are most appropriate at each level and how the stages apply to students who are learning English. In Chapter 6, I build on the developmental overview to share important research and instructional applications for English learners in the emergent stage of literacy development. I highlight essential practices in phonemic awareness, alphabet knowledge, reading sight words, and developing a concept of word in print. In Chapter 7, I present the research on the important role of phonics learning for English learners and provide examples of effective instructional practices. I describe a set of essential characteristics for implementing systematic and explicit phonics instruction, such as working at students' developmental levels and building on their home language and previous literacy skills. Phonics is an essential tool to help students develop proficient reading and writing skills. For English learners, however, phonics skills must always be taught in a way that shows students that decoding by itself is not the final goal of reading.

In Chapter 8, M. Kristiina Montero and Melanie R. Kuhn guide readers to examine the important skill of fluency. Montero and Kuhn first outline the research base in fluency garnered from native English speakers, then consider applications of this research for English learners. Next, they present a series of considerations for teachers to keep in mind in fluency instruction with English learners. Finally, they describe many practical strategies to help students develop fluency skills, taking into account the specific linguistic, cognitive, and academic needs of English learners. In Chapter 9, Cynthia Brock, Suzette Youngs, Eleni Oikonomidoy, and Diane Lapp turn the spotlight on comprehension instruction with English learners. The authors describe how three fifth-grade teachers met together in a weekly study group to read articles and view a videotaped segment of a literacy lesson that centered on one English learner's comprehension of the lesson. Through their observations and the reflective conversations based on their reading, the teachers learn how to more effectively foster reading comprehension for English learners.

To round out the series of chapters focusing on key elements in reading instruction, Shane Templeton shares ideas for vocabulary instruction with upper elementary students in Chapter 10. Templeton's chapter highlights how teachers can use cognates, or words that are related in spelling and meaning across languages, to build students' word knowledge and vocabulary. He describes ways for teachers to share the concept of spelling–meaning connections for English words and how to use Latin and Greek words to help students explore cognates; and finally, he describes a two-phase approach for cognate instruction in the classroom.

Chapter 11 addresses a question of critical importance: How can white, monolingual English-speaking teachers examine their dispositions toward linguistically and culturally diverse students in order to transform their teaching to better support the academic success of their students? Julie L. Pennington and Rachel G. Salas investigate this question, first by setting the current political context of English-only mandates and high-stakes testing. Next, they peer into the practice and reflections of a white teacher as she works with a particular Spanish-speaking student. As Pennington and Salas share suggestions from the research literature and words of wisdom from the teacher's knowledgeable colleague, readers gain numerous insights into the importance of examining their underlying beliefs about students from cultural and linguistic backgrounds distinct from their own. Readers also get ideas for ways to become more reflective practitioners in order to transform their current dispositions relating to diverse learners.

In Chapter 12, I describe many of the specific teaching practices that help students best understand and master their language and literacy studies. After sharing research on the topic, I present a schema of instructional practices that help English learners by being explicit and systematic, by engaging them in a learning community, by helping them see connections across subject matter, and by getting them to actively construct the new knowledge they are learning. I share examples of each of the effective instructional practices by highlighting teaching ideas that are presented by the authors of this volume. In this way, readers gain many illustrations of effective teaching practices to apply to their own classrooms.

In Chapter 13, I provide a summary of key points that have been presented throughout this volume, organized into six important strands. The chapter encourages readers to envision exemplary instruction for English learners and to set professional goals to help them reach that vision. Readers can reflect on the ways in which they can take the specific information in this book to improve their classroom literacy instruction with English learners and to set next steps to continue to learn about this topic with their colleagues.

Before using this book to begin your study of elementary literacy instruction with English learners, take a minute to think about your own teaching experiences in this area. First, consider the English learners you have taught. What successes have you had? Identify aspects of your instruction that seem particularly powerful. What have you learned about effective instruction with English learners from these experiences? If possible, share your ideas with a colleague or fellow student.

Next, make a list of questions you have about literacy instruction with English learners. What dilemmas have you faced, or what gaps in your knowledge base do you hope to fortify as you read this book? Keep a list of your questions as you proceed through the book, and add to it as new ideas surface. Use your list to enhance your comprehension of the information presented in each chapter, and return to your questions when you have discussion opportunities with colleagues. The final chapter of this book asks you to review and analyze the progress you have made in answering your questions and coming up with new ones.

I want to acknowledge the amazing contributions that the chapter authors provide to this volume. Their strengths as both researchers and teacher educators are evident in each chapter. The authors speak with voices that are relevant and understandable to current and future teachers. They see the big picture, yet they are able to identify manageable instructional applications for teachers to bring to their individual classrooms. I am very grateful that the chapter authors have been willing to share their expertise and insight with us in these pages.

And so, to the journey ahead.

REFERENCES

de Jong, E. J., & Harper, C. A. (2005). Preparing mainstream teachers for English-language learners: Is being a good teacher good enough? *Teacher Education Quarterly, 32*(2), 101–124.

National Institute of Child Health and Human Development. (2000). *Report of the National Reading Panel. Teaching children to read: An evidence-based assessment of the scientific research literature on reading and its implications for reading instruction: Reports of the subgroups* (NIH Publication No. 00-4754). Washington, DC: U.S. Government Printing Office.

Contents

Chapter 1	Factors Influencing Second-Language Literacy Development: A Road Map for Teachers LORI HELMAN	1
Chapter 2	Culturally Responsive Instruction: Application to Multiethnic, Multilingual Classrooms KATHRYN H. AU	18
Chapter 3	Explicit Language Instruction: A Key to Constructing Meaning SUSANA DUTRO AND LORI HELMAN	40
Chapter 4	Making Informed Decisions about the Language and Literacy Assessment of English Language Learners GEORGIA EARNEST GARCÍA AND CHRISTINA P. DENICOLO	64
Chapter 5	The Literacy Development of English Learners: What Do We Know about Each Student's Literacy Development? DONALD R. BEAR AND REGINA E. SMITH	87
Chapter 6	Emergent Literacy: Planting the Seeds for Accomplished Reading and Writing LORI HELMAN	117

Chapter 7	Opening Doors to Texts: Planning Effective Phonics Instruction with English Learners LORI HELMAN	138
Chapter 8	English Language Learners and Fluency Development: More Than Speed and Accuracy M. KRISTIINA MONTERO AND MELANIE R. KUHN	156
Chapter 9	The Case of Ying: The Members of a Teacher Study Group Learn about Fostering the Reading Comprehension of English Learners CYNTHIA BROCK, SUZETTE YOUNGS, ELENI OIKONOMIDOY, AND DIANE LAPP	178
Chapter 10	Spelling–Meaning Relationships among Languages: Exploring Cognates and Their Possibilities SHANE TEMPLETON	196
Chapter 11	Examining Teacher Dispositions toward Linguistically and Culturally Diverse Students JULIE L. PENNINGTON AND RACHEL G. SALAS	213
Chapter 12	Effective Instructional Practices for English Learners LORI HELMAN	234
Chapter 13	Literacy Development with English Learners: Concluding Thoughts LORI HELMAN	252
	Index	261

CHAPTER 1

Factors Influencing Second-Language Literacy Development
A Road Map for Teachers

Lori Helman

Of the many journeys students take, perhaps none is as important as the one to become competent readers and writers—their journey to accomplished literacy. For elementary-age students who are learning to read, write, and speak the language of instruction at the same time, this journey is likely to be complex and influenced by a variety of factors, including students' educational experiences, their cultural and linguistic backgrounds and cognitive strengths, and the type and quality of the literacy instruction they receive.

On this literacy journey teachers are called on to be planners and guides for students. Teachers craft instruction that takes many things into account: what is best practice in teaching reading and writing; what motivates students to want to learn; how to build on students' academic strengths and developmental understandings; and how to pace instruction so that it is challenging yet understandable. Over the past several decades our responsibilities as literacy educators have expanded. Because of demographic changes in U.S. classrooms, meeting the needs of all students now includes having the professional knowledge to effectively teach reading and writing to the growing number of students in our classrooms who are learning English as a new language. Teachers must know how second-language reading is the same as or different from reading in a first language, how cultural factors influence learning to read and write, and how the linguistic features of students' home languages can help or hinder learning to read in English.

At times the scope of professional knowledge that teachers require to be effective literacy instructors with students learning English may seem overwhelming. Indeed, if teaching reading really is "rocket science" (Moats, 1999), then reading instruction for English language learners (ELLs) is rocket science at an even more complex level. Thankfully, professional standards and committed educators agree that being a teacher means being a lifelong learner; as students change, so must teaching methods and materials. For this reason, teachers seek out the new learning that will be required for them to grow as professionals and effectively work with increasingly diverse student populations.

This chapter brings together both of the journeys just described—the literacy journeys of ELLs learning to read and write in English, as well as the journeys of their teachers who are developing the professional knowledge to provide appropriate and effective literacy instruction for them. Throughout this chapter I provide a road map for the multiple factors that scholars have identified as likely to influence English learners' progress on the road to becoming proficient readers and writers in their new language. Typically in the academic literature, these factors are presented as separate stories, because researchers generally study only one aspect of the topic. For example, a professional article may discuss the role of vocabulary learning in literacy development, how phonics skills are learned in a second language, or how cultural identity may influence academic progress. Rarely are all of the literacy-learning factors discussed simultaneously, and that means that teachers are left to put the road map together on their own. In contrast, this overview chapter presents a survey of the landscape of this broad field; it provides an introduction to the many topics that are explored in depth throughout the other twelve chapters of this book. I have embedded periodic reflective questions to encourage you to make personal connections and, if possible, to discuss these with colleagues or classmates. Whatever your level of background experience in teaching students who come from linguistic or cultural backgrounds distinct from your own, let this chapter get you thinking about the complexity, the challenge, and the joy of how to grow as a teacher in understanding your students even better. It is only with this added awareness that teachers can be effective planners and guides in students' literacy journeys.

FACTORS INFLUENCING SECOND-LANGUAGE LITERACY DEVELOPMENT

Take a moment to think back to your own literacy development. Do you remember when and how you learned to read and write? Was it a seamless transition for you to move from the world of oral language to written language? What bumps or difficulties did you have along the way? Were you a proficient speaker of the language you first learned to read? What do you think the challenges might be to learn to read in a language you did not speak?

Learning to read is a complex process involving psychological, linguistic, sociocultural, and educational aspects. As individuals and members of various groups (families, ethnic or cultural groups, speakers of particular languages, etc.), students bring background experiences and ways of being in the world that guide them to meet life's demands, including completing the tasks they encounter at school. When students' background experiences are similar to the challenges that are presented at school, they have a head start on knowing what to do. When their experiences are different from the educational expectations they face, extra attention and effort is required to be successful. In the following sections, I outline a variety of factors that influence literacy development for students learning to read in English at the same time they learn to speak it. A common theme in these sections is that the knowledge that students bring with them to schooling, such as their languages, cultures, and academic background experiences, has the potential to make the process of learning to read and write either easier or more complex. By becoming aware of these complexities, teachers and schools have the opportunity to design instructional settings for literacy learning that accommodate students' varying cultural and linguistic strengths.

Figure 1.1 is a graphic representation of the landscape I am presenting. It shows the four main areas I introduce in this chapter: perspectives from linguistic, psychological, sociocultural, and educational frameworks. From each of the four areas, various subcomponents branch out. Through the rest of this chapter, I describe and discuss these four areas, as well as some of the specific factors that affect the instructional context in elementary schools. My list of factors is meant to be a start, and it provides an idea of the broad framework that teachers need in order to understand their students' literacy journeys. I believe that teachers must consider multiple theoretical frameworks as they tailor effective instruction for English learners. The more lenses teachers use to view the landscape, the more comprehensive and encompassing their teaching will be.

Linguistic Factors

One of the most obvious complexities in learning to read in a new language is the fact that students need to be able to understand the language in order to make meaning from print. For this reason, linguistic factors are important to investigate and understand. Language can be looked at

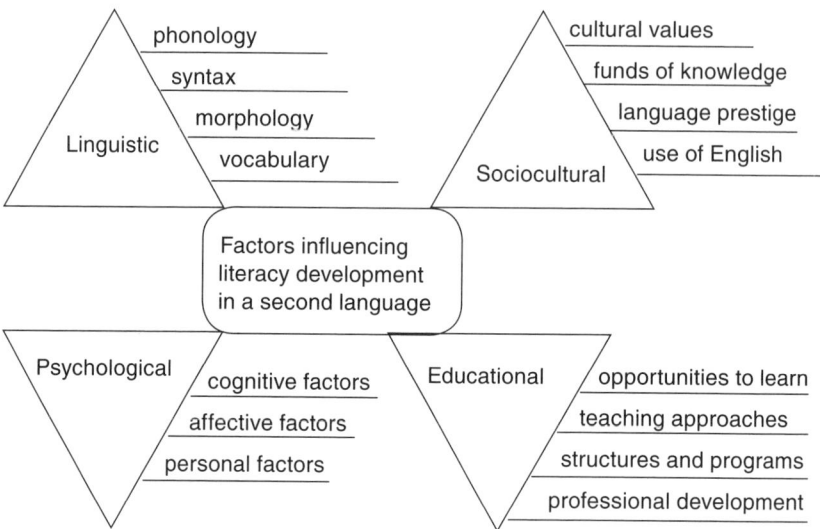

FIGURE 1.1. Factors influencing second-language literacy learning.

in a number of ways—through its sound system, its syntax, its vocabulary, its construction of words, its writing system, and its guidelines for appropriate ways of communicating interpersonally (Swan & Smith, 2001; Trumbull & Farr, 2005). Each of these linguistic areas offers challenges to a student who must apply his or her background knowledge to work in a new language. Consider for a moment your own experiences with learning a new language. What aspects of understanding the language were hardest for you: the new sounds, the vocabulary, putting sentences together, or knowing when to say what? If you were already literate in your first language, how did that help you access the new language? What impact did similarities between your native language and the new language have on how easy it was for you to communicate and understand print?

Research on literacy learning in a second language identifies several key points relating to linguistic factors. In a synthesis of the research literature on English learners in U.S. schools, Genesee and colleagues (Genesee, Lindholm-Leary, Saunders, & Christian, 2005) point out that developing oral proficiency in English is crucial to students' academic success and that there is a positive relationship demonstrated between students' oral proficiency and reading achievement. Oral proficiency in a new language takes time to develop (Genesee et al., 2005; Hakuta, Butler, & Witt, 2000; Thomas & Collier, 1997). The more similar the oral and written characteristics of a student's home language are to English, the easier it is to learn English (Dressler & Kamil, 2006). Bialystock (2001) notes that the relationship of the home language to English may either facilitate or hamper literacy learning. Research points to a multidimensional linguistic relationship that varies depending on the tasks and background languages of the students involved, much depends on characteristics of the student's home language and the language being learned, the instructional setting, and the specific demands of the literacy activities (Bialystock & Herman, 1999). Wu, De Temple, Herman, and Snow (1994) found that ELL students need to have concrete experience and practice in the target language with a given discourse activity in order to be successful. In general, oral-language proficiency correlates positively with literacy skills when larger chunks of text are involved, such as with reading comprehension and writing (Geva, 2006).

The research literature highlights cross-linguistic effects for students developing second-language oral and literacy skills (Koda, 2005). ELL students who bring literacy skills from a first language to English reading learn to read more quickly and easily than do students without native-language literacy (Genesee et al., 2005). Geva and Siegel (2000) suggest that by taking into account the specific home and school scripts students are learning, a more accurate picture of second-language reading development is presented. Susana Dutro and I discuss many aspects of language development for English learners in Chapter 3 of this volume.

I now present several important subcomponents of language and discuss how these areas may influence literacy development for English learners. Figure 1.1 presents these subcomponents, which include phonology, syntax, morphology, and vocabulary.

Phonology

Each language has a particular set of sounds that it uses to create words. Students who are learning English bring an awareness of sounds, or phonemes, from their home language to the learning of English. Developmental spelling research has shown that when sounds in English are not part of a student's home language, confusions in distinguishing and representing these sounds in text often arise (Dressler, 2002; Helman, 2004; Palmer, El-Ashry, Leclere, & Chang, 2007; Swan & Smith, 2001; Zutell & Allen, 1988). Research has also shown that students who develop phonological skills such as phonemic awareness in their home language are able to transfer that knowledge to English literacy learning (Carlisle, Beeman, Davis, & Spharim, 1999; Durgunoglu, Nagy, & Hancin-Bhatt, 1993).

Syntax

Syntax is the way words are put together into phrases and sentences. For example, in English we say, "I have a big cat." In Spanish, the adjective follows the noun, "Yo tengo un gato grande" (I have a cat big). Students learning English as a new language face syntactical challenges as they learn to speak, read, and write using different rules for syntax (cf. Chan, 2004; Swan & Smith, 2001). In a study comparing the reading development of English learners and native English speakers in Canada, ELLs were found to have greater difficulty with an oral cloze test in which their syntactic knowledge was assessed by having to supply a grammatically appropriate missing word in a sentence (Lipka & Siegel, 2007). It is easy to see how the extra difficulty English learners have with predicting possible words in sentences might influence a developing reader's ability to make accurate predictions in reading texts.

Morphology

Morphemes are the groups of letters that carry meaning within words. For example, *dog* is both a word and a morpheme; it is the smallest meaningful unit to convey the four-legged critter known as man's best friend. The word *dogs*, however, contains two morphemes: *dog* and *-s*. The *s* at the end adds the plural meaning to the word. Morphology is another layer of linguistics that students learning English may find problematic. Morphemes may be applied differently in various languages, so students may find it more difficult to learn the procedures in English, such as in showing plural or past tense. One study of morphological understanding with Spanish speakers learning English found that students were better at using morphological processes when the English word resembled the word in Spanish (Hancin-Bhatt & Nagy, 1994).

Vocabulary

Knowing the meaning of individual words in English is also an important component of literacy development. Students who do not know the meanings of the words in their reading texts have difficulty understanding them; they are also unable to use language effectively in their writing (Calderón et al., 2005; Dufra & Voeten, 1999). Research studies in this area point to the positive effects of more developed vocabularies and the negative effects of low vocabulary knowledge. García (1991) notes that students learning English often do not have the knowledge of key words in English needed to comprehend their texts. Other researchers report that poor reading comprehension for English learners is often related to low vocabulary knowledge (Jimenez, Garcia, & Pearson, 1996; Nagy, 1997; Verhoeven, 1990).

One aspect of vocabulary learning that has been researched in second-language literacy development is the learning of cognates, or words that are related in spelling and meaning across languages. An example pair of cognates is the English word *telephone* and the Spanish word *teléfono*. Research in this area shows that in languages that have close relationships and in which the cognate words have a high degree of overlap in meaning, it is possible for students to transfer their knowledge of the meanings of words in their home language to English (Dressler & Kamil, 2006). There are also pitfalls to the use of cognates, such as when cognates do not have similar meanings across languages. Application of cognate knowledge develops over time and requires that the learner has a conscious awareness that the two languages have overlap and are related (Dressler & Kamil, 2006). In Chapter 10 of this volume, Shane Templeton presents an overview of cognate instruction.

In summary, the consensus of research into linguistic influences on second-language literacy points to the importance of language knowledge on many levels. Language proficiency, including vocabulary knowledge, is highly related to comprehension of reading texts and accomplished writing. Depending on the similarities and differences between the home language and English, there may be initial confusions in the areas of phonology, morphology, and syntax as students transfer their linguistic knowledge to English.

Sociocultural Factors

Another critical theoretical perspective that is interwoven throughout this book is that of sociocultural theory (Au, 1998; Cummins, 1994; Freire, 1970; Moll, 1994; Nieto, 2002; Vygotsky, 1978). Teachers who wish to support the literacy development of their English-learning students cannot ignore the role of sociocultural aspects of teaching and learning, such as the extent to which students' backgrounds are valued in the classroom. Students bring many things from home, including a cultural heritage with norms and values, a language they speak and share with family members, ways of interacting that feel natural, and goals and aspirations. School is a social structure that embodies its own social norms and values and either reflects the larger society's status quo or consciously works to create a multicultural safe space. Issues present in the larger society, such as the prestige and status of students' home languages versus English, the values of individualism over cooperation, and the preference for mainstream middle-class behaviors, cannot help but express themselves in classroom activities.

Bear and Barone (1997) used a theoretical model developed by Bronfenbrenner to look at literacy instruction in the elementary classroom. In this model, Bronfenbrenner outlines three contexts that influence what goes on in the classroom: social aspects of the classroom, the school system that controls the classroom, and the larger social ideologies of politics, language, and culture that extend into schools and classrooms (e.g., Bronfenbrenner & Evans, 2000). The classroom world is not isolated from the world at large, and students and teachers bring in their cultures, beliefs, and expectations with them. In this brief introduction I touch on only a few of the areas that theorists have examined relating to sociocultural factors in literacy development. Chapter 2 of this volume, written by Kathryn H. Au, provides a much more complete overview. In addition, in Chapter 5 Donald R. Bear and Regina E. Smith flesh out literacy development within an ecological perspective, and in Chapter 11 Julie L. Pennington and Rachel G. Salas examine the influence that teacher dispositions toward working with multilingual and multicultural students have in supporting their literacy success.

As a teacher who brings values, beliefs, and your own cultural background into the classroom, take a moment to reflect on the following:

What is your cultural background, and how does it match the norms and practices of the personal schooling experiences you received?
Did the school environment you entered resemble your home world in language, values, and interpersonal communication styles?
As a teacher, what are some of the ways you have attempted to get to know and learn from the diversity of cultures represented by families in your classroom?
What are some of the cultural strengths that your students bring to the classroom setting?
What experiences seem new to students?

Researchers who study social inequalities and achievement inequities in school settings note numerous issues in U.S. classrooms. Included in these are mismatches among school expectations and the values, norms, and background experiences of students who do not come from middle-class, European American families. Au (2006) describes the societal patterns that are enacted in schools that *fail to build on students' cultural and linguistic backgrounds*, thereby making learning more abstract and difficult for students. Teachers are not intentionally working against students' strengths; simply, the majority of elementary school teachers are female, white, and come from middle-class backgrounds, and they may not recognize that they are bringing a different cultural framework into the classroom community (see Au, Chapter 2, this volume; Villegas & Lucas, 2002).

A related theme comes from the work of Luis Moll, who describes the strengths that students bring to school as *funds of knowledge* (Moll, 1994). When students' knowledge and background experiences, as well as their abilities, languages, and family heritage, are seen as strengths, students are empowered to be successful at school. When their cultures and experiences are not seen as contributing to school success, students are disempowered and viewed as deficient, and often their potential is underestimated. Ways to build on students' funds of knowledge are discussed throughout this book, including in particular Chapters 2 and 11.

Jim Cummins adds a political perspective to this sociocultural discussion as he describes the ways in which school settings value or devalue bilingualism and take power over students' maintenance of the home language. He connects English learners' inequitable literacy achievement to the fact that *biliteracy* has not been encouraged as an educational solution (Cummins, 2001). Cummins calls on educators to work with ELLs to develop structures for collaborative empowerment by incorporating their language and cultural values into school operations (Cummins, 1996).

Having *opportunities to use English* outside of school is also a sociocultural factor affecting students' literacy learning. Students have varying opportunities to practice their new language in the communities in which they live, and this affects their mastery of advanced English (Hansen, 1989).

Qualitative researchers have documented the presence of particular cultural values, norms, and participation styles in classrooms with diverse students; the roles of language policy, prestige, and culturally discordant instruction have also been extensively noted (Rueda, August, & Goldenberg, 2006). These factors are less directly associated with an individual student's test scores but become more apparent when large-scale data are disaggregated by demographic characteristics such as ethnicity, linguistic background, immigration status, or cultural group (Au, 2006). Sociocultural factors must always be taken into account when teachers plan for the literacy achievement of English learners.

Psychological Factors

Other factors that influence literacy development for English learners are the cognitive and affective processes that take place inside each individual's head. These processes are connected to and inseparable from sociocultural and linguistic dimensions, yet they stand apart in many ways, as well. Psychological factors may be conceptualized as what is going on in the student's memory, brain, and emotions. Cognitive researchers who study eye movements, the differences in brain functioning between bilinguals and monolinguals, and the role of motivation in literacy development would all be located in this category.

Before beginning the discussion of psychological factors, take a minute to think about the following questions: As a teacher, have you ever had the sibling of a previous student and found it hard to believe the two were related? Despite having the same linguistic and cultural background, the two students may have been unique in many ways. What differences did you notice, and why do you think those existed? Next, think about what cognitive and emotional factors might play a role in learning to read and write. What "in the head" factors played a role in your own or your own children's literacy development?

Cognitive Factors

Research has been accruing relating to the early reading development of English learners, and findings show that the same factors that are important for native English speakers learning to read also hold true for ELLs. LeSaux and Siegel (2003) found that the same cognitive and metalinguistic areas (working memory and phonological processing) predicted reading difficulties for ELLs and native English-speaking students. Word recognition development for native speakers and English learners also appears to develop in a similar way (Chiappe & Siegel, 2006; LeSaux, Koda, Siegel, & Shanahan, 2006). Bilingual students have shown some advantages in developing metalinguistic skills, and these abilities appear to aid in second-language reading comprehension (Bialystock, 1991; Carlisle, Beeman, & Shah, 1996).

Affective Factors and Personal Idiosyncrasies

It is impossible to categorize many of the factors that affect literacy development into one sole area. For example, where do motivation and personality fit in? Motivation is a complex construct, and it is dependent on many things, including the individual, his or her culture, age, experiences, the learning environment, and so on. Similarly, the idea of individual personal characteristics such as shyness or inquisitiveness seems to have a foot in the psychological area and to overlap with the cultural and educational categories as well. Whether these traits are learned or inherited, and although they may be moderated by culture, age, and classroom context, as teachers and parents we know that personal and affective factors play a role in students' literacy participation and learning. Although there is limited research with ELLs on motivation and the individual factors that affect their literacy development, this topic is worthy of consideration in the area of psychological factors. It is also present in the next section on educational factors.

Educational Factors

I turn now to the final category in my road map of factors that influence literacy development with English learners. This area is also the primary focus of this book: instructional approaches for literacy instruction. What happens in schools and classrooms matters, and the research field is beginning to form a body of knowledge relating to what constitutes effective literacy instruction with English learners (Shanahan & Beck, 2006). In each chapter of this book, the researcher/authors present both theory and methods for implementing effective instruction.

Think for a moment about your own teaching or observations you have done of other teachers in classrooms with students learning English. What kinds of learning activities, content, and teacher behaviors seem to best facilitate students' understanding? What caused students to become animated and verbal? What specific projects do you remember as being powerful for student learning? Have you witnessed a school or district that seemed to be very successful at including ELLs and their families in the educational program? What structures were in place to facilitate that connection?

Research into successful educational approaches with English learners has encompassed a variety of areas: classroom and schoolwide experiences, teaching approaches, the quality of instruction, educational expectations, and student engagement. An overarching concept that unites these educational factors is *opportunity to learn* (OTL; Brewer & Stacz, 1996). Having OTLs means that students have experienced the content and instructional strategies using sufficient instructional resources to give them equal access to the curriculum offered at their grade level. In other words, have students had qualified teachers who use quality instructional materials at a challenging academic level taught in a way that helps them understand? In a review of the research on high-stakes testing with English learners, Solórzano (2008) notes that in fact many ELLs are receiving diluted instruction that is several academic levels below their grade level, that they do not have access to critical content-area instructional strategies, and that they often have underprepared teachers and inadequate educational materials. For these reasons, it is questionable that English learners are experiencing a valid OTL.

Quality instructional approaches for English learners involve a variety of *classroom and schoolwide structures*, as well as effective *teaching approaches*. Classrooms that combine interactive approaches in which teachers engage with learners with direct instruction ensure that the content is tailored, appropriate, and meaningful for ELLs (Genesee et al., 2005). Instructional conversations, in which students have an extended dialogue with teachers in order to develop complex thinking skills, is one example of this teaching approach (Padrón, Waxman, & Rivera, 2002). In a study that investigated the use of an observation tool for effective instruction with English learners, researchers found a positive correlation with student achievement in the following instructional practices: explicit teaching, quality instruction for low-performing students, sheltered English instruction, interactive teaching, vocabulary development, and phonemic awareness and decoding instruction (Baker, Gersten, Haager, & Dingle, 2006). Other classroom instructional practices that have shown promise for Hispanic students include culturally responsive teaching, cooperative learning, cognitively guided instruction, technology-enriched instruction, and a sense of a classroom community (Padrón et al., 2002).

Although research is not substantial in this area, literacy practices found to be effective with native speakers of English are likely to be effective with English learners as well, but they may need to be *adjusted to meet the particular needs* of ELLs (Genesee et al., 2005; Shanahan & Beck, 2006). The generic literacy practices that have shown the strongest results with ELLs are generally the ones that support preliteracy and decoding skills, and there is little evidence of growth in reading comprehension for English learners based on these practices (Shanahan & Beck, 2006). In general, instructional procedures that *build on students' bilingual experiences*, such as instruction in the first language, translation, and cross-linguistic bridging, as well as the use of cognates, have been deemed productive (Genesee, 2005; Koda, 2005).

Programmatically, the most effective structures for ELL literacy development are those that involve sustained instruction in the home language (Genesee, 2005; Thomas & Collier, 2002). Biliteracy development is related to overall academic achievement (Genesee et al., 2005). Genesee and colleagues (2005) also note that programs that promote ELL students' academic success include a positive school environment, a curriculum that is meaningful and involves higher level thinking, a model of instructional enrichment, teachers with good theoretical knowledge, and a focus on student-to-student, as well as teacher-to-student, interactions. Overall, ELLs involved in specialized instructional programs are much more likely to catch up to their peers (Genesee et al., 2005). Encouraging extra experiences with English, such as at-home reading programs, has also been found to be helpful (Shanahan & Beck, 2006).

The *use of high-stakes tests* that have a strong impact on the lives of

ELLs has been called into question because these assessments do not have the psychometric properties necessary to be applied to populations of ELLs (Solórzano, 2008). Their use with students who are not proficient in English will lead to inappropriate and inaccurate evaluations (Solórzano, 2008). See Chapter 4, this volume, by Georgia Earnest Garcia and Christina P. DeNicolo for a further discussion on this topic.

In a study of critical factors in the educational success of Hispanic students, Padrón and colleagues (2002) also found that *student and community empowerment* had a positive effect on student learning. This included school-based interventions that involved the community in setting goals for students.

In terms of professional development that supports effective ELL literacy instruction, the consensus of several research studies suggests that the best approaches involve collaborative activities between researchers and practitioners to help teachers address the particular needs of ELLs (August & Calderón, 2006; Padrón et al., 2002). In addition, the research stresses the importance of helping preservice teachers understand cognitive and affective processes that influence learning, including how to use metacognition in the classroom (Padrón et al., 2002).

In summary, educational factors that influence the literacy learning of ELLs involve in-class instruction, the types and quality of lessons, involvement of the students and their communities, teacher knowledge, and students' opportunities to use language in cognitively challenging activities. Programs that are tailored to second-language learners' needs and strengths are most effective, and the use of students' home languages has proven to add to their success. Teacher professional development in this area must be cohesive and in-depth and must take place over time.

CONCLUSION

In this chapter I have presented many factors that influence English learners' literacy development by looking through the lenses of language, culture, cognition, and educational practices. Although all of these elements complicate the road map of students' literacy learning, they also provide sites for educators to enhance what takes place in the school and classroom. In the metaphoric language of this chapter, students' literacy learning resembles a journey, and the numerous strands I have described help educators find inroads to support their success. Being a teacher or educational leader means planning and guiding students' literacy development; in order to do this effectively, educators must implement research-based practices for English learners. When we use multiple perspectives, our instructional road map becomes more defined. I encourage you to keep this broad perspective in mind as you read through the instructional chapters contained in this book.

REFERENCES

Au, K. (1998). Social constructivism and the school literacy learning of students of diverse cultural backgrounds. *Journal of Literacy Research, 30,* 297–319.

Au, K. (2006). *Multicultural issues and literacy achievement.* Mahwah, NJ: Erlbaum.

August, D., & Calderón, M. (2006). Teacher beliefs and professional development. In D. August & T. Shanahan (Eds.), *Developing literacy in second-language learners: Report of the National Literacy Panel on Language-Minority Children and Youth* (pp. 555–563). Mahwah, NJ: Erlbaum.

Baker, S. K., Gersten, R., Haager, D., & Dingle, M. (2006). Teaching practice and the reading growth of first-grade English learners: Validation of an observation instrument. *The Elementary School Journal, 107*(2), 199–219.

Bear, D. R., & Barone, D. (1997). *Developing literacy.* Boston: Houghton Mifflin.

Bialystock, E. (1991). Metalinguistic dimensions of bilingual language proficiency. In E. Bialystock (Ed.), *Language processing in bilingual children* (pp. 113–140). New York: Cambridge University Press.

Bialystock, E. (2001). *Bilingualism in development: Language, literacy and cognition.* New York: Cambridge University Press.

Bialystock, E., & Herman, J. (1999). Does bilingualism matter for early literacy? *Bilingualism: Language and Cognition, 2*(1), 35–44.

Brewer, D. J., & Stacz, C. (1996). *Enhancing opportunity to learn measures in NCES data.* Santa Monica, CA: RAND.

Bronfenbrenner, U., & Evans, G. W. (2000). Developmental science in the 21st century: Emerging questions, theoretical models, research designs and empirical findings. *Social Development, 9,* 115–125.

Calderón, M., August, D., Slavin, R., Duran, D., Madden, N., & Cheung, A. (2005). Bringing words to life in classrooms with English language learners. In E. H. Hiebert & M. L. Kamil (Eds.), *Teaching and learning vocabulary: Bringing research to practice* (pp. 115–136). Mahwah, NJ: Erlbaum.

Carlisle, J. F., Beeman, M. B., & Shah, P. P. (1996). The metalinguistic capabilities and English literacy of Hispanic high school students: An exploratory study. *Yearbook of the National Reading Conference, 45,* 306–316.

Carlisle, J., Beeman, M. Davis, L., & Spharim, G. (1999). Relationship of metalinguistic capabilities and reading achievement for children who are becoming bilingual. *Applied Psycholinguistics, 20,* 459–478.

Chan, A. Y. W. (2004). Syntactic transfer: Evidence from the interlanguage of Hong Kong Chinese ESL learners. *Modern Language Journal, 88*(1), 56–74.

Chiappe, P., & Siegel, L. S. (2006). A longitudinal study of reading development of Canadian children from diverse linguistic backgrounds. *Elementary School Journal, 107*(2), 135–152.

Cummins, J. (1994). Knowledge, power and identity in teaching English as a second language. In F. Genesee (Ed.), *Educating second language children: The whole child, the whole curriculum, the whole community* (pp. 33–58). Cambridge, UK: Cambridge University Press.

Cummins, J. (1996). *Negotiating identities: Education for empowerment in a diverse society*. Ontario, CA: California Association for Bilingual Education.

Cummins, J. (2001). *Language, power and pedagogy: Bilingual children in the crossfire*. Bristol, UK: Multilingual Matters.

Dressler, C. A. (2002). Inter- and intra-language influences on the English spelling development of fifth grade, Spanish-speaking English language learners. *Dissertation Abstracts International, 63*, 145.

Dressler, C., & Kamil, M. (2006). First- and second-language literacy. In D. August & T. Shanahan (Eds.), *Developing literacy in second-language learners: Report of the National Literacy Panel on Language-Minority Children and Youth* (pp. 197–238). Mahway, NJ: Erlbaum.

Dufra, M., & Voeten, M. J. M. (1999). Native language literacy and phonological memory as prerequisites for learning English as a foreign language. *Applied Psycholinguistics, 20*(3), 329–348.

Durgunoglu, A. Y., Nagy, W. E., & Hancin-Bhatt, B. J. (1993). Cross-language transfer of phonological awareness. *Journal of Educational Psychology, 85*(3), 453–465.

Freire, P. (2000). *Pedagogy of the oppressed, 30th anniversary edition*. New York: Continuum.

Garcia, G. E. (1991). Factors influencing the English reading test performance of Spanish-speaking Hispanic children. *Reading Research Quarterly, 26*(4), 371–392.

Genesee, F., Lindholm-Leary, K., Saunders, W., & Christian, D. (2005). English language learners in U.S. schools: An overview of research findings. *Journal of Education for Students Placed at Risk, 10*(4), 363–385.

Geva, E. (2006). Second-language oral proficiency and second-language literacy. In D. August & T. Shanahan (Eds.), *Developing literacy in second-language learners: Report of the National Literacy Panel on Language-Minority Children and Youth* (pp. 123–139). Mahwah, NJ: Erlbaum.

Geva, E., & Siegel, L. S. (2000). Orthographic and cognitive factors in the concurrent development of basic reading skills in two languages. *Reading and Writing: An Interdisciplinary Journal, 12*, 1–30.

Hakuta, K., Butler, Y. G., & Witt, D. (2000). *How long does it take English learners to attain proficiency?* (Policy Report 2000-1). Retrieved May 30, 2008 from University of California Linguistic Minority Research Institute website, *http://www.repositories.cdlib.org/lmri/pr/hakuta/*.

Hancin-Bhatt, B., & Nagy, W. E. (1994). Lexical transfer and second language morphological development. *Applied Psycholinguistics, 15*(3), 289–310.

Hansen, D. A. (1989). Locating learning: Second language gains and language use in family, peer and classroom contexts. *NABE Journal, 13*, 161–180.

Helman, L. A. (2004). Building on the sound system of Spanish: Insights from the alphabetic spellings of English language learners. *Reading Teacher, 57*, 452–460.

Jimenez, R. T., Garcia, G. E., & Pearson, P. D. (1996). The reading strategies of Latino/a students who are successful English readers: Opportunities and obstacles. *Reading Research Quarterly, 31*, 90–112.

Koda, K. (2005). *Insights into second language reading.* New York: Cambridge University Press.

LeSaux, N., Koda, K., Siegel, L., & Shanahan, T. (2006). Development of literacy. In D. August & T. Shanahan (Eds.), *Developing literacy in second-language learners: Report of the National Literacy Panel on Language-Minority Children and Youth* (pp. 75–122). Mahwah, NJ: Erlbaum.

LeSaux, N. K., & Siegel, L. S. (2003). The development of reading in children who speak English as a second language. *Developmental Psychology, 39*(6), 1005–1019.

Lipka, O., & Siegel, L. S. (2007). The development of reading skills in children with English as a second language. *Scientific Studies of Reading, 11*(2), 105–131.

Moats, L. (1999). *Teaching reading is rocket science: What expert teachers of reading should know and be able to do.* Washington, DC: American Federation of Teachers.

Moll, L. C. (1994). Literacy research in community and classrooms: A sociocultural approach. In R. B. Ruddell, M. R. Ruddell, & H. Singer (Eds.), *Theoretical models and processes of reading* (4th ed.). Newark, DE: International Reading Association.

Nagy, W. (1997). On the role of context in first- and second-language vocabulary learning. In N. Schmitt & M. McCarthy (Eds.), *Vocabulary: Description, acquisition and pedagogy* (pp. 64–83). Cambridge: Cambridge University Press.

Nieto, S. (2002). *Language, culture, and teaching.* Mahwah, NJ: Erlbaum.

Padrón, Y. N., Waxman, H. C., & Rivera, H. H. (2002). Issues in educating Hispanic students. In S. Stringfield & D. Land (Eds.), *Educating at-risk students* (pp. 66–88). Chicago: National Society for the Study of Education.

Palmer, B. C., El-Ashry, F., Leclere, J. T., & Chang, S. (2007). Learning from Abdallah: A case study of an Arabic-speaking child in a U.S. school. *Reading Teacher, 61*(1), 8–17.

Rueda, R. S., August, D., & Goldenberg, C. (2006). The sociocultural context in which children acquire literacy. In D. August & T. Shanahan (Eds.), *Developing literacy in second-language learners: Report of the National Literacy Panel on Language-Minority Children and Youth* (pp. 319–339). Mahwah, NJ: Erlbaum.

Shanahan, T., & Beck, I. L. (2006). Effective literacy for teaching English language learners. In D. August & T. Shanahan (Eds.), *Developing literacy in second-language learners: Report of the National Literacy Panel on Language-Minority Children and Youth* (pp. 415–488). Mahwah, NJ: Erlbaum.

Solórzano, R. W. (2008). High stakes testing: Issues, implications, and remedies for English language learners. *Review of Educational Research, 78*(2), 260–329.

Swan, M., & Smith, B. (2001). *Learner English*. New York: Cambridge University Press.

Thomas, W. P., & Collier, V. P. (1997). *School effectiveness for language minority students*. Washington, DC: National Clearinghouse for Bilingual Education.

Thomas, W. P., & Collier, V. P. (2002). *A national study of school effectiveness for language minority students' long-term academic achievement*. Santa Cruz, CA: Center for Research on Education, Diversity and Excellence.

Trumbull, E., & Farr, B. P. (2005). *Language and learning: What teachers need to know*. Norwood, MA: Christopher-Gordon.

Verhoeven, L. T. (1990). Acquisition of reading in a second language. *Reading Research Quarterly, 25*(2), 90–114.

Villegas, A. M., & Lucas, T. (2002). Preparing culturally responsive teachers: Rethinking the curriculum. *Journal of Teacher Education, 53*(1), 20–32.

Vygotsky, L. (1978). *Mind in society: The development of higher psychological processes*. Cambridge, MA: Harvard University Press.

Wu, H., De Temple, J. M., Herman, J. A., & Snow, C. E. (1994). "*L'animal qui fait* oink! Oink!": Bilingual children's oral and written picture descriptions in English and French under varying instructions. *Discourse Processes, 18*, 141–164.

Zutell, J., & Allen, J. (1998). The English spelling strategies of Spanish-speaking bilingual children. *TESOL Quarterly, 22*, 333–340.

CHAPTER 2

Culturally Responsive Instruction
Application to Multiethnic, Multilingual Classrooms

KATHRYN H. AU

Teachers working in multiethnic, multilinguistic classrooms are faced with many complexities as they strive to provide all of their students with high-quality literacy instruction. Yet such rich diversity among students is especially common in urban districts. How can teachers rise to the challenge of bringing all of their students, including English language learners (ELLs), to high levels of literacy?

    I believe that culturally responsive instruction offers one possible avenue to success. I begin by discussing the key characteristics of culturally responsive instruction and then address three knotty issues that often seem to prevent teachers from trying to teach in a culturally responsive manner. I focus on issues of social process, or how teachers can structure interaction to promote students' active participation in literacy activities. My recommendation is that teachers offer students opportunities to participate in a variety of structures, those consistent with a diverse worldview as well as with a mainstream worldview. These recommendations are placed within the context of the readers' workshop and the writers' workshop as frameworks that lend themselves to culturally responsive literacy instruction.

SHARED ASSUMPTIONS ABOUT CULTURALLY RESPONSIVE INSTRUCTION

Researchers have used several different terms for what I am calling *culturally responsive instruction*. These terms include *culturally congruent instruction* (Au & Kawakami, 1994), *culturally relevant pedagogy* (Ladson-Billings, 1995; Osborne, 1996), and *culturally responsive teaching* (Gay, 2000). Despite these differences in terminology, certain common assumptions are shared by researchers exploring ways to build on students' cultural strengths in the classroom.

First, culturally responsive instruction resides firmly within a pluralist vision of society, in which students' cultural heritages are respected, celebrated, and seen as worthy of inclusion in the school's curriculum (Gay, 2000). Teachers who teach in a culturally responsive manner start with a high regard for the competence of ELLs and their families and recognize that the literacy demands in typical school settings may well differ from those in the community (Heath, 1983; Orellana, Reynolds, Dorner, & Meza, 2003).

Second, culturally responsive instruction aims at school success for ELLs, acknowledging that a disproportionate number of these students experience failure in school. As noted in Osborne's (1996) research, this failure is an international phenomenon. Exactly what constitutes literacy success for students of diverse backgrounds is a topic open to discussion. I have suggested that educators consider at least three purposes of literacy: for personal fulfillment, for citizenship, and for employment (Au, 2007). This last purpose, employment, should be seen in the context of globalization, including the impact of worldwide processes of communication (such as through the Internet) that have allowed the close linking of financial systems and processes of production and consumption (Burbules & Torres, 2000). To maintain a position of dominance in the global economy, a superpower such as the United States must have workers who can outthink workers in other parts of the world. One practical implication of globalization is that standards for students' literacy achievement are likely to keep rising. Globalization makes the challenge of bringing ELLs to high levels of literacy all the more urgent, to ensure that these students have the opportunities for advancement into highly paid jobs. Culturally responsive instruction is proposed as one means of closing the gap between the literacy achievement of ELLs and their mainstream peers.

Third, in order to improve the school success of ELLs, culturally responsive instruction seeks to build bridges between students' experiences at home and at school. In some cases, as in Moll's (1992) research on funds of knowledge held by Mexican American families, the approach is to change the content of the curriculum so that topics relevant to students' lives become central to classroom lessons. In other cases, as in my research on participation structures that resemble talk story (Au & Mason, 1981), the approach is to change the social processes in the classroom, or the manner in which teachers interact with students. This approach, centered on changing classroom interactions, is the focus of this chapter.

Fourth, culturally responsive instruction supports students in building, or at least maintaining, their competence in the home language and culture. The home language and culture do not simply serve as vehicles that educators can use to give students access to mainstream school processes and content; rather, the home language and culture are valued for their own sake.

Fifth and finally, culturally responsive instruction fosters social justice through an emphasis on equality of educational outcomes and the celebration of diversity. Culturally responsive instruction is aimed at righting the wrongs inherent in the present educational system, which produces a layering of test scores, with students of mainstream backgrounds in the upper layers and students of diverse backgrounds in the lower layers (see, e.g., the reading assessment results of the National Assessment of Educational Progress; Perie, Grigg, & Donahue, 2005). Culturally responsive instruction seeks to move away from a mentality of educational winners and losers toward a future in which many students from all groups achieve at high levels.

KEY ISSUES

As a result of discussing the topic of culturally responsive instruction with many educators, I know that certain issues arise time and again. Here are three issues surrounding culturally responsive instruction that many educators find confusing.

Matching to Students' Cultural Backgrounds

One source of confusion stems from the fact that much of the early research on culturally responsive instruction was conducted in classrooms in which the majority of students were from one particular ethnic group. For example, I conducted my studies in classrooms in which most of the students were Native Hawaiians (Au & Mason, 1981). Ladson-Billings's (1994) research was conducted in classrooms in which nearly all the students were African American. Philips's (1983) classic research was conducted in classrooms on the Warm Springs Reservation with students who were Native Americans.

Many teachers puzzle over how to apply the results of this research, because these studies seem to point to the need for a precise match between instructional practices and students' cultural backgrounds. These teachers reason that it is impossible for them to achieve a match, because they teach in settings in which students come from many different cultural and linguistic backgrounds. Teachers feel that they cannot possibly gain a deep understanding of a dozen or more different cultures and languages. In short, although culturally responsive instruction sounds like a promising idea, it seems impractical in the multiethnic, multilingual classroom.

Certainly, one way of looking at research on culturally responsive instruction is to emphasize the relationship between the instructional innovation and the cultural background of the students, for example, by linking the use of talk-story-like participation structures to improved reading performance in Hawaiian children (Au & Mason, 1981). However, there is another way of applying research on culturally responsive instruction to multiethnic, multilingual settings. This approach involves identifying patterns of instruction consistent with a *diverse worldview* that reflects the cultural values of many nonmainstream groups (cf. Spindler & Spindler, 1990). Teachers in multiethnic classrooms can implement culturally responsive instruction by making sure that there are times during the school day when lessons and activities are organized according to this diverse worldview, as discussed later.

Culturally responsive instruction does not involve duplicating home and community settings in the classroom. Classroom and home settings should remain distinct and different from one another, so that teachers can carry out classroom activities in a manner that promotes academic achievement and families can carry out their lives in a manner consistent with their own goals. Instead of duplication, culturally responsive instruction entails hybridity or hybrid events (Au, 2001; Manyak, 2001). In this case hybridity refers to the creative combining of elements from students' home cultures with elements typical of the classroom and academic learning. Hybrid settings depart from familiar ways of doing school while maintaining a rigorous academic focus.

Consider the following example of academic thinking by second graders of Native Hawaiian ancestry in a talk-story-like reading lesson. In talk-story-like reading lessons, teachers allow students to decide when they want to speak. This approach is in contrast to conventional classroom recitation, in which the teacher calls on the students to speak one at a time. Talk story is a Hawaiian community speech event in which speakers collaborate to recount events (Watson, 1974). Talk-story-like reading lessons are characterized by student initiation, overlapping speech, and co-narration, or the collaborative production of answers by several students.

In the example, T is the teacher, and the opening brackets indicate overlapping speech. The students had just finished reading a story entitled *Annie and the Old One* (Miles, 1985). Annie, a Navaho girl, is heartbroken when her grandmother announces that she will return to Mother Earth when the rug Annie's mother is weaving is finished. Annie behaves in a disruptive manner, believing that she can stop her grandmother from dying by preventing her mother from finishing the rug. At the end of the story, the Old One takes Annie to the desert to explain the cycle of life and death.

T: But she also compared it
[when she said—
JOEY: [The cactus.
T: OK, tell me about the cactus, Joey.
JOEY: Oh, I know about the cactus.
T: What did you find about the cactus?
JOEY: (*Reads from text.*) "The cactus did not bloom forever. Petals dried and fell to earth."
T: OK, what is she trying to tell Annie by using that analogy of the cactus?
ROS: That people die of old age. That people just don't die when they say so.
T: Well, yeah, OK, that's—that's true. But what did they mean when they said, "The cactus did not bloom forever"?
ROS: That people, they got to die.
KENT: That means that when it starts blooming a life will start, but when it falls the life will end. (Au, 1981)

Notice how Joey started to speak before the teacher was finished, indicating that he had something to say. As the teacher questioned Joey, Ross and Kent chose to jump into the discussion, elaborating on the ideas Joey had presented. By collaborating in their answers, the three boys were able to work out an interpretation of the theme of the story. The teacher skillfully asked leading questions but did not control who should answer. As this transcript excerpt illustrates, young Native Hawaiian students are able to grasp complex ideas when guided to do so within the context of talk-story-like reading lessons in which they have the opportunity to extend their ideas by collaborating with others.

Matching to Teachers' Backgrounds

A second source of misunderstanding about culturally responsive instruction is also related to the idea of matching, but this time as it concerns the cultural backgrounds of teachers, not students. Some teachers believe that they will not be able to use culturally responsive instruction because of their own mainstream cultural backgrounds, which differ from the nonmainstream cultural backgrounds of their students. Fortunately, a finding common to all the reviews on culturally responsive instruction is that teachers of mainstream backgrounds, as well as teachers of diverse backgrounds, can successfully use culturally responsive instruction and teach students of diverse backgrounds (e.g., Osborne, 1996). For example, in my study of talk-story-like reading lessons, one of the teachers, Teacher LC, was a mainstream teacher. Although initially unsuccessful in conducting reading lessons with young Hawaiian students, Teacher LC learned after a year to use talk-story-like participation structures and to link her lessons to students' interests.

Although many studies demonstrate the positive contributions made by teachers of diverse backgrounds (King, 1993), the reality is that many students of diverse backgrounds, now and in the foreseeable future, will be taught by mainstream teachers (Au & Raphael, 2000). Teachers who share their students' cultural and linguistic backgrounds can often apply their cultural knowledge to establish positive relationships with students and to teach in a culturally responsive manner. However, teachers from mainstream backgrounds can definitely learn to do the same.

Good Teaching

A third misconception about culturally responsive instruction is the notion that good teaching is universal and looks the same across settings. To begin unpacking this misconception, let's consider this explanation from Gay (2000):

> Many educators still believe that good teaching transcends place, people, time, and context. They contend it has nothing to do with the class, race, gender, ethnicity, or culture of students and teachers. This attitude is manifested in the expression "Good teachers anywhere are good teachers everywhere." Individuals who subscribe to this belief fail to realize that their standards of "goodness" in teaching and learning are culturally determined and are not the same for all ethnic groups. The structures, assumptions, substance, and operations of conventional educational enterprises are European American cultural icons. (p. 22)

In other words, to advocate a universal concept of good teaching may actually amount to advocating teaching from a European American or mainstream perspective. It is true that certain general principles of good teaching seem to be widely applicable. Examples of such principles include building on students' prior knowledge and establishing positive relationships with students. However, the way these principles are instantiated may well differ depending on the cultural backgrounds of the students. For example, Delpit (1988) suggests that indirect requests reflecting mainstream notions of politeness (e.g., "it looks like someone forgot to put away the books") may work well in some classrooms. However, in classrooms with African American students accustomed to direct requests, teachers might find their indirect requests being ignored, because students have interpreted their words as nothing more than comments or observations. According to Delpit, a savvy teacher would state the request in direct terms (e.g., "put those books back on the shelf").

I suggest that the concept of culturally responsive instruction is applicable to *all* students, those of mainstream as well as diverse backgrounds. In both cases, the idea is that students have a better chance of experiencing academic success and of reaching high levels of literacy when instruction is responsive to their cultural backgrounds. The difference is that instruction consistent with the ways we usually "do school" is responsive to the cultural backgrounds of mainstream students but not to the cultural backgrounds of students of diverse backgrounds. The prevalence of culturally responsive instruction for mainstream students but not for students of diverse backgrounds may account to some degree for the gap between the literacy achievement of mainstream and nonmainstream students.

School settings tend to reflect the values of the society's dominant group or groups, because these are the groups that control the schools, as well as other major public institutions. Researchers have identified individualism and freedom as paramount values of the dominant group (Gollnick & Chinn, 2002), shaping the way teachers teach in most schools. These values were explored in research by Spindler and Spindler (1990). In terms of individualism, they found that the dominant or mainstream point of view assumes that people can control the outcomes in their lives through their own individual efforts. Individuals are believed to advance in society through their own hard work, determination, and perseverance. Competition is viewed as a healthy process that ensures the survival of the fittest, and success is measured in material terms, such as through the acquisition of money and material goods. Freedom is seen in terms of self-reliance and independence from others. Furthermore, people are seen as separate from nature and as having the right to control nature and use its resources for their own ends.

Although a belief in individualism and freedom can be held to varying degrees by members of subordinate or nonmainstream groups, contrasting values may be preferred (e.g., Spindler & Spindler, 1990; Howard, 1974). These contrasting values contribute to what I am calling a diverse worldview. Those who hold a diverse worldview believe that people's lives may be influenced by factors beyond their control, making it best to tackle life's challenges with the support of family, friends, and colleagues. By working in concert, the whole group—family, friends, community, or another social network—can move ahead together. Cooperation allows challenges to be met more easily, as members of the group all bring their thoughts and efforts to bear. What is important is the well-being of the group, especially the family, extended family, or kinship network. In short, an orientation toward the group replaces rugged individualism. Success is measured in terms of positive relationships with others and spiritual growth, rather than in terms of material wealth. People are not separate from nature, and the natural world is viewed with a sense of wonder for its beauty and power and the gifts it has to offer. People must respect and care for the environment if nature is to continue to provide for future generations. A greater emphasis is given to interdependence—with other people and with nature—than to freedom.

As you can see, though different from the values typically reflected in schools, the diverse worldview has many positive features. In the classroom, students are likely to benefit from a hybrid environment in which they have experiences with both kinds of values—competition and cooperation, individual effort and group effort, and so on. Our goal should be to create hybrid classroom settings that give students the advantage of learning the possible benefits of both sets of values.

In many multiethnic, multilingual school settings, however, teachers may still be teaching primarily according to dominant group values (cf. the observations of Fitzgerald, 1995). In these settings conflicts may develop because the teacher and students are unknowingly operating according to two different worldviews. For example, teachers who have not previously taught young Native Hawaiian students often find themselves scolding children for not "doing your own work." No matter how often the teacher reminds them to work independently, the children continue to ask other children for help and, in turn, to offer help to others. Teachers tend to interpret the children's behavior as disobedience, but this is a mistaken assumption. Research indicates that Native Hawaiian students may be raised in households with sibling caretaking, in which children learn to rely on older siblings for help and to care for younger siblings (Gallimore, Boggs, & Jordan, 1974). Native Hawaiian children raised with sibling caretaking enter school with the habit of seeking help from peers and near-peers. The children are also predisposed to help those around them, even without being asked.

From the perspective of culturally responsive instruction, the question is how this cultural strength—seeking and offering help to peers—can be built on in the classroom. Jordan (1985) suggests that teachers allow children to work in small groups, in which they will be able to teach and learn from one another. As in any peer-tutoring situation, children do need to be taught the difference between giving another child a hint and completing the work of another child. Once these peer work groups are running smoothly, teachers can introduce the idea of special times when children will be practicing doing their own work, without help from other children. Gradually, the children will learn to distinguish between these two situations, one based on the values of cooperation and group well-being, already familiar to them from the home, and the other based on the less familiar values of competition and individualism.

As you can see, culturally responsive instruction should involve giving students experiences with cooperation as well as competition, with working for the good of the group as well as for one's own benefit. Times when individual achievement is emphasized should certainly be present, but teachers should also be aware of the benefits of cooperative learning, which may build nicely on strengths gained at home.

Culturally responsive instruction is never intended to limit students' learning only to structures for participation that they find comfortable. Teachers must also take responsibility for giving students the ability to engage successfully in structures for participation that may initially be uncomfortable. Teachers in multiethnic classrooms act as mediators in helping students of diverse backgrounds acculturate to structures for participation consistent with mainstream values and expectations. The main idea is that every student should feel "at home" in the classroom during some time in the school day.

WORKSHOP APPROACHES USING A VARIETY OF GROUPINGS

We now turn to a discussion of how culturally responsive instruction, using a variety of participation structures, is naturally built into workshop approaches for the teaching of literacy. Many teachers are familiar with the readers' workshop (Raphael & Au, 1998), which is an application of literature-based instruction, and the writers' workshop (Calkins, 1994), an application of the process approach to writing. The metaphor of the workshop comes to us from Dewey (1944) and progressive education, although Dewey and his colleagues held views of literacy quite different from those of literature-based instruction and the process approach to writing. Imagine a workshop or studio space maintained by a group of painters. If you were to visit the workshop, you might see one artist sketching a design for a new work. Another might be stretching canvas on a frame. Still another might be mixing paint to just the right color and consistency with a palette knife. Another might be brushing a few dashes of color onto a nearly finished painting. Although all of the artists in the workshop are making paintings, each might be in a different phase of work. The same thing happens in the classroom when the teacher conducts a readers' workshop or a writers' workshop. Students will all be reading and writing, but they may be in different phases of reading and writing, such as reading silently or drafting a written response to literature.

Readers' and writers' workshops typically begin with whole-class minilessons. This is followed by time for students to read and write, on their own or with a partner. While students are reading and writing, the teacher works with small groups or with individuals. In the readers' workshop, students have time to engage in discussions of literature, which may take the form of literature circles guided by the teacher or book club discussions guided by the students themselves (McMahon, 1997). In the writers' workshop, students often participate in conferences with the teacher or a peer. Both the readers' and writers' workshops conclude with whole-class activities, community share in Book Club Plus (Raphael, Florio-Ruane, & George, 2001), and the Author's Chair (Graves & Hansen, 1983) in the writers' workshop.

In the sections that follow, I discuss the different participation structures that teachers can use within the readers' and writers' workshops. For each structure, I discuss (1) the goals for literacy learning that can be met with each structure, (2) how each structure relates to the two worldviews highlighted earlier, and (3) practical guidelines that may help teachers to use each structure successfully.

Whole-Class Lessons

Whole-class literacy lessons can be an effective and efficient means of teaching content, strategies, and skills needed by all students. Both readers' and writers' workshops typically begin with whole-class minilessons, brief lessons lasting perhaps 10 to 15 minutes (Routman, 1991). For example, during the readers' workshop the teacher can introduce the whole class to a comprehension strategy, such as determining importance. During the writers' workshop teachers can teach the concept of "show, not tell," so students learn to convey their ideas through specific details that call on all five senses.

Many teachers make use of whole-class lessons particularly at the beginning of the year, so that they can familiarize students with the routines to be followed. For example, Pat Nakanishi, a sixth-grade teacher in a multiethnic classroom in Hawaii, launched the readers' workshop in her classroom by reading a novel aloud to the students (Nakanishi, personal communication, November 20, 2002). She taught students to compose different kinds of written responses to literature after each chapter was read aloud. Written responses taught included making personal connections, expressing one's feelings about the text, and walking in the character's shoes (imagining what it would be like to be the character). In addition to teacher modeling, whole-class lessons give the teacher an opportunity to present students with examples of other students' work, which can serve as positive examples. Nakanishi's students were prepared through whole-class instruction to complete written responses independently, an ability they would need when they moved into book clubs composed of four to six students, with each small group reading a different novel.

Whole-class instruction typically includes a significant component of teacher talk, with student participation being conducted according to the teacher-initiation, student-response, teacher-evaluation (IRE) structure (Mehan, 1979). The IRE structure, in which students are singled out to respond one at a time, is consistent with a mainstream worldview oriented toward individual achievement and competition. However, whole-class lessons can also be constructed to draw on elements of a worldview oriented toward the well-being of the group and cooperation. This can happen if the teacher uses whole-class lessons as a time to bring the students together as a community of learners, as in the community-share component of Book Club Plus (Raphael & Goatley, 1997). During community share, representatives share, with the whole class, what their book club discussed during their meeting that day.

Whole-class lessons usually require students to learn at the same pace and to conform to the same expectations for behavior. These expectations for conformity mean that teachers tend to rely on the IRE pattern to keep the students under tight control. The IRE pattern may create management problems for the teacher in classrooms in which students have been taught at home to value cooperation and working for the benefit of the group. Some students may feel that responding in front of the whole class is a form of showing off, bragging, or putting oneself above others. Their discomfort with the situation may lead students toward disruptive behavior. Thus, rather than being the easiest way of managing a class, whole-class lessons may become the most difficult, especially for novice teachers. This is why successful teachers in multiethnic, multilingual classrooms often use whole-class instruction judiciously, such as for minilessons. Teachers then move students into small-group instruction, in which there are usually many more opportunities for students to participate productively and for teachers to tailor instruction to meet individual students' needs as literacy learners.

To encourage the active involvement of all students during whole-class lessons, teachers in multiethnic, multilingual classrooms will want to be aware of moving away from the IRE structure. An alternative procedure involves letting students work in pairs to discuss their ideas first. One member of each pair then shares the ideas generated with the whole class. The next time around, the partner who did not share earlier has the responsibility of presenting the pair's ideas to the class. This procedure allows students to rehearse their ideas with a partner before sharing in front of the whole class. It also encourages participation by every student in the class, without individuals feeling that they have been singled out.

Teacher-Led Small-Group Lessons

In the readers' and writers' workshops, teachers usually conduct lessons with flexible skill groups. A flexible skill group is formed of students who all can benefit from instruction in a particular concept, strategy, or skill. For example, in a writers' workshop conducted in a second-grade classroom, the teacher conducted a lesson with a group of six students who all were having difficulty thinking of good titles for their stories. The teacher used one child's story as an example, demonstrating through a think-aloud how she would arrive at a title, telling what the story was about in an interesting way (e.g., "The Day I Caught My First Fish," rather than "Going Fishing"). The children took turns reading their stories aloud, and the teacher guided the group to make suggestions to help each member of the small group to think of a good title.

Teacher-led small-group lessons provide students with many opportunities to respond and to receive recognition for their efforts from both the teacher and peers. During the readers' workshop, small-group lessons can be times at which the students work together, under the teacher's guidance, to construct the theme of the text and to make their own personal connections to literature (Au, 1992). Small-group lessons often provide teachers with the most valuable instructional time, both to promote language and literacy development and to establish positive relationships with students. In a large group, the teacher must try to involve many students, so each student's response is usually quite brief. In small-group lessons, the teacher can ask questions that allow students to speak at length, and students can express more complex ideas in these extended responses. This time for students to develop ideas in a deeper and more thoughtful manner is especially important for promoting higher level thinking with text, as illustrated in the earlier example of the discussion of *Annie and the Old One*.

With students of diverse backgrounds, teachers will find it effective to structure small-group lessons following the experience–text–relationship (ETR) approach (Au, Carroll, & Scheu, 2001). In this approach, teachers help students to draw on prior knowledge or experiences related to the text, guide students point-by-point through reading of the text, and then have students draw relationships between text ideas and their own experiences. Through these lessons, students of diverse backgrounds come to see that literature contains lessons relevant to their own lives. This message is particularly important for students whose families engage in forms of literacy that do not emphasize the reading of books (cf. Guerra, 1998). During small-group lessons, teachers have the chance to help students make personal connections to books and literature.

Teachers may also use small-group lessons to promote the application of comprehension strategies introduced in whole-class lessons. Taylor, Pearson, Clark, and Walpole (2000) discovered that effective teachers in schools in low-income communities do not just provide students with explicit instruction in strategies. Rather, these teachers cue students to apply the strategies during real reading. During small-group lessons, teachers can observe students' reading performance closely and spot opportunities when students should be using comprehension strategies. They can cue students to apply these strategies until students are able to do so consistently on their own.

How small is a small group? In my experience, a small group should have no more than about six students. Groups larger than six do not work as well, because some students find it easy to avoid contributing. In groups of six or fewer, everyone usually feels obliged to make a contribution, and a lack of participation on the part of any student is readily noticed and remedied by the teacher.

As in whole-class lessons, teachers must continue to attend to issues of turn taking and pacing. Small-group, teacher-led discussions can reinforce mainstream values of competition and individual achievement when the teacher conducts these lessons following the IRE. However, if the teacher allows students to speak when they have something to say, instead of tightly controlling turn taking, small-group lessons become consistent with a worldview oriented toward cooperation and the well-being of the group. To establish a collaborative tone to the lessons, teachers strive for a conversational tone in discussions, avoiding the IRE pattern much of the time and allowing students to determine when they will speak.

Some students have ideas to offer but do not know how to enter the conversation on their own, particularly if it is fast paced. If the teacher sees that a student wants to speak but has not been able to jump into the discussion, the teacher can make a space for the student by quieting the group. For example, the teacher might say, "Excuse me, let's stop for a moment to see if Cheryl has anything to add. Cheryl, do you have an idea to share?" Students such as Cheryl realize that their contributions are valued, and over time they will gain the confidence and skill to enter the discussion on their own.

Student-Led Small Groups

Student-led small groups, in contrast to those led by the teacher, serve the purpose of allowing students to gain independence in expressing their ideas. An example of student-led small groups is seen in the book clubs in Book Club Plus (Raphael, Florio-Ruane, & George, 2001). Students prepare for the meeting of their book club by reading the assigned chapter of the novel and drafting a written response, including questions or issues for discussion. Another purpose of student-led small groups is to foster the student-to-student exchange of ideas, with little or no scaffolding by the teacher. Students develop their ability to participate in the literate community and to relate to peers, often becoming skillful at managing interactions, elaborating on the responses of others, and drawing quiet members into the conversation.

Student-led small groups can be organized in a manner that fosters the development of these social interactional skills, in keeping with a worldview oriented toward the well-being of the group and cooperation. This orientation can be supported when the teacher guides students to set the ground rules to be followed during small-group discussions. For example, the fourth graders in Torry Montes's class agreed that everyone should participate and that shy students would be invited to join the conversation (Montes & Au, 2003). Rules such as these promote collaboration rather than competition among students within the group and help to prevent one or two students from dominating the conversation.

Student-led small groups in the form of book clubs can be used to promote higher level thinking about text. Teachers can take a number of steps to enhance students' ability to engage in thoughtful discussions about novels and so make good use of the time in book clubs. Teachers should make sure all students have access to the text, for example, by having struggling readers engage in partner reading or giving them access to a listening center in which they can hear the book on audiotape or CD. Teachers need to make sure that students know how to prepare written responses by providing whole-class instruction along the lines followed by Pat Nakanishi. In general, teachers should model the kinds of comments students might make about the text, such as offering interpretations or making personal connections, as well as giving students help with learning how to ask open-ended questions. Teachers can have students observe and comment on live or videotaped book club discussions so that students see the difference between productive and unproductive conversations about literature.

Pairs, Partners, and Peer Tutoring

I seldom observe teachers having students work in pairs. However, this participation structure can be highly valuable. The use of pairs or partners is usually associated with the diverse worldview and the value of cooperation rather than competition. Because many students in multiethnic, multilingual classrooms find it comfortable to learn from a peer, this structure provides students with a way to rehearse their answers and to gain knowledge in a low-stakes, nonthreatening environment. Students are more likely to take risks with language and literacy when their audience is just another student rather than a whole class, a small group, or the teacher. With only two participants, all but the most recalcitrant student is likely to be actively involved, with numerous opportunities for participation.

As part of the readers' workshop, children in the primary grades can discuss with a partner a story read aloud by the teacher. Older students can discuss chapters in a novel with a partner. As Cole (2003) points out, it is easy to enter a discussion of literature when the only competition is one other person.

Teachers can also use partner work to build students' independence in the use of comprehension strategies as a step between whole-group guided discussion and individual, independent work (Raphael, Highfield, & Au, 2006). In this context, pair or partner work has an important place in the gradual release of responsibility. Too often, teachers provide lessons in strategies and skills and then expect students to use the strategy on their own. For teachers in all classrooms, and especially multiethnic ones, this can be an unrealistic expectation, especially for struggling readers and writers. When students work with partners, they can discuss the strategy and how it is to be applied, and they can learn together. After completing a number of tasks with partners, students will be better prepared to work on their own.

As part of the writers' workshop, students may engage in peer conferences. Peer conferences may take place for the purposes of planning, especially for identifying a topic. Later, one student may read a first draft to another student to get ideas for revision. Peer editing conferences can occur as well, with students following a checklist of skills drawn from minilessons the teacher has conducted. The teacher may appoint peer editors, but the students who have a good command of Standard English spelling, punctuation, and grammar are often known to the class and sought after anyway. The teacher may want to designate an area for peer conferences (a table and chairs off to one side of the room, or a corner away from where other students are working) so that the ensuing conversations do not disturb others. A chart with the steps to be followed in peer conferences can be posted in the area, and checklists or other forms to be completed during the conference can be kept nearby.

Teachers in multiethnic, multilingual classrooms should adopt the attitude that the room is filled with teachers. Not only other adults, but also each student in the class, is a potential teacher. This attitude is important in multiethnic classrooms in which there are many struggling readers and writers, because the teacher will never have enough time to provide each of these learners with all the help needed. Some of that help must come from other students. Teachers sometimes wonder whether peer tutoring may be detrimental to the academic progress of capable students. Studies suggest that peer tutoring is beneficial to the learning of both the tutor and the target student. Peer tutoring helps to build the community of learners by showing students that they can and should contribute to the progress of others as readers and writers.

A caution is that teachers must also give proficient students ample opportunity to engage with challenging texts and literacy tasks. For this reason, it may be important to vary the basis for assigning students to work with partners. At times it may be beneficial to form pairings that consist of a proficient reader and a struggling reader for the purposes of peer tutoring. At other times, pairings might match students who are similar in terms of reading proficiency, so that proficient students have the chance to address challenges at their own instructional level and struggling students have the chance to gain independence.

Individual or Independent Work Time

What about time for students to work on their own? The ability to complete academic tasks independently is valued in school settings that are oriented toward individual achievement and competition and that emphasize standardized or state tests. Realistically speaking, to meet school expectations, students in multilingual, multiethnic classrooms do need to learn to work on their own and to demonstrate their academic knowledge without relying on others.

The key to successful independent work time is to make sure students are well prepared to complete their work successfully. In a kindergarten classroom I observed one March, the teacher began each day with a minilesson. Then she placed the children in pairs and had them discuss with their partners what they planned to write about. The children who knew what they wanted to write about returned to their seats to start, while the few who had not identified a topic remained on the carpet to speak with the teacher. After she had attended to these children, the teacher made a quick circuit of the classroom, checking on the whole class. A card with the letters of the alphabet was taped at each child's place, and children referred to these cards as they wrote. The teacher had taught children to say a word slowly, to peel off the initial consonant sound, and to look for the letter that could be used to represent it. At this point in the year, most of the children could use a combination of drawing and initial consonants to put their messages down on paper. The teacher called the few children who still needed help with this task to work with her at a table to one side of the classroom. I noticed that she guided the children but did not do any of the writing for them. Some of the other children went up to the front of the room to refer to charts listings the names of all the children in the class; commonly used words such as *mother, father, brother*, and *sister*; and action words such as *running, playing*, and *swimming*.

During the 30 minutes of writing time, most children composed stories several sentences long. I knew this was quite an accomplishment, because few children in this class had attended preschool. Several had never used a pencil or crayon before coming to kindergarten.

During a discussion following my observation, I learned that the teacher had used minilessons to teach the children the elements to be included in their stories, such as characters, setting, and action. She had started the year by helping the children who had some knowledge of letter sounds to use initial consonant sounds to represent words. These children served as examples to others at their tables. Slowly but surely, the teacher had worked her way through the class until only two children still needed her support to draft their messages. At the same time, the teacher had worked with the children to develop the lists at the front of the room and had taught them to refer to the lists when they were unsure about how to spell a word. As you can see, the teacher made sure that the children were provided with a great deal of scaffolding, so that they gradually came to meet her expectations for independent writing. She used a combination of whole-class minilessons, partner work, small-group instruction, and individual assistance to support children.

Teachers in multiethnic, multilingual classrooms must be careful about making assumptions, even about independent activities that seem to involve straightforward procedures, such as sustained silent reading (SSR). SSR has the purpose of promoting students' interest in reading. During SSR, students read books of their own choosing. However, some students have not had the opportunity to develop their tastes and interests as readers and do not know how to find books they will enjoy reading. For example, a Native Hawaiian fifth-grade student told me during an interview that he would go to the library and "grab any book." This particular community did not have a public library or any stores where children's books were sold. For many families, children's books may be a luxury that is difficult to afford. Reyes (1991) observed that two girls with Southeast Asian backgrounds did not know how to choose books and consequently did not benefit from the time set aside for SSR. Precious time for independent reading was wasted because their teacher did not realize that they needed help selecting appropriate books.

Teachers can help students find books they will enjoy by conducting an interest inventory, by giving book talks and encouraging students to do the same, and by showing students how to find books they will enjoy. Teachers in multiethnic classrooms who want to make a strong impression on reluctant readers should consider lending these students books to read from their own personal collections. Students appreciate such gestures of understanding and caring from their teachers.

Philips (1983) provides another insight about individual work time. She observed that Native American students used this time to approach the teacher for help with their work. These students preferred to receive assistance from the teacher individually and in private, rather than during whole-class or small-group lessons. Her study suggests that teachers in multiethnic classrooms may want to make themselves available for individual conferences with students at some time during the school day. The teacher may have students sign up for these conferences in advance, as during the writers' workshop, or students may simply come over to the teacher's desk when no other student is there.

In short, teachers in multiethnic, multilingual classrooms have the challenge of organizing to create a place for these five participation structures over the course of a week, if not a day. Teachers who conduct literacy instruction within the context of readers' and writers' workshops will find that these approaches readily provide opportunities for all five structures. A variety of participation structures is necessary if students of diverse cultural backgrounds are to engage successfully in literacy learning, at least part of the time. Some structures will likely be comfortable for students at the beginning of the school year, whereas others may require time and practice. As the year progresses, teachers enable students to participate effectively in structures that may initially have been unfamiliar or uncomfortable. Teachers achieve this goal by explaining the rules for different structures, by giving students reasons that these structures are being used, by modeling appropriate behaviors, and by coaching students in the use of these behaviors. The opportunities for literacy learning available to students of diverse backgrounds increase as they begin to engage successfully in all the structures for participation commonly found in school, those consistent with a worldview oriented toward competition, as well as with a worldview oriented toward cooperation.

CONCLUSION

This chapter focused on culturally responsive instruction in multiethnic, multilingual classrooms. I began by addressing assumptions shared by advocates of this approach, which aims to improve students' literacy learning by building on strengths they bring from the home. The key characteristics of culturally responsive instruction were addressed, including the idea that this approach does not require an exact one-to-one match between characteristics of students' home cultures and classroom practices. Rather, I suggested that teachers in multiethnic classrooms should be aware of two contrasting worldviews, one based on mainstream values of competition and individual achievement and the other based on the values of cooperation and the well-being of the group emphasized by many diverse cultural groups. To implement culturally responsive instruction, teachers will want to provide students with learning opportunities within a variety of participation structures, taking care to ensure that these structures reflect both worldviews. I suggested that teachers look to the readers' workshop and the writers' workshop as frameworks that already incorporate a variety of participation structures involving the whole class, small teacher-led groups, small student-led groups, pairs and partners, and individual work. The idea is to allow students to learn literacy in school through participation structures already familiar to them from the home, while at the same time teaching them to learn within previously unfamiliar participation structures. Every student in a multiethnic, multilingual classroom should feel "at home" during some part of the school day. Building from this base, students can gradually gain the ability to participate in new structures and attain proficiency as readers and writers. Culturally responsive instruction aims to give students the best of both worlds, showing respect for their home cultures and languages while preparing students to take advantage of opportunities offered by the larger society.

REFERENCES

Au, K. (1981). Comprehension-oriented reading lessons. *Educational Perspectives, 20*(1), 13–15.

Au, K. H. (1992). Constructing the theme of a story. *Language Arts, 69*(2), 106–111.

Au, K. H. (2001). Culturally responsive instruction as a dimension of new literacies. *Reading Online, 4*(8). Retrieved November 16, 2008, from *http://www.readingonline.org/newliteracies/lit_index.asp?HREF=au/index.html.*

Au, K. (2007). Culturally responsive instruction: Application to multiethnic classrooms. *Pedagogies, 2*(1), 1–18.

Au, K. H., Carroll, J. H., & Scheu, J. A. (2001). *Balanced literacy instruction: A teacher's resource book* (2nd ed.). Norwood, MA: Christopher-Gordon.

Au, K. H., & Kawakami, A. J. (1994). Cultural congruence in instruction. In E. R. Hollins, J. E. King, & W. Hayman (Eds.), *Teaching diverse populations: Formulating a knowledge base* (pp. 5–23). Albany: State University of New York Press.

Au, K. H., & Mason, J. M. (1981). Social organizational factors in learning to read: The balance of rights hypothesis. *Reading Research Quarterly, 17*(1), 115–152.

Au, K. H., & Raphael, T. E. (2000). Equity and literacy in the next millennium. *Reading Research Quarterly, 35*(1), 170–188.

Burbules, N. C., & Torres, C. A. (2000). Globalization and education: An introduction. In N. C. Burbules & C. A. Torres (Eds.), *Globalization and education: Critical perspectives* (pp. 1–26). New York: Routledge.

Calkins, L. M. (1994). *The art of teaching writing* (2nd ed.). Portsmouth, NH: Heinemann.

Cole, A. D. (2003). *Knee to knee, eye to eye: Circling in on comprehension.* Portsmouth, NH: Heinemann.

Delpit, L. (1988). The silenced dialogue: Power and pedagogy in educating other people's children. *Harvard Educational Review, 58,* 280–298.

Dewey, J. (1944). *Democracy and education: An introduction to the philosophy of education.* New York: Free Press.

Fitzgerald, J. (1995). English-as-a-second-language reading instruction in the United States: A research review. *Journal of Reading Behavior, 27,* 115–152.

Gallimore, R., Boggs, J. W., & Jordan, C. (1974). *Culture, behavior and education: A study of Hawaiian-Americans.* Beverly Hills, CA: Sage.

Gay, G. (2000). *Culturally responsive teaching: Theory, research, and practice.* New York: Teachers College Press.

Gollnick, D. M., & Chinn, P. C. (2002). *Multicultural education in a pluralistic society* (6th ed.). Upper Saddle River, NJ: Merrill Prentice-Hall.

Graves, D., & Hansen, J. (1983). The Author's Chair. *Language Arts, 60*(2), 176–183.

Guerra, J. C. (1998). *Close to home: Oral and literate practices in a transnational Mexicano community.* New York: Teachers College Press.

Heath, S. B. (1983). *Ways with words: Language, life, and work in communities and classrooms.* Cambridge, UK: Cambridge University Press.

Howard, A. (1974). *Ain't no big thing.* Honolulu: University of Hawaii Press.

Johnson, D. W., Johnson, R. T., et al. (1993). *New circles of learning: Cooperation in the classroom and school.* Washington, DC: Association for Supervision and Curriculum Development.

Jordan, C. (1985). Translating culture: From ethnographic information to educational program. *Anthropology and Education Quarterly, 16,* 105–123.

King, S. H. (1993). The limited presence of African-American teachers. *Review of Educational Research, 63*(2), 115–149.

Ladson-Billings, G. (1994). *The dreamkeepers: Successful teachers of African American children.* San Francisco: Jossey-Bass.

Ladson-Billings, G. (1995). Toward a theory of culturally relevant pedagogy. *American Educational Research Journal, 32*(3), 465–491.

Manyak, P. C. (2001). Participation, hybridity, and carnival: A situated analysis of a dynamic literacy practice in a primary-grade English immersion class. *Journal of Literacy Research, 33*(3), 423–465.

McMahon, S. I. (1997). Book clubs: Contexts for students to lead their own discussions. In S. I. McMahon & T. E. Raphael (Eds.), *The book club connection: Literacy learning and classroom talk* (pp. 89–106). New York: Teachers College Press.

Mehan, H. (1979). *Learning lessons: Social organization in the classroom.* Cambridge, MA: Harvard University Press.

Miles, M. (1985). *Annie and the old one.* New York: Little, Brown Young Readers.

Moll, L. C. (1992). Literacy research in community and classroom: A sociocultural approach. In R. Beach, J. L. Green, M. L. Kamil, & T. Shanahan (Eds.), *Multidisiplinary perspectives on literacy research* (pp. 211–244). Urbana, IL: National Conference on Research in English and National Council of Teachers of English.

Montes, T. H., & Au, K. H. (2003). Book Club in a fourth-grade classroom: Issues of ownership and response. In R. L. McCormack & J. R. Paratore (Eds.), *After early intervention, then what? Teaching struggling readers in grade 3 and beyond* (pp. 70–93). Newark DE: International Reading Association.

Orellana, M. F., Reynolds, J., Dorner, L., & Meza, M. (2003). In other words: Translating or "para-phrasing" as a family literacy practice in immigrant households. *Reading Research Quarterly, 38*(1), 12–34.

Osborne, A. B. (1996). Practice into theory into practice: Culturally relevant pedagogy for students we have marginalized and normalized. *Anthropology and Education Quarterly, 27*(3), 285–314.

Perie, M., Grigg, W., & Donahue, P. (2005). *The nation's report card: Reading 2005* (Document No. 2006-451). Washington DC: U.S. Department of Education, National Center for Educational Statistics.

Philips, S. U. (1983). *The invisible culture: Communication in classroom and community on the Warm Springs Indian reservation.* New York: Longman.

Raphael, T. E., & Au, K. H. (Eds.). (1998). *Literature-based instruction: Reshaping the curriculum.* Norwood, MA: Christopher-Gordon.

Raphael, T. E., Florio-Ruane, S., & George, M. (2001). Book Club Plus: A conceptual framework to organize literacy instruction. *Language Arts, 79*(2), 159–168.

Raphael, T. E., & Goatley, V. J. (1997). Classrooms as communities: Features of community share. In S. I. McMahon & T. E. Raphael (Eds.), *The book club connection: Literacy learning and classroom talk* (pp. 26–46). New York: Teachers College Press.

Raphael, T. E., Highfield, K., & Au, K. (2006). *QAR now: A powerful and practical framework that develops comprehension and higher-level thinking in all students.* New York: Scholastic.

Reyes, M. (1991, April). *The "one size fits all" approach to literacy.* Paper presented at the annual meeting of the American Educational Research Association, Chicago.

Routman, R. (1991). *Invitations.* Portsmouth, NH: Heinemann.

Spindler, G., & Spindler, L. (1990). *The American cultural dialogue and its transmission.* London: Falmer Press.

Taylor, B. M., Pearson, P. D., Clark, K., & Walpole, S. (2000). Effective schools and accomplished teachers: Lessons about primary-grade reading instruction in low-income schools. *Elementary School Journal, 101*(2), 121–165.

Watson, K. A. (1974). Transferable communicative routines: Strategies and group identity in two speech events. *Language in Society, 4*, 53–72.

CHAPTER 3

Explicit Language Instruction
A Key to Constructing Meaning

SUSANA DUTRO
LORI HELMAN

Ms. Wright shows an illustrated book about the farm to her first-grade students. "The tractor went up and down the rows of corn," she reads. Later in the morning, she checks in with her students about the story and finds that at least one of her English learners has an image of the tractor bouncing up and down like a ball on the ground.

Ramón, a fourth-grade student, studies his reading passage intently to understand the sentence, "The cat knew nothing besides hunting birds and mice." He wonders, "Wouldn't it be dangerous for the birds and mice to be beside the cat?"

The previous two vignettes demonstrate the importance of a deep knowledge of English vocabulary and grammatical structures in order for students to be successful in their literacy learning. Literacy achievement in English is highly dependent on a rich language foundation that allows students to comprehend the words, sentences, and passages of the texts they are reading and writing. This chapter examines the complexity of language development for English learners, helps teachers gain insights into their students' language abilities, and provides them with ways to incorporate powerful instructional routines for teaching and practicing essential language skills.

Over the past two decades there has been a tremendous rise in the number of English learners in U.S. elementary schools, increasing from 2 million students in 1993–1994 to 3 million in 1999–2000; in the 2003–2004 school year, 13.3% of enrolled elementary public school students were classified as limited English proficient (LEP; Strizek, Pittsonberger, Riordan, Lyter, & Orlofsky, 2006). Because of this growth, many teachers now serve students who are learning English as a new language. Each teacher deserves support in understanding the skills and needs of his or her students and in using effective teaching strategies. Today, vast majorities of English learners are taught to read using the same instructional materials as their native English-speaking peers and are held to the same achievement expectations. Often, students are assessed on standardized tests in English regardless of their level of English proficiency and after only a short period of time in American schools (Solórzano, 2008). Increased accountability measures add pressure to accelerate achievement in English. For all students to meet high academic expectations, it is critical that teachers have a wide range of tools that help them match instruction to students' current skills and push students ahead to meet established benchmarks.

English learners face a daunting task. While learning grade-level subject-matter content, they must gain a multifaceted knowledge of the English language, including:

- Phonology, rhythm, cadence
- Vocabulary (basic, general utility, low utility/content specific)
- Syntax (word order)
- Language forms (structures, verb tenses, grammar)
- Functions of language use for both social and academic purposes
- Formal and informal discourse styles for speaking and writing
- Cultural contexts

Students learning English as a second language must learn every word and sentence combination that native English speakers have spent thousands of hours internalizing during their early childhoods. This must be done in a condensed time frame, and often only during the hours a student is in school. Additionally, students must learn the content language being taught in their reading and writing materials. This includes not only the conceptual and concrete language taught in the current year but also the foundational vocabulary taught in each previous year. Consider what it takes to learn abstract concepts such as "plot," ideas such as "loyalty," and techniques such as "predicting" in a second language.

English is rich in idioms and figurative language. English learners must learn both the literal and idiomatic meanings of hundreds of sayings and expressions that native English speakers use on a daily basis, such as "knowing the ropes" or "put your best foot forward," which pepper everyday speech, literature, and informational text. They must do this while keeping pace with native English-speaking peers who are rapidly increasing their knowledge of the English language inside and outside the classroom and applying that knowledge to subject-matter learning.

In examining research on the reading performance of English learners, Genesee, Lindholm-Leary, Saunders, and Christian (2005) found that students with well-developed oral skills in English experience greater success in English reading. National data highlight the fact that a disturbing number of students learning English do poorly in literacy tasks requiring academic language proficiency; for example, results from the National Assessment of Educational Progress show that 72% of LEP students are performing below the basic level on the fourth-grade reading assessment (U.S. Department of Education, 2003). And the gap in achievement between English learners and peers who are native speakers of Standard American English persists through the secondary schools. This has led many to conclude that quality content instruction in English is not sufficient to ensure that English learners gain academic proficiency (Saunders, Foorman, & Carlson, 2006). Without explicit instruction in English and how it works—vocabulary, word usage, grammatical features, and syntactical structures—the most effective support for content learning may be insufficient. Academic achievement will be accelerated when students are proficient in English. We suggest that, like other complex learning, this requires systematic and explicit instruction. Educators and districts report a continuing need for cohesive information about how to plan, teach, and monitor progress in meeting the needs of their linguistically diverse students (Datnow, Lasky, Stringfield, & Teddlie, 2005).

This chapter is designed to provide background information about the importance of academic language instruction and to help educators design effective programs to teach English learners the language that they will not learn outside of schools, may not be taught in other subject areas, and need to be able to use every day.

LEARNING ENGLISH

How quickly and efficiently an English learner progresses in developing proficiency in a second language depends on a number of factors, including his or her level of language and literacy development in the primary language, time spent in U.S. schools, type of instructional program, age, individual experiences, and, very importantly, *quality of instruction* (Genesee et al., 2005; Geva, 2006). It is common for many students to have acquired a great deal of oral English through experiences in school and the community and to appear fluent. They have gleaned some important vocabulary, grammatical structures, conventions, and rules of discourse from many interactions. But these students often have tremendous gaps in knowledge of how the English language works.

Academic Language

As students move up through the grades, the language demands increase rapidly. Sentence constructions are longer and more complex, vocabulary less concrete. Problems in reading and writing in the later grades often stem from limited vocabulary and syntactic knowledge of English (Garcia, 2000). Even children who are quite skilled orally in social situations can have these gaps. They are missing a deep and rich vocabulary and proficiency in the structures and vocabulary needed to compare, describe, predict, and persuade in English; students are unable to easily select a word appropriate to an academic topic they are discussing. In short, they need to develop the language to express their conceptual thinking—the language of academic success. Cummins (2003) contrasts academic language proficiency with conversational fluency, based on the use of less frequent vocabulary words, complex syntax, and abstract expressions unlikely to be heard in everyday conversations. Without this deep understanding of English, students are constrained academically, frustrating themselves and their teachers. This can be especially problematic in how we understand students of immigrant backgrounds who have attended U.S. schools for years, appear acculturated, and are comfortable using English in most settings. These students do not on the surface appear to need specific instruction in language. However, their verbal fluency often masks their instructional needs.

Who Are English Learners?

English learners may be characterized by a number of different profiles—recent arrivals, long-term learners, and learners of standard forms of English. Recent arrivals to the United States may bring strong literacy skills in their home languages, and these languages may be quite similar to, or very different from, the English writing system. Other recent immigrants may bring very limited literacy skills in their home languages and little to no formal schooling experiences. Long-term English learners may include students who have lived their entire lives in the United States. Some of these students possess strong English language and literacy skills with a few gaps. Others have low literacy skills, and although they seem to have strong oral English skills, there are many holes in their academic language repertoires. Finally, learners of standardized English include students who are primarily English speaking but have been designated Limited English Proficient (LEP) or English-only students who speak a nonstandard dialect. The range of skills and background experiences of students must be taken into account when considering the types of instructional programs that will be most effective with students learning English.

Key Ideas in Understanding Students' English Language Development

Before describing our suggestions for how to structure explicit language instruction in elementary classrooms, we would like to share several foundational concepts in language development theory on which our ideas rest. These include the multiple facets of language that students are required to internalize and the importance of both instruction and opportunities for practice when learning a new language.

Language may be thought of as being composed of many different aspects: (1) phonology, how the individual sounds are expressed in a language; (2) morphology, the way meaningful chunks make up individual words; (3) syntax, how words are put together into sentences; (4) semantics, how meaning is communicated; and (5) pragmatics, the social/interaction aspects of language (Trumbull & Farr, 2005). Much of how we learn to speak our home language happens effortlessly and almost invisibly. It is only when we manipulate a new language that many of these subcomponents of language take center stage; for example, when we have difficulty sounding like native speakers (phonology), putting words in the correct order (syntax), or using the appropriate language in a certain social context (pragmatics). Each language also has a lexicon, or corpus of words, that it contains. Knowing the meanings of these individual words, or vocabulary knowledge, is another important component of language development that continues to grow throughout our lifetimes.

Another way to look at language development is through the model of *communicative competence* (e.g., Canale & Swain, 1980). Communicative competence implies that a person is able to effectively use language for specific purposes in particular settings, using the words, the grammar, the social knowledge, and the discourse competence to put all of the linguistic information together. For example, communicative competence might be demonstrated by ordering food at a restaurant, by discussing a book you read, or by writing a paper on the migration patterns of geese. Communicative competence will likely look very different depending on the task at hand. As educators, it is our goal to prepare students to demonstrate communicative competence with academic reading, writing, speaking, and listening tasks that match the expectations of the grade-level curriculum standards.

Many models of second-language acquisition exist that help us understand the complexity of learning a new language from various perspectives: cultural, social, cognitive, and linguistic (Trumbull & Farr, 2005). Research on effective instructional models for second-language acquisition is sorely lacking. In their review of the literature, Genesee and colleagues (2005) found only one empirical study examining the effects of instructional practice on students' oral English proficiency. They did, however, describe the self-perpetuating nature of English language development: The more students learn, the more they use what they know, and, in turn, the more possibilities exist for learning more through language interactions. Their research review also studied language use in and outside of school and found that there is little evidence that merely being exposed to English is a sufficient way for students to develop advanced levels of English language proficiency (Genesee et al., 2005). For this reason, explicit instruction to help students *learn*, as well as structured opportunities for them to *practice*, English are crucial for developing academic language proficiency with second-language learners.

STRUCTURING LANGUAGE LEARNING

Academic success depends on learning to read well. Learning to read well depends on rich language knowledge. Explicit language instruction helps ensure that English learners gain the knowledge they need to be academically successful. By academic success we mean that the reader must extract meaning and information from texts; evaluate evidence and relate it to other ideas and information; recognize and analyze textual conventions used in various genres; and use textual cues to interpret and infer authors' intentions. These academic benchmarks make it clear that achieving full proficiency in English includes far more than mere fluency in conversation or everyday uses of language. Proficiency means that students must know English well enough to be "fully competitive in academic uses of English with their age equivalent, native-speaking peers" (Hakuta, Butler, & Witt, 2000; p. 3).

According to Title III requirements, regardless of the type of program in which an English learner is enrolled, each student must receive instruction in English at his or her level of English proficiency, as well as meaningful access to grade-level academic content (*Castañeda v Pickard*, 1981). We know this, but how do we put it into practice?

Important questions surface concerning how to provide appropriate accommodations for students not yet academically proficient in English. There are several approaches to increasing success in subject-matter content taught in English. One short-term method is to incorporate sheltered instructional techniques to make the material understandable (cf. Echevarria, Vogt, & Short, 2000; Díaz-Rico & Weed, 2002). Another related strategy is to explicitly teach the academic language that students need to express content learning orally and in writing (Dutro & Moran, 2003).

We propose an *instructional blueprint for English learners* that provides a comprehensive view of instruction and outlines a model to ensure that English learners are taught appropriately *throughout* the day. In this model there are two purposes for instruction: English language development (ELD) and explicit language for content. Planning a lesson always begins with the end in mind: What is the purpose of communication, or the language function, to be practiced in the lesson? English-as-a-second-language instruction driven by the proficiency level of the student is taught during dedicated *Systematic ELD Instruction* time. Additionally, English is taught in the context of each subject area through *explicit language for content*. This language instruction is driven by the need of the content area—that is, the language that enables students to think, discuss, read, and write about the topic at hand. Comprehensible delivery ensures that content instruction is clear, sequential, and scaffolded.

The types of instruction outlined in the blueprint must be provided within an inclusive, culturally responsive learning environment that recognizes and builds on the value of the language, culture, and experiences of each student (see also Chapters 2 and 11, this volume). Each component of the instructional blueprint is essential to a well-designed program for English learners. None is sufficient on its own: Systematic ELD instruction supports success in content areas by strengthening language skills, but on its own it will not ensure meaningful access to the curriculum. Explicit language for content does not provide sufficient language instruction to ensure a solid foundation because it does not follow a scope and sequence of language skills and may leave gaps in language knowledge. In the rest of this chapter, we describe how the instructional blueprint provides a framework for explicit language and literacy instruction in elementary classrooms, and we present several sample activities.

FOCUSED APPROACH TO EXPLICIT LANGUAGE INSTRUCTION

A focused approach to explicit language instruction involves attention to three critical strands: functions, forms, and fluency. *Functions* of language are the tasks that learners must engage in as they use English purposefully (Halliday, 1973). These include social tasks such as participating in conversations or asking for directions, as well as academic tasks such as drawing conclusions or making generalizations. The *forms* of language are the discourse and grammatical tools necessary for communicating at many levels in English (Doughty & Williams, 1998). These tools include using the correct word order, subject–verb agreement, verb tenses, pronouns and articles, and so on. We refer to *fluency* as the accurate and fluent use of language that English learners develop when they have numerous opportunities to practice. Fluency is enhanced with clear modeling of vocabulary and language patterns, structured peer practice with the language being taught, and frequent and varied opportunities to apply the new language both orally and in writing.

Vocabulary knowledge can be considered a component of the language *tool*. Students need familiarity with a wealth of words in order to communicate in school settings. Some vocabulary words can be described as "brick" words—they are the words needed to talk about a topic (Dutro & Moran, 2003). Brick words range from basic to general use to highly specialized, such as the words *dry, arid*, and *evapotranspiration*. To continue with the construction metaphor, "mortar" is the functional language that is required to generate connected speech and print (Dutro & Moran, 2003). It is grammar in action and helps humans move beyond speaking in single words and phrases. Figure 3.1 presents examples of brick and mortar words and illustrates their importance within the focused approach.

Students need to be able to use functional, or mortar, words to express relationships and construct sentences. Mortar words and phrases are the parts of the sentence that organize the bricks to express an intended meaning. Mortar words and phrases may describe attributes or locations, such as *have, are usually, next to*; they may express actions, such as *is, was, weren't*; they may help us inquire, such as *what, when, why is*; and much more. Without the mortar, we have a list of vocabulary words (or a pile of bricks). Once we decide what we want to communicate, we use our knowledge of grammar and syntax to construct sentences and paragraphs that convey our meaning.

To understand brick and mortar words better, we examine a young readers' story that is included in the third-grade component of a common basal textbook. The text, *Seal Surfer*, tells the story of a relationship that develops between a boy and a seal in an ocean town over the course of several years (Foreman, 2003). In order to understand this story well, a student needs to know many basic brick words (e.g., *beach, grandson, seal, fish, sun, wind*, etc.), many general brick words (e.g., *injured, hunting, upward, plunged, surface*, etc.), and some specialized brick words (e.g., *mussels, Beethoven, corkscrewing, buffeted, quay*).

In addition to understanding the meaning of the words in the story, English learners also need to decipher complex syntactical structures that are included. Take, for example, the following sentence: "As he con-

Language Functions

Purposes for using language to:

- Perform cognitive tasks
- Express thinking orally and in writing
- Inform text structure (common are bolded below)
- Engage in social and academic conversation

Relevance to EL instruction:

What are some of the communicative purposes English learners must be able to navigate? What language functions do cognitive tasks require? What text structures must students comprehend?

- Participate in discussions
- Express social courtesies
- Give/follow directions
- Predict
- Express action and time relationships
- Express needs, likes, and feelings
- Draw conclusions
- Clarify
- Classify and compare/contrast
- Describe, explain, and elaborate
- Make generalizations
- Sequence
- Express cause/effect
- Proposition/ support
- Summarize

Language Tools

What language tools are needed to communicate for different purposes? What language is needed to comprehend text and express thinking orally and in writing?

Mortar	Bricks
Functional words and phrases in sentence structures that allow us to generate a range of statements and questions for different functions. Requires knowledge of grammatical features, syntax, conventions for formal/informal use, and the ability to use varied and complex sentences. A few examples:	**Topic-specific words** and phrases needed to talk about that topic. This vocabulary may include specific nouns and adjectives, verbs and adverbs related to a theme or subject. These words and phrases may be basic, general use, or specialized, such as:
would have liked to / has been / was beginning to / given that *are usually/tend to / may have been / didn't have/want/ know / in the case of*	*Basic: tree, elbow, art, force, shoes, skull, dry, donate* *General: debate, government, arid, empathy, mammal* *Specialized: War of Independence, incisor, germinate, archetype, integer, carburetor*

Instruction & Application

After analysis, how are language tools introduced, modeled, and practiced using I/We/You Do It? What opportunities for structured interaction are provided for students to practice the language they are learning? How are students supported in gaining oral and written fluency?

Goal: Accurate and fluent use of language	• Ease of comprehension (listening and reading) and production (speaking and writing) • Automaticity in reading and writing • Facility of language use for a wide range of purposes • Appropriateness of discourse style and register demanded by situation

FIGURE 3.1. A focused approach: Features of explicit language instruction. From Dutro (2008). Copyright 2008 by E.L. Achieve. Reprinted by permission.

centrated on watching her, the wave he was riding suddenly broke and plunged him headfirst off his board" (Foreman, 2003, p. 58). We see that, even focusing on a single sentence of the story, students are required to disentangle meaning not only from the numerous brick and mortar words but also from complex sentence structures and verb tenses. To comprehend the passage, students need to break the sentence into several simpler meaningful phrases, such as, "He concentrated on watching her. The wave broke (crashed). This caused him to plunge head first off of his board." Students need to know that a surfer can "ride" a wave, that this wave can "break" or crash, and that it can cause a person to be "plunged" deep into the water. Clearly, knowledge of the *forms* of language is critical to students' literacy achievement.

To be successful, students must first be able to accurately and automatically decode the text. They must have knowledge of the word meanings and be able to follow the sentence structure. Often, students need specialized background knowledge to make sense of a text, in this case, knowledge about the ocean, its waves, and the context of surfboarding. Students also must be motivated to read the text for a purpose, whether personal or academic. Teachers are wise to examine each text that is presented to English learners and consider what linguistic, academic, and motivational knowledge students will need to bring to the task.

Students bring a wide range of oral English knowledge with them to the classroom. This proficiency is often measured with a standardized assessment such as the Language Assessment Scales—Oral (LAS-O; DeAvila & Duncan, 1994) or the California English Language Development Test (CELDT; California Department of Education, 2003). Based on the results of their oral assessment, students may be classified at the beginning or early-intermediate proficiency level, the intermediate proficiency level, or the advanced proficiency level (California Department of Education, 1999). Table 3.1 provides an overview of some of the characteristics and instructional objectives for students at each of these levels of oral proficiency. As noted in Table 3.1, students progress from very limited expressive skills in English at the beginning level to an understanding of the subtleties and purposes of complex language use by the advanced proficiency level. One of the roles of the teacher is to facilitate students' language production across various levels of proficiency. In other words, teachers identify what language is essential for students to further develop their language proficiency. Teachers then find appropriate sentence frames to help students practice the topical language at increasingly more challenging linguistic levels based on students' capabilities in English. For example, while studying how to distinguish fact from opinion, a teacher might set up three linguistic structures to aid students at varying levels of English proficiency. To answer the question "What facts and opinions

TABLE 3.1. English Proficiency Levels and Objectives

Proficiency level	Characteristics	Objectives for student language use
Beginning to early intermediate	• Progress from having little receptive or productive English to a basic use • Have limited use of written English, primarily using high-frequency words and previously learned material • Need many repetitions and concrete experiences to internalize vocabulary, language patterns, and concepts	• Move from nonverbal to single-word or short-phrase responses to longer oral responses • Replicate language structures that have been taught and practiced, such as survival/functional vocabulary, present, progressive, or negative verbs and descriptive adjectives
Intermediate	• Comprehend information on familiar topics and can engage in expanded conversation • Can work independently with a variety of print • Can write basic information and extended responses, especially with sentence frames as scaffolds	• Develop longer oral and written responses • Build sentences with adjectives and adverbs • Work with compound sentences • Expand the use of verb tenses, including future, past, and perfect
Advanced	• Use English in complex academic arenas • Comprehend detailed information in abstract topics with limited contextual clues • Have advanced vocabulary knowledge • Recognize language subtleties in multiple contexts and for varied social and academic purposes	• Expand the use of verb tenses, including the past perfect and conditional tenses • Build complex sentences with transitional phrases and conjunctions, as well as prepositional phrases • As appropriate to developmental level, work with morphological layers of the language, including Greek and Latin roots

were presented in this book about wolves?", an advanced learner might be presented with the sentence frame: "In this book we learned the fact that _____ and the opinion that some hold that _____." (*In this book we learned the fact that wolves live in packs and the opinion that some hold that wolves are always hungry.*) An intermediate learner might be asked, "What are some facts and opinions about wolves?" "Facts about wolves are that they _____ and _____. Opinions about wolves are that they _____ and _____." (*Facts about wolves are that they live in packs and eat meat. Opinions about wolves are that they are always hungry and are very smart.*) A beginning/early-intermediate learner might be asked, "What is a fact about wolves? What do some people think about wolves?" "A fact is that _____. Some people think wolves _____." (*A fact is that wolves eat meat. Some people think wolves are mean.*) By scaffolding the language frames to match students' linguistic abilities, teachers provide all students the opportunities to engage in the academic content (fact vs. opinion) at a comprehensible level.

Another example of providing linguistic support and challenge to students at varying levels of proficiency is demonstrated in the following writing task for a cooking project. Students are asked to write a note about what they need to conduct the project. Advanced learners are provided with the sentence frame, "In order to make _____, we need the following items: _____." (*In order to make pancakes, we need the following items: flour, milk, and eggs.*) Intermediate learners are provided with the sentence frame, "We need to buy _____ to make _____." (*We need to buy flour, milk, and eggs to make pancakes.*) Beginning/early-intermediate learners are provided with the sentence frame, "We need _____ and _____." (*We need flour, milk, and eggs.*)

Some Essentials of Language Teaching

How do teachers structure their classroom lessons to help English learners access the content and also practice important language structures? First, clarify the purpose of the lesson. Consider whether the lesson is part of a Systematic ELD program or an example of explicit language for content. For example, a Systematic ELD lesson will progress along a scope and sequence of language skills determined by students' current level of proficiency, such as using prepositions *inside, outside*, and *next to*. An explicit-language-for-content lesson will focus on bridging students' English language knowledge with the demands of an upcoming lesson, such as learning the brick-and-mortar vocabulary associated with an informational text on electricity that students will read and write about. An explicit-language-for-content lesson may also focus on scaffolding the content so that students can understand given their current level of English proficiency, such as the teacher's helping students write a short biography of a favorite author. Depending on which type of lesson is being designed, the objectives will vary.

We share an example of an explicit-language-for-content lesson. One purpose of this type of lesson is to front-load language and background knowledge to help students meet the cognitive and linguistic demands of the upcoming content instruction. For this kind of lesson the teacher will most likely be working with instructional materials that have been adopted by the school to meet the academic standards in literacy. Let's say the lesson involves reading a nonfiction book about food chains and food webs. The teacher's manual points out that during this lesson students will learn about a common expository text structure—sequence and time relationships. To plan an explicit-language lesson that will help the students understand the forthcoming content instruction, the teacher first considers the function of the language in the content instruction: Will it be used to perform a cognitive task, to express thinking, to inform text structure, or to engage in academic conversation? In our current example, the purpose of the lesson is academic; the focus of the language being studied is sequence and time relationships (as evidenced within a text structure). Understanding that expository text frequently describes sequence and time relationships is an important concept for tackling new texts and will help students be more discerning readers and writers.

Next, the teacher examines the language demands of the lesson: What is the purpose or function of the language? To classify or compare characteristics, describe actions, show a sequence, express cause and effect, or support a proposition? In this case, it is to express sequence. In the analysis of the language demands, we need to start with the function, then move to the topic vocabulary. In the text on food chains and webs, students will need to know some key vocabulary that may be unfamiliar, such as *habitat, organism, predator*, and *prey*, or to understand new meanings for known words, such as *producer* or *consumer*. They will be asked to express the sequence of who eats what in what order, so sequencing words such as *first, second, third, next*, and so forth, will be very important. The teacher plans to front-load sentence frames such as "First, the _____ eats the _____. Second, the _____ eats the _____. Third, the _____ eats the _____. And so on." (*First the beetle eats the grass. Second, the small bird eats the beetle. Third, the hawk eats the small bird. And so on.*)

To implement an explicit-language lesson, teachers:

- Set the scene by engaging students in a meaningful context for language learning: "We will be finding out about how animals survive by finding the food they need to eat, and figuring out what happens first, second, and next."
- Link to prior knowledge by building on students' experiences or previous academic learning: "What animals have you seen or studied about? What do they eat? What eats them?"

- Teach and practice "brick" vocabulary: "A predator is the hunter, a prey what it catches to eat. The hawk is a predator of smaller birds and mice."
- Provide opportunities for students to practice the vocabulary: "Tell your partner about a predator and a prey that you know."
- Teach and practice language patterns: "Look at the chart we made about a food chain. Tell us what the animals eat in the order of smallest to biggest. First the _____ eats the _____. Second the eats the _____. And so on."
- Provide a real-life context for students to apply the new vocabulary and language patterns: "Draw a picture of a food chain. Write about what each animal eats underneath its picture. Share your chart with a friend."

To plan an explicit-language instruction lesson, consider following the format of "I do—We do—You do." Table 3.2 provides an overview of the components and their pacing. As noted in Table 3.2, the "I do" section of the lesson involves explicit teaching, during which time the teacher models and explains how to use the new language. The "We do" section allows students to practice the new language in a structured context, with close monitoring by the teacher. In the "You do" section of the lesson students work more independently to apply the language patterns in more natural contexts.

Tools for Explicit Language Instruction

Teachers need many tools in their repertoires to support them in conducting meaningful language instruction in literacy. In the next section, we outline three examples of teaching practices that are useful in delivering effective language lessons.

Visuals for Topic Vocabulary

One way to support students in reading and writing as they learn new vocabulary is to create a posted collection of topic vocabulary words matched with illustrative sketches called an *Illustrated Word Bank*. The purpose of Illustrated Word Banks is to comprehensibly teach vocabulary and concepts while creating a resource for students to use throughout ELD lessons on that topic. By connecting a visual to the vocabulary taught, teachers provide the context to help students remember new words. An example of an Illustrated Word Bank is a chart of common businesses in the community. In this business-oriented Illustrated Word Bank, there might be pictures of a department store, a music store, a jew-

TABLE 3.2. The Flow of a Lesson

Component	Pacing	Procedure
Setting the context	4–6 min	Set the scene by engaging students in a meaningful context for language learning. Link to prior knowledge by building on students' experiences or connect to the previous lesson
I do	5–7 min	Model how to use the vocabulary and language patterns with support of graphic organizers and sentence frames
I–We do	8–12 min	Model and monitor students for accuracy as they practice in small groups and with partners Use structured routines to engage students and ensure that everyone is participating
You do	10–15 min	Provide opportunities for student-generated language practice in small groups, partnerships, and individually
Wrap-up and reflection	3–5 min	Ask students to summarize what they have learned and restate the lesson objective

elry store, a hair salon, a shoe store, a bookstore, and a bakery. The word bank could also include pictures of items that might be purchased at each business, such as a dress, a book, a necklace, a pair of shoes, a CD, a loaf of bread, and a bottle of shampoo.

Students refer to the Illustrated Word Bank when they need to be reminded of the vocabulary word for each place, or when they need to write the word. The Illustrated Word Bank may also be used as a framework for an explicit-language lesson when language patterns for asking and answering questions are added. In our example, a note card is posted that provides the following question and answer: "What do people buy at _____? They buy _____ at _____." (*What do people buy at a music store? They buy a CD at a music store.*) Another language pattern that could be used with this Illustrated Word Bank is: "Where is (are) you (he, she, they, it, we) going to go? _____ going to go to the _____." (*Where is he going to go? He's going to go to the bookstore.*) Additional scaffolding is provided by color-coding a list of words (*I'm, you're, he's, she's, we're, they're*) and highlighting the spot in the language pattern at which one of these words belongs. For students at more advanced levels of English proficiency, the language pattern for this Illustrated Word Bank may be: "Why is (are) he (you, she, it, they, we) going to go to _____? Because _____ is (are) going to buy _____." (*Why are we going to go to the bakery? Because we are going to buy bread.*)

To prepare an Illustrated Word Bank, first identify a list of words or concepts to be taught and gather pictures of the target words. You can use pictures from magazines, make photocopies, draw them yourself, or take photographs. Identify a spot to hang your Illustrated Word Bank. You can put a piece of butcher paper on the wall or put picture cards in a hanging pocket chart. Have tape or pins ready for posting or cards with the labels printed if you are using a pocket chart. You may also want to make extra word cards for students to use when practicing the language patterns with each other.

To teach vocabulary using the Illustrated Word Bank, consider the following procedures:

1. "*I do it.*"—Introduce each word orally and *either* post the picture and label it *or* tape the picture onto the butcher paper and write its label nearby. As you do this, explain the meaning of the word or phrase in student-friendly language and give an example or two to provide context. Students chorally repeat key words and phrases after each one is posted or traced.

2. "*We do it.*"—For *intermediate* and above students, stop periodically and prompt the students to turn to a partner and tell what they have learned so far, as you monitor their exchanges. A prompt may be "Tell your partner what _____ means," or provide them a sentence stem to complete, such as "A department store is a place that sells _____." For *beginners* and *early-intermediate* students, you might have them chorally complete a sentence with a familiar pattern, such as "This is a _____," "I see/have/know a _____," or "A _____ has/can _____." Then have them repeat to a partner (first Partner A, then B).

On subsequent days, you may revisit the Illustrated Word Bank with labeled picture cards or word/phrase cards (depending on grade level of students) in different ways. Distribute one word card to each student, reading each one as you go. Review the vocabulary on the Illustrated Word Bank, having students listen for their word and put their card over the matching one on the chart. Some suggestions, listed by increasing difficulty, are:

- *Beginning*—Say the word/phrase (e.g., *bookstore*)
- *Early intermediate*—Provide a prompt with a sentence stem: "My card is a _____." Or "I have a _____. What do you have?" Or "This is a _____."
- *Intermediate*—"This is a _____ because it has _____ and _____." Or "This is a _____, not a _____." Or whatever other familiar language pattern best suits the context.
- *Advanced*—"_____ is related to _____ [tell to what and how]." Or "A characteristic [attribute] of _____ is _____."

3. *"You do it."*—As Illustrated Word Banks become part of the functional language environment, encourage students to use them as resources when using language orally or in writing independently.

Sentence Construction Charts

A sentence construction chart provides a frame for a specific language pattern in English and offers sample words or phrases that can be placed into the pattern. Students can refer to a sentence construction chart to find choices of words by parts of speech within a given pattern.

Figure 3.2 shows an example of a simple sentence construction chart with the pattern "The _____ can/cannot _____." Sentences that may be constructed from this chart include: *The dog can play outside* or *The dog cannot sleep inside.*

By providing sentence stems and frames, teachers give students the opportunity to learn and practice new language patterns. Sentence construction charts allow students to construct grammatically correct sentences at a level of complexity beyond that which they could generate independently. Using topic vocabulary from Illustrated Word Banks, word walls, and charts, students can produce their own sentences based on the stem or frame.

Sentence stems provide the opening word(s), phrase, or clause of a sentence, leaving the rest to be completed:

"There are...." (*There are books in the classroom.*)
"I was surprised when...." (*I was surprised when I saw her wearing a hat.*)

Sentence frames leave one or more portions of the sentence blank; these can be at the beginning, middle, and/or end of a sentence:

"The _____ went _____." (*The man went home.*)
"I like to _____ and _____, but not _____." (*I like to run and skip, but not swim.*)
"_____ are _____-er than _____." (*Cars are faster than bicycles.*)

Sentence stems and frames are appropriate for written or oral responses and may be used for all types of language functions.

To prepare a sentence construction chart, first identify the sentence stem or frame you want to work with. It is important to select useful and

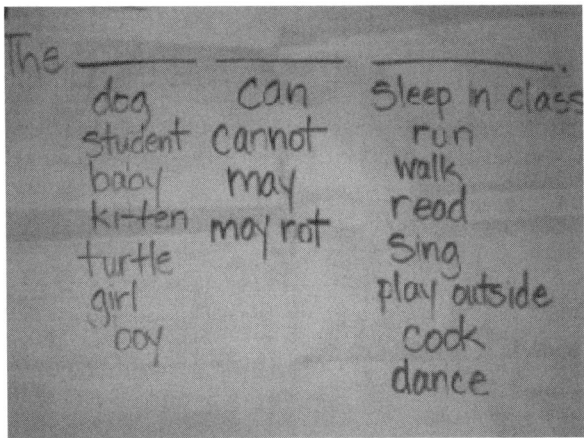

FIGURE 3.2. A simple sentence construction chart. Contributed by Linda Palomino and Robyn Lee-Giuseffi. From Dutro (2008). Copyright 2008 by E. L. Achieve. Reprinted by permission.

meaningful sentences and to add the purpose of the sentence frame to the side, such as:

- Express action: "The _____ went _____." (*The mouse went under the house.*)
- Express preferences: "I like to _____." (*I like to swim.*)
- Compare: "_____ and _____ are _____er than _____." (*Moose and elk are bigger than horses.*)

When possible, provide several variations of the language pattern. For example, when creating sentences that are used for comparing, you might demonstrate the following sentence variations:

"_____ and _____ are similar because they both _____." (*Cars and buses are similar because they both have engines.*)
"Both _____ and _____ are/have/can _____." (*Both cars and buses have engines.*)
"_____ and _____ have _____ in common." (*Cars and buses have engines in common.*)

Write the sentence stems or frames using the new language pattern(s) on chart paper or on strips of plain paper to use in a pocket chart. It is helpful to build sentences with topic vocabulary from Illustrated Word Banks or other visual support materials. Use a different color of marker for each category of word; for example, the subject of the sentence may be written in blue; the verb, red; and so on. During the lesson, students may suggest other words to add to the list.

To teach language patterns using the sentence construction chart, consider the following procedures:

1. "*I do it.*"—Introduce the sentence frame(s). Read the initial familiar sentence to the students, then explain the purpose of the sentence (its function). Use sample words on the list(s) to show how they can be substituted to create new sentences. Model how to generate sentences by using the stem or frame and adding well-known topic vocabulary or words from familiar sources to generate sentences. Put a sticky note by the words that you are changing.

2. "*We do it.*"—Students repeat with you the sentences you model. Then individual students suggest sentences, placing sticky notes by their word choices. The rest of the class repeats the new sentences. Mix it up by asking and answering questions or by changing the subject of the sentence (first to third, singular to plural) or tense, as appropriate to students' level of proficiency.

3. "*You do it.*"—Give students an opportunity to independently generate sentences using a structured format for practicing the language patterns with each other. Examples of structured formats include *think, pair, share* with a partner, or *Talking Stick,* in which students take turns in a small group (see the following description). After extensive oral practice, students can use the sentence construction chart to compose written sentences in structured small-group formats such as *pass the pen* for writing practice.

Sentence construction charts have the potential to be used at all levels of language development. Figure 3.3 illustrates an example of a more advanced sentence construction chart that not only represents a more complicated syntactical pattern but also provides a wonderful opportunity for enriched vocabulary development.

Talking Stick Activity for Structured Language Practice

This activity supports students' use of increasingly precise and varied language for interesting purposes. In order to internalize new vocabulary and develop grammatical accuracy, students need lots and lots of practice. It is important to develop automatic and fluent accuracy, so attention must be paid to correctness—not just what is said but also *how* it is

Explicit Language Instruction

An	enormous	bald eagle	soared	over the forest.
	descriptive adjective	Noun (who, what)	Verb (did what)	prepositional phrase (where)
A	powerful		soared	on the rock
Some	fast		dove	over the ocean
Seven	majestic		flew	in the sky
A few	strong		propelled	around the treetops
Many	bold		devoured	
Several	large		fished	
Dozens	brown		tore	
			screamed	

FIGURE 3.3. An advanced sentence construction chart.

said. Structured language practice routines ensure that each student practices new language multiple times during every lesson. Fifty percent of each Systematic ELD lesson should be dedicated to structured language practice, with the teacher monitoring accuracy and providing corrective feedback.

One example of structured language practice is an activity called *Talking Stick*. In this participation strategy, students work in small groups and take turns addressing a prompt from the teacher. This routine allows every student to have the opportunity to speak several times and encourages more reflective or reticent participants to take a turn.

To prepare for the Talking Stick activity, first gather some sentence frames or a graphic organizer that students will use to practice their language patterns. Be ready with a list of brick vocabulary that relates to your current study. Divide your class into groups of approximately four students and have enough sticks (or erasers, stuffed animals, or any other designated objects) so that there is one per group. Go over the procedures for Talking Stick with the students: Students sit in a circle. The stick is passed around clockwise at first. Students can only "pass" (decline to respond) one time.

To use the Talking Stick activity for structured language practice, consider the following procedures:

1. "*I do it.*"—Display the sentence construction chart, graphic organizer, or other material that you will be working from. Model an example of a word or sentence using the structure and vocabulary you want to practice. For example, with students who are practicing the language structure "I am _____" (*I am eating*), the teacher might say, "I am sitting. I am talking."

2. *"We do it."*—The teacher asks a question or gives a prompt, then passes a talking stick to one student in each group. The student with the object speaks, following the pattern the teacher has presented (e.g., "I am _____"). Everyone listens, then the student passes the talking stick on to the next person. The process continues until everyone in the group has a turn speaking or until the teacher gives a signal to return the talking stick.

3. *"You do it."*—To extend the activity, once everyone in the group has had a turn speaking, anyone in the group may ask for another turn by saying, "Please hand me the talking stick."

The Talking Stick activity can be adapted for students from all levels of language proficiency. For example, students at the beginning levels of English proficiency may be asked to give a one-word response, such as to name a verb, an animal, or another familiar object. If desired, the other students can repeat the word each individual gives. Students at the intermediate levels may be asked to give comparative adjectives, such as *big, bigger, biggest; smart, smarter, smartest; funny, funnier, funniest*; or a new verb tense, such as *I eat, I am eating, I was eating, I ate, I will eat*. Students at the advanced levels of English proficiency can practice gaining fluency and correctness with complex language patterns and advanced vocabulary, such as in the sentence *He was the president who wrote a famous speech*.

CONCLUSION

For English learners to achieve at high levels in literacy tasks in their elementary school classrooms, it is crucial that they receive support in learning the structures and vocabulary of academic English. Developing this proficiency requires explicit language instruction that builds on what students can currently do and stretches them to attain ever more complex language patterns. In this chapter we have provided a foundation for understanding the importance of language in literacy and academic achievement. We outlined the challenges that English learners face in achieving academic success and discussed the need for all teachers to be adequately prepared to provide explicit language instruction for their students.

English learners enter American classrooms at a variety of proficiency levels in English and with widely varied background and schooling experiences. Key to meeting their academic needs is an understanding of the background language and literacy strengths they bring and their current levels of oral and written English. Once students' language skills are identified, teachers can structure appropriate learning opportunities through an instructional blueprint for English learners. According to this blueprint, students receive two kinds of explicit language instruction: Systematic ELD instruction and explicit language for content. This double-focused approach ensures that students (1) develop an increasingly strong foundation in the complex structures and vocabulary of the English language, (2) learn the academic language that they need to engage with the literacy content of their classroom and to express their personal understanding, and (3) comprehend the grade-level materials that are presented in class.

Throughout this chapter, we have guided readers with a focused approach to explicit language instruction. Students must always be aware of the communicative purposes of classroom tasks, or *functions*, so that they see how what they are learning is connected to language use in the real world. Students are explicitly taught the *forms* of both the vocabulary—brick and mortar words—and the syntactical patterns of English. Finally, students are provided many opportunities to try out the language that they are learning to develop *fluency* in the accurate use of language.

We closed the chapter by providing in-depth instructions in how to implement three tools for explicit language instruction: Illustrated Word Banks, sentence construction charts, and Talking Sticks for structured language practice. These teaching methods offer ways to provide visual support to students in their language learning, to scaffold their knowledge of increasingly complex language patterns, and to provide opportunities to get guided practice and feedback from the teacher. It is our hope that these three examples serve as stepping stones for teachers to try out more and more explicit language instruction in their own classrooms.

Literacy achievement in English is dependent on a rich language foundation that allows students to comprehend the texts they are reading and writing and to communicate their personal understandings orally and in print. This chapter has provided important tools and concepts to help teachers plan for explicit language instruction that allows students to construct meaning in their reading and writing classrooms.

REFERENCES

California Department of Education. (1999). *Content standards: English language development, English version*. Retrieved May 29, 2008, from *www.cde.ca.gov/be/st/ss*.

California Department of Education. (2003). *California English Language Development Test (CELDT)*. Monterey, CA: CTB/McGraw-Hill.

Canale, M., & Swain, M. (1980). Theoretical bases of communicative approaches to second language teaching and testing. *Applied Linguistics, 1,* 1–47.

Castañeda v. Pickard, 648 F.2d 989 (U.S. App. 1981).

Cummins, J. (2003). Reading and the bilingual student: Fact and friction. In G.G. García (Ed.), *English learners: Reaching the highest level of English literacy* (pp. 2–33). Newark, DE: International Reading Association.

Datnow, A., Lasky, S. G., Stringfield, S. C., & Teddlie, C. (2005). Systematic integration for educational reform in racially and linguistically diverse contexts: A summary of the evidence. *Journal of Education for Students Placed at Risk, 10*(4), 445–453.

De Avila, E. A., & Duncan, S. E. (1994). *Language assessment scales.* Monterey, CA: CTB Macmillan/McGraw-Hill.

Díaz-Rico, L. T., & Weed, K. Z. (2002). *The crosscultural, language, and academic development handbook: A complete K–12 reference guide.* Boston: Allyn & Bacon.

Doughty, C., & Williams, J. (Eds.). (1998). *Focus on form in classroom second language acquisition.* Cambridge, UK: Cambridge University Press.

Dutro, S. (2008). *A focused approach to Systemic ELD instruction* (2nd ed.). San Marcos, CA: E.L. Achieve.

Dutro, S., & Moran, C. (2003). Rethinking English language instruction: An architectural approach. In G. G. García (Ed.), *English learners: Reaching the highest level of English literacy* (pp. 227–258). Newark, DE: International Reading Association.

Echevarria, J., Vogt, M. E., & Short, D. J. (2000). *Making content comprehensible for English language learners.* Boston: Allyn & Bacon.

Foreman, M. (2003). *Seal surfer. Horizons* (Level 3.2). Boston: Houghton Mifflin.

Garcia, G. E. (2000). Bilingual children's reading. In M. L. Kamil, P. B. Mosenthal, P. D. Pearson, & R. Barr (Eds.), *Handbook of reading research.* (Vol. III, pp. 813–834). Mahwah, NJ: Erlbaum.

Genesee, F., Lindholm-Leary, K., Saunders, W., & Christian, D. (2005). English language learners in U. S. schools: An overview of research findings. *Journal of Education for Students Placed at Risk, 10*(4), 363–385.

Geva, E. (2006). Second-language oral proficiency and second-language literacy. In D. August & T. Shanahan (Eds.), *Developing literacy in second-language learners: Report of the National Literacy Panel on Language-Minority Children and Youth* (pp. 123–139). Mahwah, NJ: Erlbaum.

Hakuta, K., Butler, Y. G., & Witt, D. (2000). *How long does it take English learners to attain proficiency?* (Policy Report 2000-1). Santa Barbara, CA: University of California Linguistic Minority Research Institute.

Halliday, M. (1973). *Explorations in the functions of language.* London: Edward Arnold.

Saunders, W. M., Foorman, B. R., & Carlson, C. D. (2006). Is a separate block of time for oral English language development in programs for English learners needed? *Elementary School Journal, 107*(2), 181–198.

Solórzano, R. W. (2008). High stakes testing: Issues, implications, and remedies for English language learners. *Review of Educational Research, 78*(2), 260–329.

Strizek, G. A., Pittsonberger, J. L., Riordan, K. E., Lyter, D. M., & Orlofsky, G. F. (2006). *Characteristics of schools, districts, teachers, principals, and school libraries in the United States: 2003–04 Schools and Staffing Survey I* (NCES 2006-313 Revised). Washington, DC: U.S. Government Printing Office.

Trumbull, E., & Farr, B. (2005). *Language and learning: What teachers need to know*. New York: Christopher-Gordon.

U.S. Department of Education. (2003). *National Assessment of Educational Progress (NAEP 2003 reading assessment)*. Retrieved from *www.nces.ed.gov/nationsreportcard*.

CHAPTER 4

Making Informed Decisions about the Language and Literacy Assessment of English Language Learners

GEORGIA EARNEST GARCÍA
CHRISTINA P. DENICOLO

Jada Bluson had taught second grade for 4 years at Castle Elementary School and was well liked by students, parents, and staff. She was considered a very successful teacher in the midsized community where she lived and worked, and she was known for her creativity, passion for learning, and effective teaching practices. Entering her fifth year of teaching, she felt it would be her best year yet, as she had spent the summer aligning her lesson plans with the state and district standards for second grade. At the start of the school year, Jada learned that she would have many more students identified as English language learners than in previous years in her second-grade classroom. She was excited about the opportunity to work with linguistically diverse students and their families, but she began to worry that she did not know enough to be a truly effective teacher for all her students.

The purpose of this chapter is to provide an overview of standardized assessments used to evaluate the language and literacy performance of English language learners (ELLs) and authentic assessments designed to inform instruction. Similar to Jada Bluson in the preceding vignette, teachers across the United States are striving to align instruction with state standards and feel the need to further their understanding of how assessment can support the decisions surrounding the teaching of bilingual and multilingual students.

ELLs participate in a variety of language and literacy assessments. Language proficiency assessments, for example, are used by educational personnel to determine students' language dominance; their classification as limited English proficient (LEP); their placement in bilingual education, English as a second language (ESL), or all-English classrooms; and their progress in acquiring English. Depending on their age, ELLs also may participate in literacy assessments in English and/or their native language to inform the placement and/or exiting decisions. If they are in a bilingual education or ESL program, students generally will participate in literacy achievement assessments to help determine when they should be exited from ESL or bilingual education. According to No Child Left Behind (NCLB, 2001), ELLs who have been in U.S. schools for more than 12 months and who are in grades 3–8 also have to participate in an annual reading/language arts assessment to show their yearly progress and attainment of reading and language arts.

We begin this chapter by first reviewing what is known about the different types of wide-scale language and literacy assessments that are used for various purposes with ELLs. We define wide-scale assessments as tests that are administered to large groups of students and that do not involve any variation in the individual test's format and administrative and scoring procedures. Next, we focus on Jada Bluson and her classroom context. We provide a narrative to show how Jada learned to integrate assessment with her instruction to evaluate and inform her instruction of ELLs. We conclude the chapter by presenting a set of recommendations for the appropriate selection, design, and use of language and literacy assessments with ELLs.

THE USE OF WIDE-SCALE LANGUAGE AND LITERACY ASSESSMENTS WITH ELLs

Currently, states and school districts use wide-scale language and literacy assessments with ELLs for a variety of purposes. Some of the assessments are norm-referenced, whereas others may be standards-based. Norm-referenced assessments usually are commercially produced and indicate how a student performs in relationship to other students. The test items specifically are chosen to help distribute student performance according to a bell curve distribution. The results sort students so that only a small number of students score in the top and bottom percentiles, with the majority in the middle percentiles. Standards-based assessments involve establishing performance-based expectations or standards at different levels of performance (e.g., *needs improvement, basic, proficient*, and *advanced*) and evaluating student performance according to the attainment of the standards. Because every student who meets a standard or criterion is scored at that specific level, the tests are criterion-referenced.

Both norm-referenced and standards-based assessments are judged according to their validity (whether the assessment content appropriately reflects the construct being measured), reliability (how well the assessment results match those of similar measures of the same construct for the same students), and fairness (absence of linguistic and cultural biases in the construction of the test, test items, scoring and reporting procedures; Messick, 1994; Rivera & Collum, 2006; National Clearinghouse for English Language Acquisition [NCELA], 2006). According to the National Clearinghouse for English Language Acquisition (NCELA, 2006), current federal rhetoric emphasizes the use of standards-based assessments to inform teacher instruction because the standards and assessments are supposed to be aligned with the teacher's curriculum and instruction. In contrast, norm-referenced tests are viewed as sampling student performance. Next we discuss the varied uses of norm-referenced and standards-based assessments with ELLs.

Language Proficiency Assessments

When children in the United States come from homes in which languages other than English are spoken, federal law requires school personnel to evaluate the entering children's English language proficiency (NCLB, 2001). School personnel are supposed to ask the children's parents or guardians to complete a home language survey, in which the responsible adults indicate the languages spoken in the home and identify whether their children speak the languages (see Figures 4.1 and 4.2 for examples from the state of Illinois). If the home language survey indicates that the child may be an ELL, then the child is supposed to be given a language proficiency test to determine his or her classification as a student who is LEP. Each state determines the type of test that can be used and the level of language proficiency that warrants classification as a LEP student and placement in a bilingual-education, ESL, or all-English classroom (NCELA, 2006). Once a child is designated as LEP, NCLB requires that his or her annual progress and attainment of English language proficiency be evaluated and reported on an annual basis (NCELA, 2006).

According to NCLB (2001), the proficiency test(s) selected or developed by the state to classify students as LEP and to monitor their progress in acquiring English must be aligned with state standards in English language proficiency and must measure students' receptive (listening and

The state requires the district to collect a Home Language Survey for every new student. This information is used to count the students whose families speak a language other than English at home. It also helps to identify the students that need to be assessed for English language proficiency.

Please answer the questions below and return this survey to your child's school.

Student's Name: _____
1. Does anyone in your home speak a language other than English?
   Yes ____
   What language? _____
   No ____
2. Does your child speak a language other than English?
   Yes ____
   What language? _____
   No ____

If the answer to either question is yes, the law requires the school to assess your child's English language proficiency.

_____ _____
Parent or Guardian Signature Date

FIGURE 4.1. Home language survey in English from the Illinois State Board of Education. Copyright © 2005–2008, Illinois State Board of Education. Republished with permission. All rights reserved.

reading) and productive (speaking and writing) skills in English. Although the assessment is supposed to include academic language proficiency by determining "conversational and academic English necessary to function on grade level, in both productive and receptive skills, in all-English classrooms," it is not to overlap with the required reading/language arts standards-based assessment in English that typically is administered to ELLs in grades 3–8 (NCELA, 2006).

Standards-based language proficiency assessments are new to the assessment scene and have not been well investigated. At this point in time, we do not know how well they indicate students' actual language dominance and development, inform their instruction in English, reflect their progress in acquiring English, indicate their academic language proficiency, or predict their academic performance in all-English classrooms (García, McKoon, & August, 2006a, 2006b, 2008). Although NCLB calls for standards-based language proficiency assessments that evaluate the English language development of ELLs at specific developmental stages, this is an accomplishment that publishers of commercial language proficiency tests have not been able to attain (García et al., 2006a).

Researchers who have examined commercial language proficiency tests have warned that there are at least three reasons that school districts

모국어 조사

주에서는 각 학구가 모든 새로운 학생에 대해 모국어 조사를 실시하도록 요구하고 있습니다. 이 정보는 가정에서 가족들이 영어 이외의 언어를 사용하고 있는 학생들을 파악하기 위한 것입니다. 또한 학교 당국이 이중언어와 제2영어 교육 서비스 실시의 필요를 파악하는 데에도 도움이 됩니다.

아래의 질문들에 답해서 이 설문지를 자녀가 다니고 있는 학교로 반송해 주십시오.

학생 이름: _____

1. 가정에서 영어 이외의 언어를 사용하는 사람이 있습니까?
   ____ 예
      어떤 언어를 사용합니까? _____
   ____ 아니오

2. 귀하의 자녀는 영어 이외의 언어를 사용합니까?
   ____ 예

   어떤 언어를 사용합니까? _____

   ____ 아니오

위에 나온 두 질문 가운데 하나에라도 '예'라는 대답이 나온 경우, 학교는 귀 자녀의 영어 능력을 평가하게 됩니다. 학교 당국은 귀 자녀의 듣기와 말하기 능력을, 2학년에서 12학년 학생인 경우 읽기와 쓰기 능력을 측정하게 됩니다.

서명 _____
   부모 또는 보호자

FIGURE 4.2. Home language survey in Korean from the Illinois State Board of Education. Copyright © 2005–2008, Illinois State Board of Education. Republished with permission. All rights reserved.

should not rely solely on the use of a single language proficiency assessment to determine children's classification as LEP; their instructional placement in bilingual, ESL, or all-English classrooms; their attainment of English; or their reclassification as fluent English-proficient learners and exit from bilingual or ESL programs (García & Pearson, 1994; García et al., 2006a, 2006b, 2008). Given that we know very little about the validity, reliability, and fairness of the standards-based language proficiency assessments required under NCLB (2001), we strongly recommend that users of the state assessments also heed the following concerns. First, language proficiency tests frequently emphasize skills that are related to the oral use of a language, such as phonology (knowledge of the sound system), morphology (knowledge of meaningful word units, such as past tense markers or use of *-ed* as in *she died*), syntax (knowledge of grammar), and lexicon (vocabulary knowledge). As a result, their ability to indicate how well students marshal the individual skills to actually communicate in real-life and academic settings is limited (García et al., 2006a).

Second, although language proficiency tests generally sample how well students produce (speak and write) and comprehend oral and written language (listen and comprehend), they do not evaluate how well students use a language to understand academic instruction or to learn in an academic setting (García & Pearson, 1994; García et al., 2006a, 2006b, 2008). Two sets of researchers reported the limited ability of a commercial language proficiency test, the Language Assessment Scales (LAS; DeAvila & Duncan, 1990; Duncan & DeAvila, 1988), to predict the academic English reading of ELLs. Laesch and Van Kleeck (1987) investigated how well the LAS scores of third-grade Mexican American students enrolled in bilingual education predicted their scores on a standardized reading comprehension test, the California Test of Basic Skills (CTBS). Although the LAS classified the third-graders as fluent English speakers, the students' scores on the LAS did not significantly correlate with their scores on the CTBS. In a study with seventh-grade ELLs enrolled in sheltered social studies classrooms, another set of researchers (Stevens, Butler, & Castellón-Wellington, 2000) reported a significant but low-magnitude correlation between the students' LAS reading test scores in English and their performance on the social studies section of the Iowa Test of Basic Skills (ITBS), a standardized academic test. In fact, the students' LAS performance only accounted for 20% of the ITBS variance. Both sets of researchers warned that educational personnel should not use commercial language proficiency tests to evaluate students' academic language proficiency.

Third, language proficiency tests tend to be brief because they are administered individually or in small groups and are time-consuming (NCELA, 2006). Due to their brevity, they do not present a very complete picture of the oral- and written-language use or development of ELLs. By combining data from other sources with the student's language proficiency test scores, a more complete picture of the student's language proficiencies in English and the native language is obtained. According to Kindler (2002), prior to the implementation of NCLB, three-fourths of the states or governing bodies (e.g., Guam, Puerto Rico) in the United

States reported that their districts used a range of measures for the eligibility decision. For example, they reported that to determine which children were LEP and should be placed in bilingual or ESL education, their school districts used a commercial language proficiency assessment—such as the LAS, IDEA Language Proficiency Tests (IPT; IDEA, 1994), or Woodcock–Muñoz Language Survey (Woodcock & Muñoz-Sandoval, 1993)—in combination with other sources of information, such as language samples, a normed- or criterion-referenced achievement test, a parent report, student grades and/or records, teacher interviews and/or observations, and referrals by educational personnel.

In terms of reclassifying a student as a fluent English-proficient learner and the decision to exit the student from a bilingual or ESL program into an all-English classroom, the NCLB Act (2001) actually specifies that, in addition to the state standards-based language proficiency assessment used to evalute students' attainment of English, states may include other criteria. According to NCELA (2006), the federal government anticipates that most states will add an achievement measure of some type. Prior to NCLB, it was common for states and governing bodies to use a range of assessments. For example, Kindler (2002) wrote that states and governing bodies reported using commercial and state-developed achievement tests, information from parents and other educational personnel, oral proficiency measures, student records and grades, and teacher interviews and observations. Some districts were known not to move students into the all-English classroom until the students indicated that they could perform at grade level by scoring at the 50th percentile on a standardized reading or language arts achievement test in English.

English Reading/Language Arts Achievement Tests

Although a number of cultural and historical test biases have been reported that could affect the use of norm-referenced and standards-based tests with students from diverse linguistic and cultural backgrounds (see García & Pearson, 1994), due to space limitations, we have decided to focus only on biases specific to ELLs. For example, a serious problem in evaluating the English reading/language arts performance of ELLs is knowing when students are proficient enough in English to participate appropriately in wide-scale reading/language arts achievement tests in English (Butler & Stevens, 2001; García et al., 2006a; Hakuta & Beatty, 2000). Butler and Stevens (2001) warn that when students are in the process of acquiring English, it is difficult to know whether their test scores on English tests accurately reflect their domain knowledge and skills or their limited English proficiency. The Standards for Educational and Psychological Testing (American Educational Research Association,

American Psychological Association, & National Council on Measurement in Education, 1999) emphasize that the validity of a test may be questioned when ELLs participate in a test that has been designed for fluent English speakers:

> The test user should investigate the validity of the score interpretations for test takers believed to have limited proficiency in the language of the test [because] the achievement, abilities, and traits of examinees who do not speak the language of the test as their primary language may be seriously mismeasured by the test. (p. 118)

The Standards further state that significant test bias occurs when ELLs participate in assessments normed on native English speakers:

> Test norms based on native speakers of English either should not be used with individuals whose first language is not English or such individuals' test results should be interpreted as reflecting in part current level of English proficiency rather than ability, potential, aptitude, or personality characteristics or symptomatology. (p. 91)

Unfortunately, few, if any, norm-referenced reading/language arts or vocabulary tests in English include ELLs as part of the norming populations (García & Pearson, 1994; García et al., 2006a).

Researchers who have investigated the reading achievement test performance of ELLs have reported that their performance on English assessments may be misleading for a number of reasons. Several researchers have noted that due to differences in receptive and productive development, ELLs may reveal greater comprehension of English texts when they are allowed to answer questions or write their answers in their native language (García, 1991; Lee, 1986). Others have reported that second-language learners, as compared with monolingual learners, may need more time to complete reading tests in their second language because they tend to process text more slowly (García, 1991; Mestre, 1984). Still others have shown that the frequency of vocabulary items differs across languages and across regional dialects of the same language, so that the use of a vocabulary test in only one language may underestimate the vocabulary knowledge of bilingual students because they sometimes know different items in each of their languages (Fernández, Pearson, Umbel, Oller, & Molinet-Molina, 1992; Sattler & Altes, 1984). In a study that focused on the differential test performance of Spanish-speaking and monolingual English-speaking fifth and sixth graders who had been enrolled in the same classrooms, García (1991) reported a number of testing bias issues that resulted in the Spanish-speaking students' test performance underestimating their English reading comprehension. For example, she found significant differences in the two groups of students' prior knowledge for the test passages and performance on questions that required students to integrate their prior knowledge with test information to answer the questions correctly. When differences in prior knowledge were statistically controlled, then there was no significant difference between the two groups' performances on the test passages, although low and average readers from the Spanish-speaking group still performed more poorly on the questions that involved prior knowledge integration. The Spanish-speaking students knew significantly less of the vocabulary included in the test passages and questions, but even when they could figure out unfamiliar vocabulary in the passages, they frequently missed related questions because they did not know the paraphrased vocabulary in the test items. When students were asked the test questions in Spanish, then they revealed much greater comprehension of the English test passages.

In 2006, updated regulations on NCLB (U.S. Department of Education, 2006) stated that ELLs who have attended school in the United States for more than 12 months and who are in grades 3–8 must take the annual, standards-based reading/language arts test in English used by the state. However, if ELLs have attended school in the United States for less than 12 months, they may be exempt from taking the test in English on one occasion, although schools still are required to report how many students have been exempted. Also, in determining the annual scores of LEP students, states and schools now may include the reading/language arts scores of former LEP students who are considered to be fluently English proficient for up to 2 years after their reclassification.

Testing Accommodations

To offset some of the linguistic and cultural biases noted earlier, a number of states have experimented with testing accommodations. According to Rivera and her colleagues (2006), testing accommodations involve changes to a test or to its testing context that do not make the test content or construct invalid. Testing accomodations are supposed "to provide support to ELLs in processing the language of the test without providing help on the test's content" (p. 6). Most important, the accommodation should not result in a "demonstrable advantage" for those who use it as compared with those who do not (p. 7). Most of the research on accommodations has involved simplification of the linguistic structure (e.g., reduced sentence complexity or simplification of non-content-oriented vocabulary), dictionaries (with simple definitions of noncontent words in English or definitions of noncontent words in the native language) and bilingual glossaries, dual-language tests (with side-by-side versions of the test in the two languages), the oral reading of the instructions or test items in English or the native language, allowing students to respond in the native language, and allowing additional time to take the test. At this point in time, most of the accommodations have occurred with tests of mathematics or science (García et al., 2006b; Rivera, Collum, Shafer, Willner, & Sia, 2006).

According to NCLB (2001), ELLs should be tested in language arts and reading with the "same academic assessments to measure the achievement of all students ... [and] should be provided reasonable accommodations, including, to the extent practicable, assessments in the native language and form most likely to yield accurate data." Whether providing students with accommodations will help to offset their limited English proficiency while reading in English still is not known. Certainly, providing ELLs with instructions in their native languages or with glossaries or dictionaries for unfamiliar vocabulary in the instructions may help, as may extending the amount of time given for ELLs to complete the assessment or orally reading the assessment in English or the native language. However, it may be difficult to use the two accommodations most frequently cited with mathematics and science tests—simplified syntax and vocabulary—because these two constructs are an essential part of reading. Also, it is very doubtful that an assessment primarily based on monolingual native English-speaking students, even with accommodations, will be able to identify students who demonstrate the features of strong bilingual or second-language readers (see Jiménez, García, & Pearson, 1995, 1996). Whether the standards-based assessment developed for monolingual native English speakers can effectively inform the instruction of ELLs also can be questioned due to the underlying assumption of "one size fits all" (Reyes, 1992). Reyes compares the use of teaching methods and curriculum for all students to one-size-fits-all clothing. If the clothing is too big or small, the assumption is that there is something wrong with the person. If the instruction is not implemented based on an understanding of what specific types of students know and need to learn, the underlying assumption is that the students are lacking.

The requirements outlined here cover the assessments that states must use according to NCLB (2001). We now return to the vignette at the beginning of the chapter. We present a dialogue betweeen Ms. Bluson and her mentor, Ms. West, as a way to examine classroom assessment practices that inform instruction by providing insight into linguistically diverse students' language and literacy development.

THE CLASSROOM CONTEXT: HOW JADA BLUSON INTEGRATED ASSESSMENT WITH INSTRUCTION

To prepare for the school year, Jada Bluson decided to meet with her former teaching mentor, Ms. West, for guidance on how to address the fact that in her second grade she would be teaching monolingual English-speaking students along with ELLs from several different language backgrounds. As she had always struggled with managing assessment requirements, she decided to ask Ms. West to focus on effective assessment practices for students learning English as a second or third language.

Jada looked overwhelmed, so Ms. West sensed it was time to validate the progress she had made toward learning how to improve her instruction and assessment methods. "Let's review what we have covered so far. I think you have a good understanding of the required information and assessments used at the start of the school year: home language surveys, English language proficiency assessments, and yearly evaluations of reading and math. In order to measure the progress of English language learners in literacy you have to establish a systematic way to collect, document, and communicate the progress students are making in reading and writing, as well as academic-language proficiency in English across content areas. Doing this will lead to more effective instruction, because your instructional planning will not be based on curricular guides and tests that are developed for monolingual English-speaking students. I think you will feel more confident when you know that you have a way to understand the exact progress students are making toward the English language proficiency, literacy, and content standards."

Jada agreed. "It would be a big help because in the past, when I was grading the unit tests that come with the language arts program for students who are monolingual English speakers, I was not sure if students misunderstood what the question was asking, the terminology, or the concept. I can only imagine how this will be magnified when I have students with a greater range of English proficiency levels."

"Exactly!" Ms. West exclaimed, "That is why we can never rely on one assessment to measure a student's learning. If the student is learning English at school, it becomes even more imperative that we do not rely on only one form of assessment." Ms. West explained that authentic assessment is the evaluation of student progress toward learning goals while engaging in activities that reflect everyday uses of knowledge. She told Jada that authentic assessments of English language proficiency would involve assessing student's use of English when working with peers, responding to class discussions, or presenting information that is part of a project (O'Malley & Pierce, 1996). Jada nodded enthusiastically as

Ms. West continued, "There are several forms of assessment that provide essential information regarding the overall literacy development of bilingual students because they do not limit assessment to the evaluation of a narrow set of skills or processes. Instead, authentic assessments look at students' language and literacy knowledge across languages and contexts. The more you gain experience working with English language learners, the more you can expand on the assessment framework. For this school year, I recommend that you add three assessment practices to your instructional plan: retellings, anecdotal records, and the provision of explicit feedback."

Retellings

Jada jumped in. "I already use retellings to assess students' comprehension of story elements, but what I am not sure about is how to do that if they are more proficient in another language. I want to understand more about what you just mentioned regarding students' prior learning, linguistic abilities, and ways to work with families."

Ms. West agreed. "In discussing retellings we will also talk about the value of students using their first or home language in the classroom and the role of assessment in supporting biliteracy development. The degree of home-language use may change as students develop proficiency in English and depends on the instructional goals and the individual student."

"So, I am guessing the first step would be to learn about students' prior learning experiences and literacy knowledge?" Jada asked.

"Yes, if you do not speak the same language as your students, it will be more difficult to determine their level of comprehension when reading. Speaking with family members can provide information that will help you more accurately interpret a student's participation level and assist you as you plan for instruction. When families speak languages other than English at home, you will need to find ways to support home–school communication and to develop an understanding of your students' prior schooling experiences. If the school does not provide translation services, you can seek translation help from colleagues, district-wide parent liaisons, community agencies, older siblings, or relatives. Once a relationship is established, you can provide explanations of reading and writing goals in the native language and allow students to respond to activities in their home language. This also builds on one of your current teaching practices, connecting with community funds of knowledge [Moll, Amanti, Neff, & González, 1992]. Think about English language development as an extension of what you are already doing. You work hard to ensure that your teaching, curriculum, and parental involvement reflect and respect the cultural backgrounds of your students by dedicating time to get to know people in the community and identifying key elements of students' home culture that align with the curriculum. At the start of every school year, you interview family members to gain insight into the funds of knowledge or networks of information, resources, and practices that they maintain in their homes and communities [Moll et al., 1992]. This information guides you in selecting instructional themes for the school year. This is a very time-consuming process, but it has enabled you to develop such a deep level of understanding of each of your students by drawing on knowledge that each student may not have had the opportunity to share in school."

Ms. West continued. "In addition to learning about the forms of knowledge that exist in the community, interviewing family members can provide valuable information to ensure that you accurately assess the progress your bilingual students are making. Having a clear understanding of students' literacy knowledge better prepares you to support students' transfer of knowledge from their first language to the second or third language [Cummins, 1996]. Ideally, instruction and assessment support the development of metalinguistic awareness by addressing the identification of cognates, false cognates, and differences in letter–sound correspondences across languages. Taking note of how students incorporate metalinguistic awareness as they read and write across content areas helps assess their biliteracy development [Valdés, 2001]. Assessment that promotes student use of their home language or dialect can provide teachers with valuable information regarding students' reading and writing. It is important to note the strategies students utilize to comprehend a passage or unfamiliar word or when students use knowledge from one language to inform work in their developing language. Documenting the strategies and sharing them with students promote higher order thinking, not simply information recall. You can think of authentic and classroom assessment as a way to braid together students' prior knowledge, use of strategies, and English language development to provide a more complete view of student's abilities."

Ms. West further explained, "Retellings are one form of authentic assessment that can be done in the native language or in both the first and the second languages. When students provide an oral or written account of what they have read, it is referred to as a retelling. Retellings provide teachers with insight into students' comprehension of text and ability to identify story elements. Teachers can use the retelling to pose additional questions or readdress aspects of the story that were not accurately represented. Garcia [1994] stresses the range of possibilities that exist with retellings. Teachers can have students retell with partners, respond using more than one language, or record retellings in the home language so teachers can later seek translation support for the recording" (García, 1994).

Jada responded enthusiastically. "I will definitely use retellings for reading comprehension assessment, but I have to tell you that I am not sure that I know what to do if students use their native language, aside from having someone else translate their responses. Could I encourage students to draw illustrations to accompany retellings that are not in English?"

Ms. West explained that students might have the oral-language skills in English to discuss their retellings. She suggested that, in addition to drawing, students could act out what they had written. Before moving on, Ms. West had one more bit of advice on native-language use. "Jada, keep in mind that when you encourage students to use their native language, you acknowledge the interconnectedness of culture, language, and learning. By inviting your students to teach you the languages they speak and/or taking language classes, you demonstrate your commitment and the value you place on bilingualism [Nieto, 2002]. This sends a powerful message to all of your students and most likely will inspire your monolingual students to do the same!"

Anecdotal Records

"Jada," Ms. West asked, "Remember how we were discussing the aspects of your teaching that will be very important for working with English language learners? Talk to me about how you think instructional themes and building community will support your bilingual students."

Jada took out her plan for the year. "We talked about thematic instruction, and how that allows me to teach vocabulary words that students will work with across content areas. It also provides more opportunities for students to form connections with prior learning because they are working on the topic over time. From the first day of school, I strive to develop a real sense of community in the classroom and establish routines throughout the school day. Those are two areas that I think will support all of the students in my classroom."

Ms. West agreed. "The consistency and sense of safety developed will allow your second-language learners to feel comfortable because they will know what to expect throughout the school day and the norms for participation in the classroom. When students dedicate less attention to wondering what will happen, they will be able to focus on the language being used. Thematic instruction and routines also provide opportunities to monitor social and academic-language development across content areas, but it requires planning; so you document language use and incorporate that information into lessons" (Stiggins, Arter, Chappius & Chappius, 2004).

Jada added, " One thing I could do is to start taking weekly anecdotal records of the informal talk during transitions and then use that for lesson planning on oral-language development during calendar time."

Ms. West rephrased Jada's suggestion. "Documenting students' social and academic-language development by observing them as they participate in a range of activities can help you identify language use and the range of literacies they possess."

"I am not sure I understand what you mean by literacies," Jada responded, starting to feel overwhelmed once again.

Ms. West explained, "English language learners are extremely diverse, representing a wide range of experiences in school, varied levels of proficiency in English, and different home experiences [Zentella, 2005]. Many were born in the United States, and others may have just arrived in the country. Some students may have been enrolled in a bilingual program in another school. I want you to keep in mind that although students may be identified as being part of one cultural group, such as Latino, that does not mean they have similar home experiences or backgrounds."

"Of course," Jada replied. "Every family has its own practices and culture."

"Yes, just as we cannot assume that families all engage in the same cultural practices, we cannot assume that reading, writing, or talking has the same process or purpose across families. When we discussed your literacy block, we talked about the underlying ideologies that guide how individuals engage in literacy practices across the different areas of their lives. *Literacy* is a commonly used word, but it does not mean the same thing for everyone. Not all families engage in similar practices, but this does not mean they do not engage in literacy. You will be better able to understand your students' reading and writing abilities by observing their engagement in authentic literacy practices, activities that are meaningful and purposeful to the students. The language arts curriculum often centers on the skills that are necessary for reading and writing in English. Many multilingual students use very complex forms of literacy knowledge in their homes and communities. The work of Orellana, Reynolds, Dorner, and Meza [2003] shows that many students translate complex documents and conversations for family members and yet rarely have the opportunity to build on these abilities in school. What are some literacy practices that you implement?"

"Well," Jada pointed out, "one example is literature discussion groups, where students discuss their comprehension of texts. I follow Daniels's [1994] model, in which students select a text and utilize roles to engage in reading strategies such as forming connections, facilitating discussions, and highlighting significant events. I have found that when I provide a range of literature that is representative of the cultures in the classroom, students are highly motivated to participate in literature discussions."

Ms. West was thrilled with Jada's understanding of culturally relevant texts. "In addition to the level of motivation, students are more apt to use their cultural and linguistic resources to support comprehension; this creates the opportunity for you to observe language use in the home language and English across all domains [Fránquiz & Reyes, 1998]. Children's literature that is relevant to students' lives can serve as a vehicle to promote student identification of critical encounters in text, events in the story that have a high level of importance or impact on students, leading to longer discussions with periods of extended discourse [DeNicolo & Fránquiz, 2006]. When students hold these discussions you can then take note of students' language use, comprehension of text, and oral- and academic-language development."

Jada realized that she would really need to systematically observe students while they were engaged in independent or group activities. "How will I keep track of all that during literature discussion groups? As much as I train students on how to work collaboratively, I still need to check in periodically with each group to keep them on track."

Ms. West explained that with a checklist she could sit with each group and take note of parts of the conversation; she could record the discussions once a week and collect the students' role sheets. "You could plan for what you would note from each form of assessment. Documentation that is systematic will provide you with a deeper understanding of ways that students interact with text because you can observe patterns of language use and inconsistencies between written and oral discourse [Pérez & Torres-Guzmán, 2002]. This will also give you a range of evidence of what they have not yet mastered" (Nathenson-Mejía, 1992).

Jada still looked doubtful, and Ms. West was prepared once again to provide her with guidance. "Based on what I have read, I suggest creating an anecdotal record chart that is designed for observation of the strategies or skills being covered in instruction or that are ongoing, such as prior knowledge and language use. The anecdotal notes are recorded under the corresponding section. You could focus on a small number of students each day, covering the entire class each week [Pierce, 2001]. You may also at times choose to use anecdotal records to focus on specific students, writing longer narratives regarding their engagement and participation across a range of literacy activities." Ms. West showed Jada an abbreviated anecdotal record for three students (Figure 4.3) that another teacher had used to document the students' language use in a dialogue journal.

1/15/2008: Tuesday	Language Use in Dialogue Journals
Han	Wrote English caption for drawing using invented spelling: sbmrn [*submarine*].
Alfredo	Code-mixed in English while writing caption in Spanish for drawing. Used the word *snow*.
Soo Joung	Wrote in Korean about the drawing. Translation: We went to a birthday party at our church.

FIGURE 4.3. Abbreviated anecdotal record.

Provision of Explicit Feedback

"Okay," said Jada, "I am going to use retellings for reading comprehension and anecdotal records for documenting social and academic language development, as well as taking note of students' strategy use. What do you recommend for writing?"

"Well, let's look at how you can develop a high level of cognizance regarding each student's progress in writing, ensuring that students are aware of their own learning. I know it was difficult last year to have a writer's workshop, but conferences are a great time for providing explicit feedback, which is critical to the academic progress of bilingual students [Reyes, 1992]. One of the criticisms of the writing process approach is that students are expected to improve their writing by discussing their work with peers and their teacher. Students who are learning English as a second language at school may not view suggestions for improving their writing as instruction. If teachers take off points without explaining exactly what was incorrect, students may unknowingly assume that their language use is correct and/or fail to question what could be improved in their writing. It is crucial that teachers identify errors or miscues in students' reading, writing, and comprehension and explain why the error is an error. In writing instruction, for example, students, with the assistance of their teachers, can develop an understanding of their own patterns, misunderstandings regarding word meaning, or negative transfer from their home language. In this approach, assessment once again becomes a tool to develop awareness regarding language when students can identify how and why they are using a particular word, letter combination, or grammatical construct. Students could have individual checklists with their most frequent errors and use that as a form of self-assessment."

Jada said, "As much as I would love to talk about self-assessment and other forms of authentic assessment such as portfolios, I may have to hold off until second semester! For now, I am going to incorporate what we have talked about into each student's profile: retellings in the first language and English; anecdotal records on prior language use, comprehension strategies, and English language proficiency; checklists to keep track of language use during transitions, vocabulary use across content areas, and feedback specific to each child. As I compile all the data on students at the end of each week, it will not only make lesson planning easier, I will have a wealth of information to share with students, parents, and other teachers."

RECOMMENDATIONS

We have organized our recommendations so that we first discuss the selection and use of language and literacy assessments (wide-scale, classroom-based, and authentic) for high-stakes decisions about the education of ELLs (e.g., their identification as LEP, instructional placement, annual progress in attaining English, reclassification and exiting decision from bilingual or ESL education, and annual reading/language arts achievement). In the following section of our discussion, we provide additional recommendations for the integration of authentic assessments with instruction.

The Selection and Use of Assessments for High-Stakes Decisions

1. Although NCLB (2001) requires states to use an assessment tied to English language proficiency standards to identify LEP students, evaluate their English language proficiency for placement decisions, and assess their annual attainment of English, due to the limitations of any single measure, we strongly encourage educational personnel to combine the findings of the standards-based assessment with those of other assessments (e.g., parental report, scores on commercial language proficiency assessments and achievement tests, anecdotal records, and language samples of students' writing, speaking, and reading performance) for those purposes. Because students' proficiency in their native language also is a factor that needs to be taken into account in the placement decision and in helping to determine whether students have acquired appropriate content/domain knowledge that can be transferred to English, we strongly encourage educational personnel to also base their decisions and evaluations on results from native-language measures (commercial language proficiency and achievement tests, anecdotal records, and language samples of students' writing, speaking, and reading performance).

2. For exiting decisions, it is imperative for educational personnel to

make their decisions on more than the standards-based language proficiency assessment. Because it is difficult to know from any one assessment how well ELLs will do in all-English classrooms, we recommend that educational personnel rely on achievement measures (norm-referenced and standards-based), as well as classroom-based and authentic assessments. Students' reading, writing, listening, and speaking performance in English and their domain performance (in the native language, when in bilingual education, and in English) all need to be taken into account.

3. Educational personnel need to understand the strengths and weaknesses of the wide-scale assessments (norm-referenced and standards-based) that are available. For this reason, we recommend that, in selecting assessments, educational personnel first read the evaluations of specific assessments published in the *Mental Measurements Yearbook* (Geisinger, Spies, Carlson, & Plake, 2007). The evaluations will indicate the validity, reliability, and appropriateness of various assessments and to what extent they have been norm-referenced or based on the performance of various subgroups, such as ELLs. We also recommend that district and state personnel insist on a federal research agenda that investigates the validity, reliability, and fairness of standards-based language and reading/achievement arts assessments designed and/or selected by the various states.

4. Even though standards-based reading/language arts achievement assessments used by the states are supposed to be aligned with curriculum and instruction, it is important for educational personnel to realize that the standards are based on the instruction and performance of monolingual native English-speaking students. As such, these tests do not tell teachers how to teach this material so that it is comprehensible for ELLs. Also, because the tests cannot differentiate between students' developing proficiency in English and their reading performance in English, it is important for educational personnel to use appropriate testing accommodations. Because NCLB specifies that it is possible to use reading/language arts tests in the native language, states and districts should include a measure of students' reading/language arts achievement in the native language, especially when instruction in the native language occurs. The latter may mean that states will have to be encouraged to design standards-based reading/language arts assessments in the native language.

5. Educational personnel need to take advantage of the 1-year English reading/language arts testing exemption for ELLs in grades 3–8 who have been in the United States for less than 1 year and also be sure to include in their annual report the English reading/language arts test scores of fluent English-proficient students for up to 2 years after they were classified as ELLs.

Integrating Authentic Assessment with Instruction

1. The classroom environment provides many opportunities for authentic assessment. A classroom environment in which students are encouraged to take risks in language use across domains (literacy and content areas) supports the exchange of feedback, the role of evaluation, and the use of student cultural and linguistic resources. When students see that information gained from observations, retellings in the first and second language, and student response to explicit feedback are informing the teacher's instructional decisions, they will see evaluations as opportunities for learning.

2. It also is important to remember that authentic assessment requires authentic instruction; that is why it is essential for classroom teachers to develop an understanding of the languages their students speak, the literacies they engage in at home, and the networks of support that exist in the community.

3. Similarly, because authentic assessment and authentic instruction should reflect a school-wide commitment to identifying and serving the educational needs of all students, it is imperative for the entire school staff to receive training and preparation in educating ELLs. Ideally, students will have access to native-language instruction. However, shortages of bilingual teachers, political initiatives, and demographic shifts all contribute to the fact that some students may not have bilingual education as an option. Schools that have a bilingual or ESL program also will benefit when all of the teachers become more knowledgeable about second-language acquisition, culture, and instructional methods, such as sheltered instruction, so that they will be better able to work with all students and collaborate with the bilingual or ESL teachers.

CONCLUDING REMARKS

In closing, we encourage all teachers to approach their work with ELLs with the same enthusiasm and quest for knowledge as Jada Bluson has. Just as Ms. West guided Ms. Bluson through the aspects of her instruction that would enable her to develop assessments to monitor language and literacy development as well as content learning, parents and community members should be accessed as resources to guide teachers on how to incorporate community literacy, wisdom, and practices into the classroom. When educational personnel take the time to learn about ELLs, then it is much easier for them to make informed decisions about language and literacy assessments.

REFERENCES

American Educational Research Association, American Psychological Association, & National Council on Measurement in Education. (1999). *Standards for educational and psychological testing 1999*. Washington, DC: American Educational Research Association.

Butler, F. A., & Stevens, R. (2001). Standardized assessment of the content knowledge of English langauge learners K–12: Current trends and old dilemmas. *Language Testing, 18*(4), 409–427.

Cummins, J. (1996). *Negotiating identities: Education for empowerment in a diverse society*. Ontario, CA: California Association for Bilingual Education.

Daniels, H. (1994). *Literature circles: Voice and choice in the student-centered classroom*. York, ME: Stenhouse.

DeAvila, E., & Duncan, S. (1990). *Language Assessment Scales—Oral*. Monterey, CA: CTB McGraw-Hill.

DeNicolo, C. P., & Fránquiz, M. E. (2006). "Do I have to say it?": Critical encounters with multicultural children's literature. *Language Arts, 84*(2), 157–170.

Duncan, S., & DeAvila, E. (1988). *Language Assessment Scales—Reading and Writing* (2nd ed.). Monterey, CA: CTB McGraw-Hill.

Fernández, M. C., Pearson, B. Z., Umbel, V. M., Oller, D. K., & Molinet-Molina, M. (1992). Bilingual receptive vocabulary in Hispanic preschool children. *Hispanic Journal of Behavioral Sciences, 14*(2), 268–276.

Fránquiz, M. E., & Reyes, M. de la Luz. (1998). Creating inclusive learning communities through English language arts: From *Chanclas* to *Canicas*. *Language Arts, 75*(3), 211–220.

García, G. E. (1991). Factors influencing the English reading test performance of Spanish-speaking Hispanic children. *Reading Research Quarterly, 26*(4), 371–392.

García, G. E. (1994). Assessing the literacy development of second-language students: A focus on authentic assessment. In K. Spangenberg-Urbshat & T. Pritchard (Eds.), *Kids come in all languages: Reading instruction for ESL students* (pp. 180–205). Newark, DE: International Reading Association.

García, G. E., McKoon, G., & August, D. (2006a). Synthesis: Language and literacy assessment. In D. August & T. Shanahan (Eds.), *Developing literacy in second-language learners: Report of the National Literacy Panel on Language-Minority Children and Youth* (pp. 583–596). Mahwah, NJ: Erlbaum.

García, G. E., McKoon, G., & August, D. (2006b). Language and literacy assessment of language-minority students. In D. August & T. Shanahan (Eds.), *Developing literacy in second-language learners: Report of the National Literacy Panel on Language-Minority Children and Youth* (pp. 597–624). Mahwah, NJ: Erlbaum.

García, G. E., McKoon, G., & August, D. (2008). Language and literacy assessment. In D. August & T. Shanahan (Eds.), *Developing reading and writing in second-language learners: Lessons from the Report of the National Literacy Panel on Language-Minority Children and Youth* (pp. 251–274). New York: Routledge, Center for Applied Linguistics, and International Reading Association.

García, G. E., & Pearson, P. D. (1994). Assessment and diversity. In L. Darling-Hammond (Ed.), *Review of research in education* (Vol. 20, pp. 337–392). Washington, DC: American Educational Research Association.

Geisinger, K. F., Spies, R. A., Carlson, J. F., & Plake, B. S. (Eds.). (2007). *Mental measurements yearbook* (17th ed.). Highland Park, NJ: Gryphon Press.

Hakuta, K., & Beatty, A. (2000). *Testing English language learners in U.S. schools*. Washington, DC: National Academy Press.

IDEA language proficiency tests (1994). Brea, CA: Ballard & Tighe.

Jiménez, R. T., García, G. E., & Pearson, P. D. (1995). Three children, two languages, and strategic reading: Case studies in bilingual/monolingual reading. *American Educational Research Journal, 32*, 31–61.

Jiménez, R. T., García, G. E., & Pearson, P. D. (1996). The reading strategies of bilingual Latina/o students who are successful English readers: Opportunities and obstacles. *Reading Research Quarterly, 31*(1), 90–112.

Kindler, A. L. (2002). *Survey of the states' limited English proficient students and available educational programs and services, 2000–2001 summary report*. Washington, DC: National Clearinghouse for English Language Acquisition and Language Instruction Educational Programs.

Laesch, K. B., & Van Kleeck, A. (1987). The cloze test as an alternative measure of language proficiency of children considered for exit from bilingual education programs. *Language Learning, 37*(2), 171–189.

Lee, J. F. (1986). Background knowledge and L2 reading. *Modern Language Journal, 70*, 350–354.

Messick, S. (1994). The interplay of evidence and consequences in the validation of performance assessments. *Educational Researcher, 23*(2), 13–23.

Mestre, J. P. (1984, Fall). The problem with problems: Hispanic students and math. *Bilingual Journal*, 15–20.

Moll, L. C., Amanti, C., Neff, D., & González, N. (1992). Funds of knowledge for teaching: Using a qualitative approach to connect homes and classrooms. *Theory into Practice, 31*(2), 132–141.

Nathenson-Mejía, S. (1992). Helping young writers working in Spanish: Informing instruction through analysis of writing in Spanish. *Bilingual Research Journal, 16*(3&4), 53–67.

National Clearinghouse for English Language Acquisition. (2006). *Resources about assessment and accountability for ELLs*. Washington, DC: Author. Retrieved November 13, 2007, from *www.ncela.gwu.edu/resabout/assessment/index.html*.

Nieto, S. (2002). *Language, culture and teaching. Critical perspectives for a new century*. Mahwah, NJ: Erlbaum.

No Child Left Behind Act of 2001, 20 U.S.C. 6301 et seq. (2002).

O'Malley, J. M., & Pierce, L. V. (1996). *Authentic assessment for English language learners.* New York: Addison Wesley.

Orellana, M. F., Reynolds, J., Dorner, L., & Meza, M. (2003). In other words: Translating or "para-phrasing" as a family literacy practice in immigrant households. *Reading Research Quarterly, 38*(1), 12–34.

Pérez, B., & Torres-Guzmán, M. E. (2002). *Learning in two worlds. An integrated Spanish/English biliteracy approach.* Boston: Allyn & Bacon.

Pierce, L. V. (2001). Assessment of reading comprehension strategies for intermediate bilingual learners. In S. R. Hurley & J. V. Tinajero (Eds.), *Literacy assessment of second language learners* (pp. 64–83). Needham Heights, MA: Allyn & Bacon.

Reyes, M. de la Luz. (1992) Challenging venerable assumptions: Literacy instruction for linguistically diverse students. *Harvard Educational Review, 62*(4), 427–446.

Rivera, C., & Collum, E. (2006). Introduction: Including and accounting for English language learners in state assessment systems. In C. Rivera & E. Collum (Eds.), *State assessment policy and practice for English language learners: A national perspective* (pp. xxxiii–xlvii). Mahwah, NJ: Erlbaum.

Rivera, C., Collum, E., Shafer Willner, L., & Sia Jr., J. K. (2006). An analysis of state assessment policies addressing the accommodation of English language learners. In C. Rivera & E. Collum (Eds.), *State assessment policy and practice for English language learners: A national perspective* (pp. 1–173). Mahwah, NJ: Erlbaum.

Sattler, J. M., & Altes, L. M. (1984). Performance of bilingual and monolingual Hispanic children on the Peabody Picture Vocabulary Test—Revised and the McCarthy Perceptual Performance Scale. *Psychology in Schools, 21*(3), 313–316.

Stevens, R. A., Butler, F. A., & Castellón-Wellington, M. (2000). *Academic language and content assessment: Measuring the progress of English language learners* (CSE Technical Report No. 552). Los Angeles: University of California, National Center for Research on Evaluation, Standards, and Student Testing.

Stiggins, R., Arter, J., Chappuis, J., & Chappuis, S. (2004). *Classroom assessment for learning: Doing it right—Using it well.* Portland, OR: Assessment Training Institute.

U.S. Department of Education. (2006, September 13). *Secretary Spellings announces final limited English proficiency regulations* [Press release]. Retrieved October 25, 2007, from *www.ed.gov/adminis/lead/accfount/lep-factsheet.html.*

Valdés, G. (2001). *Learning and not learning English: Latino students in American schools.* New York: Teachers College Press.

Woodcock, R., & Muñoz-Sandoval, A. (1993). *Woodcock–Muñoz language survey.* Itasca, IL: Riverside.

Zentella, A. C. (Ed.). (2005). *Building on strength: Language and literacy in Latino families and communities.* New York: Teachers College Press.

CHAPTER 5

The Literacy Development of English Learners
What Do We Know about Each Student's Literacy Development?

DONALD R. BEAR
REGINA E. SMITH

ISABEL

In Isabel's writing about her perfect vacation (Figure 5.1), she told her teachers about her social world, and the *way* she wrote told them about her literacy development. Effective teachers learn about students' social and developmental worlds, and they shape their instruction accordingly. This chapter shows you how to determine a developmental level for each student and how to plan developmental instruction based on this assess-

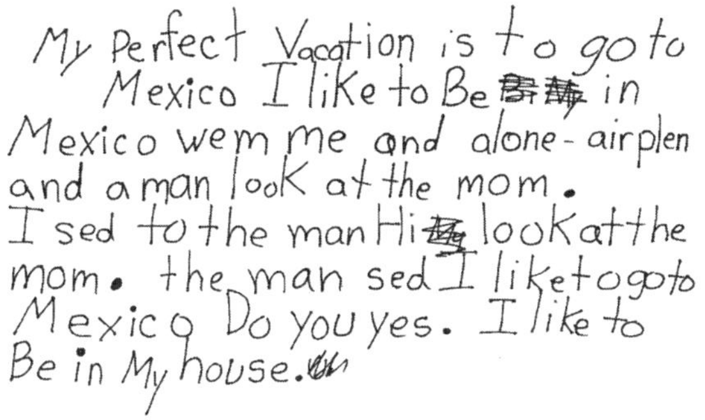

> My Perfect Vacation is to go to
> Mexico I like to Be ~~BM~~ in
> Mexico wem me and alone-airplen
> and a man look at the mom.
> I sed to the man Hi~~s~~ look at the
> mom. the man sed I like to go to
> Mexico Do you yes. I like to
> Be in My house.

FIGURE 5.1. "My Perfect Vacation."

ment. First, we provide a bird's-eye view of the developmental model and then delve into each of the five stages of development. We touch base with the literacy development of five learners throughout the chapter, including Isabel, and share what these artifacts say about literacy development.

What Does Isabel Teach Us about Development and Instruction?

Determining a developmental level is a matter of bringing together what teachers see and hear students do. In the area of literacy, Isabel's teachers gathered information about reading, writing, and orthographic or word knowledge. They knew how much the children read and how they used their knowledge of phonics, spelling, and vocabulary. The vacation piece in Figure 5.1 was a prompted second-grade writing assessment conducted throughout the school in February. The writing sample shows that Isabel's *language basket* is filled shallowly with English words, and there is the feel in the writing that she wants to obtain some sense of verbal fluency and expression. If only there were more English words in her basket, or if there were the possibility for her to tell stories in school in Spanish, what stories she might have told.

Isabel had begun the school year in the latter part of the emergent stage; she knew several letters of the alphabet, and she was beginning to point to words as she read. Periodic informal reading inventories were administered as part of the core program assessments. By early February, Isabel was reading early to middle kindergarten-level texts at an instructional level. Isabel was a word-by-word reader who read without expression and slowly. She pointed to the words as she read, and she read aloud when she read to herself. Isabel collected a few sight words after three or four rereadings of text at an independent or instructional level. In the developmental model that we walk through in the next section, these reading behaviors are associated with beginning reading. The teacher, Ms. Roberts, continued to use repetitive texts, chants, and rhymes during instructional activities and was able to increase the complexity and length of the texts.

Isabel's teachers also used the results of periodic spelling inventories and oral-reading analyses to quickly learn a little more about her developmental word knowledge. As can be seen in Figure 5.2, Isabel moved from being a late emergent speller in July, the beginning of the school year, to a middle letter name speller in February of second grade. She became proficient in spelling beginning and final consonants, many words with short vowels, and many beginning consonant blends. Isabel

Correct Spelling	July Assessment	February Assessment	May Assessment
1. fan	fan	fan	fan
2. pet	parr	pet	pet
3. dig	dena	dig	dig
4. rob	roro	rob	Rob
5. hope	Pinsp	hop	hopp
6. wait	tinor	wat	watt
7. gum	gins	gum	gum
8. sled	Siroz	sid	sedd
9. stick	Spin	siy	stick
10. shine	piszi	shin	sin
11. dream	giors	dem	dem
12. blade	borrs	Ban	bladl
13. coach	Tisr	cot	ckosh
14. fright	fars	fit	fitt
15. chewed	tosro	toe	choe
16. crawl		col	ckole
17. wishes		wishs	whish
18. thorn		son	chon
19. shouted		shati	satid
20. spoil		soy	spoll
21. growl		gaagl	grall
22. third		srd	thrd
23. camped		cap	ckap
24. tries		tis	chris
25. clapping		vape	chapen
26. riding		rdte	Riding

FIGURE 5.2. Isabel's spelling during second grade (July, February, May).

began to spell some consonant digraphs correctly, as well as sounds that do not exist in Spanish, such as *s*-blends and digraphs. She spelled the /ch/ in *coach* and *chewed* with a T as TOE, substituting a plosive /t/ for a more difficult, affricate sound, the /ch/, a sound that exists in both Spanish and English. The difficulties with the *th*, with SRD for *third* and SON for *thorn*, may relate to immature speech and delay in learning to say /th/. *Camped* was spelled CAP, with the *-ed* omitted. Isabel regularly included a vowel, though the spelling of vowels was inconsistent. During this time, Ms. Roberts continued to use picture vowel sorts with Isabel's group and began to teach same-vowel word families (e.g., *-at* vs. *-an*) and mixed-vowel word families (e.g., *-at* vs. *-ot*).

English learners do not make up a single, homogeneous group. Students have unique social and language backgrounds, and teachers bend instruction to help students resolve what confusions there might be between students' primary languages and English (Bear, Helman, & Woessner, in press). Isabel's teachers wanted to know more about her so that they could plan instruction. Her teachers in February were pleased that Isabel had made significant progress, and they created a rich profile of Isabel's development, triangulated across many measures of literacy performance. They could see that Isabel's growth was consistent with the developmental model across reading, writing, and spelling. What was confusing to the teachers was why she had not made greater progress, nor was it clear when she would read at grade level. You will meet Isabel again in this chapter during the presentation of beginning reading, the second stage of literacy development.

In this chapter, we explore the influences of students' language and literacy experiences in English. In particular, we consider how English learners from different language backgrounds think about the writing system, the orthography. The way they think about words is integral to their learning to read and write. You will see how literacy develops at the different stages and how this model of development guides instruction with English learners. The question to keep in mind is: What do we know about each student's literacy development?

A MODEL OF LITERACY DEVELOPMENT

The developmental model is presented in Figure 5.3, and was developed by Edmund Henderson when he was a reading professor at the University of Virginia (Henderson, 1981). This figure illustrates the integration or *synchrony* among reading, writing, and spelling, and we use this developmental model to determine a stage of development for each student.

LAYERS OF THE ORTHOGRAPHY FOR ENGLISH:		
ALPHABET / SOUND	PATTERN →	MEANING →

Reading and Writing Stages:

Emergent →	Beginning →	Transitional →	Intermediate →	Advanced
Early Middle Late	Early Middle Late	Early Middle Late	Early Middle Late	Early Middle Late

Pretend read
Directionality
Concept of Word (COW)
No COW Partial Full

Read aloud, word-by-word, fingerpoint reading; ~10–200+ sight words; ~40–60 wpm instructional rate

Approaching fluency, phrasal; some expression in oral reading; ~60–100 wpm oral instructional rate; Wright Brothers of reading Approaching fluency; more organization; several paragraphs

Read fluently, with expression; develop a variety of reading styles; vocabulary grows with experience reading ~100–200 silent, ~150–250 silent, instructional rate

Fluent writing; build expression and voice; experience different writing styles and genres; writing shows personal problem solving and personal reflection

Pretend write
Increasing use of letters
Beginning consonants

Word-by-word writing; writing starts with a few words to paragraph in length

Spelling Stages:

Emergent →	Letter Name–Alphabetic →	Within-Word Pattern →	Syllables and Affixes →	Derivational Relations
Early Middle Late	Early Middle Late	Early Middle Late	Early Middle Late	Early Middle Late

Examples of spellings:

	Early	Middle	Late	Early	Middle	Late	Early	Middle	Late	Early	Middle	Late	Early	Middle	Late
bed		MST	B	ft	bd	bad	bed								
ship		TFP	S	jn	sp	shep		ship							
float		SMT	F	kd	fot	sep	flote	floaut	flowt	float					
train		FSMP	G	slr	jan	flot	teran	traen	trane	catol					
cattle			K	p jr	tan	flott				train					
cellar			S		catl	chran	tran	catel	seler	cattel	cattle				
pleasure					salr	cadol	seler	celer	plesher	seller	cattle				
confident					plasr	celr	plejer	pleser		pleser	seller	pleser	pleasure	pleasure	
opposition						plager				confident	plesher	plesour	confident	confedent	confident
										opasishan	confiednet	opositian	oposision	opposition
												oppasishion		

FIGURE 5.3. The synchrony of literacy development.

Looking among reading, writing, and spelling behaviors as we do in Figure 5.3, there are distinct literacy behaviors that are developmental hallmarks to determine a stage of development for each student. This unified or integrated model of development and learning does rely, particularly during the first three stages, on the centrality of *orthographic knowledge*, the knowledge students have of the structure of words as evidenced in their reading and spelling (Henderson, 1992). Orthographic knowledge is like an engine that makes fluent traverses through text possible. Orthographic knowledge makes for rapid word recognition that then makes it possible to chunk text into phrases.

Take a moment to examine the top row in Figure 5.3 for reading. Underneath the heading "Beginning," the reading behaviors characteristic of beginning readers such as Isabel are presented; they read in a word-by-word fashion, fingerpoint read, and read aloud to themselves. In the next column, transitional reading and its characteristics are noted. Transitional readers are approaching fluency; they have just enough word knowledge and automaticity in word knowledge to read many unfamiliar words in phrases with modest fluency. This is the period of time in which students move from reading partly orally and partly silently to reading mostly silently by the end of the stage.

In synchrony with the reading, consider the spelling stages presented in the bottom half of Figure 5.3. First there are squiggles of emergent writing, and then there are misspellings under the levels of letter-name–alphabetic spelling. Students in the letter-name stage of spelling and the beginning stage of reading learn how to spell short vowel patterns. A letter-name speller might spell *float* as FLOT. In contrast to letter-name spellers, students in the within-word pattern stage are in the transitional stage of reading; they often spell *float* as FLOTE or FLOWT, they have learned to spell short vowel patterns accurately, and they are experimenting with how to spell long vowel patterns.

The differences in orthographic or word knowledge observed in spelling accounts for the differences in reading between beginning and transitional readers. The word knowledge of beginning readers is insufficient for fluent reading without repeated practice. In the transitional stage, fluency is accomplished as students' word knowledge advances. In the stage-by-stage discussion that follows, we discuss word knowledge and reading fluencies and highlight the synchronies—the timing of development—across various measures. We have found that the literacy learning of English learners follows the same developmental sequence as that of native speakers, but with a twist: Their learning is tempered by what they know about languages and other literacies (Helman & Bear, 2007).

A CONCORDANCE OF LEVELS: HOW DO YOU DESCRIBE YOUR STUDENTS' LEARNING?

Before we introduce you to English learners who illustrate the five stages of literacy development, consider in what ways teachers, and particularly you, think about development and students' learning. Many teachers discuss students' reading development in terms of grade-level achievement informally (below, on, or above grade level) or more formally with a standardized test score (e.g., 3.2, or how many words read in a minute), and students are described by the levels at which they read aloud leveled texts with good accuracy (reads at level D, etc.) or by an accumulation of state-prescribed learning standards. Table 5.1 presents a concordance, or agreement, to locate different ways to describe development and achievement.

Try finding your students' grade level in the far left column, and then look across that level to see whether the developmental stages and other descriptors match. The information in concordances such as this assists in triangulating data and guiding teachers in the selection of instructional-level materials. What levels of reading, writing, and spelling would you expect of students? For example, starting with the second part of second grade, look at the developmental reading and spelling ranges established in the third and fourth columns. Obviously, all students are not reading on grade level. Compared with a grade-level designation, a developmental perspective can be more appealing and more pertinent in describing learning to teachers, parents, and students. This concordance, developed with the advice of colleagues, is referred to later in regard to matching reading materials with developmental levels.

When determining a stage, some overlap exists between two adjacent stages (Is the student a late beginning reader or an early transitional reader?). In most instances, the more conservative assignment is a better choice for instruction. The boundaries between stages and levels are fuzzy boundaries, and there is gradual growth across stages and levels. Assessment processes provide multiple signs and signals that show a gradual movement across stages, and there are times when students are between stages and show behaviors characteristic of more than one stage.

The column on the far right of Table 5.1 includes Ehri's description of development by phases (Ehri & McCormick, 1998). Like Ehri, other researchers have explored the idea of stages or phases and have presented a sequence of development that fits well with Figure 5.3 (Invernizzi & Hayes, 2004; Wolf, 2007). These models, like the

TABLE 5.1. Concordance of Developmental Stages of Reading, Spelling and Reading and Program Levels

Grade Level	Reading Level	Reading Stages	Spelling Stages	Instructional Levels - Letters	Instructional Levels - Numbers	Ranges of Instruction Rates, oral/silent (wpm)	Lexiles	Reading Phases (Ehri)
Pre-K	Readiness	Early emergent	Early emergent	—	—	Support read	NA	Prealphabetic
K	Readiness	Early emergent to middle emergent	Early to middle emergent	A	1	Support read	NA	Prealphabetic
K/1st	Readiness	Middle emergent to late emergent	Middle to late emergent	B	2	Support read	NA	Prealphabetic
K/1st	PP	Late emergent to early beginning	Late emergent to early letter name	C	3	Familiar Read	NA	Partial alphabetic
1st	PP2	Early to middle beginning	Early to middle letter name–alphabetic		4	Familiar read	NA	Partial alphabetic
1st	PP3	Middle beginning	Middle letter name–alphabetic	E	6 and 8	40–60 wpm	NA	Partial alphabetic
1st	Primer	Late beginning	Late letter name–alphabetic	F and G	10 and 12		200L–400L	Full alphabetic
1st/2nd	First	Early transitional	Early within-word pattern	H and I	14 and 16		200L–400L	Full alphabetic
2nd	Second	Middle transitional	Middle within-word pattern	J and K	18 and 20	60–100/60–100	300L–500L	Consolidated alphabetic
2nd/3rd	Second	Late transitional	Late within-word pattern	L and M	24 and 28		300L–500L	Consolidated

Grade	Stage	Spelling Focus	Text Level	Number	WPM	Lexile	Fluency
3rd/4th	Third Early intermediate	Early syllables & affixes	M, N, O, P	30, 34, 38		500L–700L	Consolidated
4th	Fourth Middle intermediate	Middle syllables and affixes	P, Q, R	40		650L–850L	Automatic
5th	Fifth Intermediate to advanced	Middle syllables and affixes to early derivational relations	S, T, U	50	80–100/ 100–180	650L–850L	Automatic
6th	Sixth Intermediate to advanced	Middle syllables and affixes to middle derivational relations	V and higher	60	80–120 100–200	650L–850L	Automatic
7th	Seventh Early to middle advanced	Early to middle derivational relations	Y/Z	70	100–120 150–250	850L–1000L	Automatic
8th	Eighth Middle advanced	Middle derivational relations	Z and up	80		850L–1000L	Automatic

Note. Rates vary by the difficulty of the text, students' background knowledge, and development within a stage. (An advanced [teenage] reader may hit 160 wpm orally in easy text; an early beginning reader may read relatively difficult material at 40 wpm.)

developmental model described in this chapter, are based on behaviors teachers see every day. With these behaviors in mind, teachers learn to see and hear development, and as they teach, they assess to optimize instruction that is differentiated for students' independent and instructional levels.

THE INFLUENCES OF STUDENTS' PRIMARY LANGUAGES

Before we examine ways to assess students' development, consider the language and literacy backgrounds of English learners. Two questions about English learners' primary languages may be asked: How do students use their primary language and literacy? And how do students' first languages influence their learning of English?

Teachers want to know about all students' language and literacy development. English learners bring their primary languages and literacies to learning to read and write in English. The more they know about language and literacy in one language, the better prepared they are to learn to read and write in English. Although there are genuine differences among literacies, there are also many commonalities across writing systems, even between Chinese and English. What all written languages share are the three layers presented at the top of Figure 5.3: *alphabet/sound*, *pattern*, and *meaning*. Students' reading and writing show us what they know about these three layers of English.

How Do Students Use Their Primary Languages and Literacies?

To understand students' connection with another language, teachers learn more about language and literacy in students' lives; for example, what they read at home, whom they talk to in this language, and simple daily routines with language, such as in what language the students prefer to view television. Teachers benefit from knowing more about the educational milieu at home, the education of family members, and the types of literacy used at home.

At school, teachers observe students talking in different social settings—on the playground, when students come into the classroom and chat with friends, and in instructional settings, including whole-class, small-group, individual, and partner activities. To know students' language use, teachers can listen to students talking in social situations in which the students are fluent and expressive. What are their vocabularies like in their primary languages? When meeting with parents, teachers want to know what parents have noticed about children's language and literacy development. This is all information necessary to better understand the use of language and literacy in students' social worlds, or their *social ecologies*. Additional aspects of students' language and literacy development are their learning and health histories; for example, illnesses, attendance, schools, and special services. Knowing about students' social ecologies makes it easier to relate to them as readers and writers and to choose materials and activities that motivate them personally (Bear & Helman, 2004).

How Do Students' First Languages Influence Learning English?

To answer this question, teachers can investigate the structure of students' primary languages and then compare the language structures of their primary languages with English. These are the same comparisons students make as they learn to speak and read English. There are structures in each of the seven language systems: phonemics, phonology, syntax, semantics, morphology, prosody, and pragmatics on the language side, and the orthography in the written areas. Differences in syntax between English and other languages are easy to hear, as when an adjective follows a noun ("It is a waterfall beautiful") or when the *-ed* is deleted in speech and writing for past-tense endings because the structure is unfamiliar to many English learners.

Students' orthographic knowledge is something they use when they read and spell. Their orthographic knowledge draws on their knowledge in several of the language systems, including sounds, syntax, and morphology, the meaningful structures of words. For example, in the area of comparing phonemes, or the sounds, between languages, it is worth knowing that students who speak Spanish know 24 distinct sounds. To learn the 44 sounds of English, students who speak Spanish compare their sound system with that of English, and they make substitutions in reading and writing that are applications of what they know in Spanish (Helman, 2004). By knowing the sounds of Spanish, teachers understand what differences to focus on in word study activities. For example, after students who speak Spanish have learned most beginning sounds, they compare the /b/ and /v/ sounds of English, because in Spanish, these two sounds are said in the same manner. Perusal of online resources such as Wikipedia provides an overview of the structures of different languages and their writing systems; or refer to texts such as *Learner English* (Swan & Smith, 2001).

THE SYNCHRONY OF DEVELOPMENT

Reading, writing, and spelling develop in synchrony; they unfold and grow in a timed sequence. Development is seen socially in the reciprocal interactions with others that become increasingly more complex (Bronfenbrenner & Morris, 1998). A reciprocal process may also be seen in the way students learn about words. Reading and writing feed each other; as students study word structures and spelling, their word reading skills improve. As they do more reading, their word knowledge grows. *Reading informs writing*, and *writing informs reading* (*reading ↔ writing*; Ehri, 1997; Stanovich, 2000; Templeton & Morris, 2000). Find a great writer who is not a voracious reader! Great writers become great by doing lots of reading. Many writers describe how they studied their beloved authors, rereading what they wrote, copying out favorite parts, and imitating their styles.

The Slant of Development between Reading and Spelling

Reading development is ahead of spelling development when correctness is the way development is measured. The measure of correctness creates a *slant of development*: (spelling/reading). Reading unfolds before the behaviors in spelling are learned; for example, students read more words accurately than they spell.

Feature analyses of reading and spelling errors paint a more integrated and unified picture of development and demonstrate what students are learning and what to teach in word study. Teachers want to know what students are trying to learn next. In reading, *orthographic competencies*, what students know about words, are observed in what students say when they read words presented in isolation and when they read texts. In spelling, an analysis of spelling errors lets teachers know from what word study instruction students will benefit. In addition to what students do correctly, analyses of what strategies students use when they do not know how to spell are quite valuable. What particular features of the orthography students are experimenting with, what they are using but confusing, shows their instructional levels for learning (Invernizzi, Abouzeid, & Gill, 1994).

Later in this chapter, the focus children illustrate the slant of development. To illustrate the relationship between reading and writing, consider students in the transitional stage of reading. On the developmental model in Figure 5.3, transitional readers are "approaching fluency." Even though transitional readers read most single-syllable and many two-syllable words correctly, in their spelling they are still learning about long vowel patterns. To illustrate, in reading, students decode fairly frequently occurring polysyllabic words such as *happily* and *mistake* easily, yet in spelling they are learning long vowel patterns, such as the CVCe, CVVC, CVV patterns (*name, rain, bay*) and complex vowel patterns (*brought, weight*). English learners demonstrate the same slant of development in their reading and writing regardless of age or grade level (e.g., third graders may be beginning readers, and sixth graders may be transitional readers).

In summary, spelling is a conservative measure of what students know about words. The inverse of the idea that students read more words than they spell is that if students can spell a word, it is highly likely that they can read the word. Furthermore, they can read even more difficult words, and this is the slant of development we look for when assessing students. Given the power of spelling as a measure of word knowledge, a qualitative analysis of students' spelling is an assessment that not only assesses spelling but also suggests what reading levels students might have achieved. We explore this notion in the next section.

ASSESSMENT AND THE CREATION OF INSTRUCTIONAL GROUPS

When the school year begins, teachers assess students to determine their instructional levels, a step that leads to differentiated instruction. Given the powerful relationship between reading and spelling development that Henderson integrated as five stages of reading and spelling (Henderson, 1981), teachers may also use informal spelling inventories to understand students' orthographic knowledge. In contrast, many teachers conduct an individually administered informal reading inventory (IRI), which begins with an informal test of word recognition in isolation (WRI) using graded word lists. Then they proceed to have students read selections of graded or leveled passage reading. Beginning with a spelling inventory instead of an individually administered WRI may offer efficiencies when organizing instructional groups. Why not use an easily administered assessment to begin the literacy assessment of students' orthographic and word knowledge? In the assessment process, some teachers use the results of the spelling inventory to prioritize the selection of students for further assessment and only later go to a WRI or IRI with passage selections for oral or silent reading.

Spelling Inventories and Analyses as a First Look at Instructional Groups

Most spelling inventories include a list of 20–25 words, and teachers usually administer the inventory in small groups or with the whole class.

An inventory is chosen because of the potential of students to show what they know about words. Students need to misspell enough of the words to determine a spelling stage. To illustrate the integration of literacy learning and the slant of development, consider students in the within-word pattern stage of spelling who are transitional readers. These students may spell *rain* as RANE as they learn to spell CVCe words; and in reading, based on the slant of development, they may read instructional-level texts that include easy polysyllabic words.

Feature guides in qualitative spelling inventories lead to scores and indicate what spelling or orthographic features students know and what features they are misspelling and are approaching understanding. A feature guide may also indicate what spelling stages students are in and whether or not they are at the beginning, middle, or end of the stage (Bear, Invernizzi, Templeton, & Johnston, 2008).

An initial spelling assessment is often a source of motivation for teachers because it provides a concrete view of the range of spelling abilities in their classrooms and helps them see how much about literacy development can be learned from looking at a student's spelling, beyond simply whether or not words are spelled correctly. In some schools, to mark students' progress in word knowledge, spelling inventories are administered three or four times over the school year.

The misspellings at the bottom of Figure 5.3 are characteristic of each stage of spelling development. Examining a collection of as few as six to twelve errors from an inventory or writing sample makes it possible to assign a stage for each student. Sometimes, English learners do not know the words they are asked to spell. A spelling inventory that includes pictures helps them to know what words they are being asked to spell (Bear, Helman, Templeton, Invernizzi, & Johnston, 2007).

Once a spelling stage has been determined, teachers know what types of orthographic features to teach. The spelling assessment is also a data point to triangulate with other reading and writing behaviors; knowing a spelling stage makes it possible to hypothesize a students' reading level. With a stage of spelling in mind, developmental groups such as the one presented in Figure 5.4 are created. Forming these groups may start with a brief spelling assessment and then be further shaped by other measures and diagnostic touchstones of reading and writing development, as described in Figure 5.3.

Analyzing English Learners' Spelling: Six Types of Spelling Errors

We have described six types of spelling errors characteristic of English learners, and when the error types are taken into consideration, unusual

Spelling Stages -->	Emergent			Letter Name–Alphabetic			Within Word Pattern			Syllables & Affixes		
	Early	Middle	Late	Early	Middle	Late	Early	Middle	Late	Early	Middle	Late
					Lilianna	Isabel	Casey	Alex	Cheyenne			
					Veronika	George	Alina	Chris	Ignacio			
						Jesus	Loren	Heather	Jorge			
						Brian	David	Jason				
						Jake	Devin	Kristian				
						Jennifer	Ana	Kevin				
							Liz	Marlena				
								Sarah				
								Taylor				
								Tye				
								Natasha				

FIGURE 5.4. February spelling-by-stage classroom organization chart in a second-grade classroom.

spelling errors make more sense (Helman & Bear, 2007). These six error types provide a framework for analyzing spelling development:

1. English learners progress through the same stages of spelling development as they learn about the three layers of the orthography—sound/alphabet–pattern–meaning—and, as they are also learning a new language, they need more time and experience to develop.

2. Misspellings can mirror minimal phonemic contrasts between students' primary languages and English. For example, look for vowel substitutions that match the vowels in students' primary languages (spelling *hot* as HAT because the short o in *hot* is spelled with an *a* in the student's first language). In the case of consonants, look for consonants in English that are difficult to discriminate or pronounce that do not exist in students' first languages (Bear et al., 2007). For example, the nasal sounds of English, such as the /ng/ in *sing* compared with the /n/ in *fan*, are difficult for many English learners to distinguish. To analyze spelling errors, keep in mind, first, standard developmental errors and, second, the errors that reflect the interaction between students' languages and English.

3. Look for whole-word substitutions and the similarities in the features of the target words and the misspellings. English learners are often predisposed to memorize some sight words, and as they ponder the sound–symbol relationships of English, they plug in a word that is similar in some way(s). A student who wrote FISH for *fences* may have drawn on the first sound for comparison. English learners may be older learners as they progress through the stages, and they may memorize strings of letters and proceed to more difficult patterns without making generalizations about the orthographic patterns that underlie the words they have memorized.

4. English learners often do more sounding out, such as in the spelling of BLEID for *blade*. Why English learners do more sounding out is probably most often related to the way they understand their primary oral and written languages. Spanish, the predominant primary language among students, is described as a surface or transparent orthography; the orthography lends itself to being sounded out. Spanish is also an open-syllable language—most syllables end with a vowel. Students may do more sounding out because they expect there to be a vowel at the end of syllables, so the word *bat* may be spelled BATA.

5. There is greater variability in the spelling of English learners. English learners have so much to learn about the 44 sounds of English, and it often takes them more time to learn the numerous vowel sounds. There is greater variability in the vowel substitutions that students make until they internalize the vowel sounds of English.

6. Students may omit ending and middle syllables. For example, *marched* may be spelled MARCH. This is an example of an error that is related to structural differences between English and students' primary languages. The *-ed* at the end of *marched* is a grammatical, past-tense, inflectional ending, and this grammatical ending, pronounced in one of three ways (*walked, called, waited*), may be unrecognized by English learners and thus omitted in their spelling.

Instructional Groups in the Classroom

Once the teacher has completed an analysis of students' spelling samples and has determined a stage of spelling for each student, instructional groups emerge. These groups may meet formally on a regular basis with the teacher or may be considered for ordering materials and for choosing activities.

In a second-grade classroom, the team teachers, Ms. Roberts and Ms. Husband, took the information about students' spelling to plan their initial guided reading instruction and to pinpoint children whom they want to immediately study further (Bear, Invernizzi, Templeton, & Johnston, 2008, DVD). Figure 5.4 is the grouping pattern that emerged from a qualitative spelling assessment conducted in February, the seventh month in their Title I school. A sizable amount of the explicit literacy instruction for the 29 students was delivered in small groups. The nine English learners were integrated into the class, and two of the students received some pullout instruction with the English-learner specialist.

The teachers had four instructional literacy groups, as seen in Figure 5.4. There was some slight mixing and rearranging of students into groups after reviewing the results of their core program's IRI. Ms. Roberts taught one group of students in the letter-name–alphabetic stage and the group in the early within-word pattern stage. Ms. Husband taught the students in the two higher groups of within-word pattern spellers/transitional readers.

Ms. Husband presented 10-minute lessons to the 15 students from the two highest groups of within-word pattern spellers seen in Figure 5.4. They met to introduce new sorts, review concepts, clarify misconceptions, and add words that fit with the sort they studied. Once she explained to students what they would do independently, such as review their sorts, enter more words in their word study notebooks, or play word study games, Ms. Husband divided the 15 students into two groups: Students in one group went to their desks to complete the word study activity for the day, and the other group of students met with Ms. Husband at the reading table for reading and word study instruction. When children were not working with their teachers in small groups, they participated in center activities or worked on independent tasks at their desks. In these individual and center activities, students extended and applied concepts taught explicitly in reading groups. Activities included independent sorts, writing sorts, word study games, speed sorts, drawing and labeling, and charting, or recording in word study notebooks words that fit the patterns they were learning. Reading tasks included independent reading in the classroom library, computer activities, and reading and rereading familiar texts in their personal readers (Bear, Caserta-Henry, & Venner, 2004). The children completed some of these activities in a word study center that matched color folders assigned to instructional groups.

LITERACY DEVELOPMENT: STAGE BY STAGE

Assessment with the developmental model in mind has shown what stages students are in and how to best match instruction to students' perceptual understandings. Literacy instruction is then provided in each of the five essential reading components described by the National Reading Panel (2000): phonemic awareness, phonics, fluency, vocabulary, and comprehension. Classroom organization to teach these essential components is also influenced by the contexts of the school and district. Ms. Husband and Ms. Roberts organized homogeneous groups for guided reading and word study, and they presented writing and read-alouds in whole-class and heterogeneous groups. In the discussion that follows, we focus primarily on reading with students in instructional level reading and word study activities. These two types of activities are most dependent on making the perceptual match between what students know and the materials and activities chosen for instruction.

Emergent Stage Development

There are plenty of emergent readers and writers in kindergarten and first-grade classrooms. Some primary-age newcomers do come to second and third grade as emergent learners, and, like the English learners in kindergarten and first grade, their word knowledge can be investigated informally in meaningful language experience activities. What books are their favorites? In what languages have they experienced literacy? Students' experiences in listening to stories and being involved actively in language and literacy activities and communities are paramount as a foundation for learning to read and write.

Early Emergent Reading and Spelling

It is common for early emergent writers to write their names with wide scribbles, and they may tell a story as they scribble. Gradually, they learn how to hold a crayon or large marker. Preschool emergent readers have plenty to say, they learn to listen to stories, and they enjoy movement to accompany songs. Emergent readers play with the alphabet, thumb through cloth books, tub books, and cardboard books, and listen to short books with soothing, rhythmic language. They name objects as in picture books, act out movements of their favorite characters, make lists for menus, to-do lists, and lists of rules (Helman, Bear, Johnston, Invernizzi, & Templeton, 2009). The activities are not focused on formal phonics instruction. It is never too early to provide a rich language environment and to create opportunities for students to talk to try out the language they hear (McGee & Schickedanz, 2007).

Middle and Late Emergent Readers and Spellers and Concept of Word in Print

During the second half of this stage, students' writing begins to look more like real writing, and in reading, students begin to sit and try to read a book from which they have memorized some lines. Students in the latter part of the emergent stage know the letters and can recite the alphabet. They hear the salient sounds and feel them articulatory gestures, and may write a few corresponding letters on the page.

Students may know a few letter–sound correspondences and are close to being able to read in a conventional sense, at which point they begin to learn easy phonics and acquire sight words. Stated quite directly, students who do not have a concept of word in print (COW) are emergent readers who need close support as they learn to fingerpoint read and track text accurately. Students who do not have a COW are not expected to learn sight words, and they will not make the same phonic generalizations that are the natural result when students learn sight words from reading. It is not a simple skill for students to manage their pointing as they recite a memorized text. Teachers and researchers have found that students who do not have a COW lose their beat and their place in pointing (Flanigan, 2007; Morris, Bloodgood, Lomax, & Perney, 2003). In English, it is important to assess COW with texts that have a two-syllable word on each line, preferably toward the middle of the line. The two-syllable words make it possible for students to demonstrate whether they are going to be thrown off in their pointing. For example, in reading with support of memory the line "1, 2, buckle my shoe," students who do not have a COW are thrown off pointing with the second syllable of *buckle*, /kle/.

Activities to Support Middle and Late Emergent Readers and Spellers

The way to assess COW is the way to teach COW. Sentence strips, two-line poems, level A books, and personal dictations about their experiences become the reading material of emergent readers. Children continue to play with the alphabet and sing the alphabet song. By desire and familiarity, middle and late emergent learners acquire a few sight words, and they practice writing a few favorite words ("How many times will my child write the word *love*?" a parent of a kindergartner asked).

Concept sorts are a way for English learners to learn vocabulary; in these picture sorts they take picture cards and arrange them conceptually by a theme, in an order that makes sense to them (plants, animals). After sorting individually or with a partner, they discuss their sorts in small groups. The pictures in the sorts make it easier for them to describe what they did. Students may be able to sort pictures by a few beginning sounds as they move to the letter name–alphabetic stage of spelling.

Beginning Reading and Letter Name–Alphabetic Spelling Stage Development

We return to Isabel, the second grader whose description of a perfect vacation and an airplane ride to Mexico opened this chapter. The study of Isabel's learning is compelling because of the mixed feelings teachers had about her success and development at the end of second grade. As illustrated here, Isabel made significant progress, and yet her learning missed the benchmark even as teachers planned carefully developmental instruction over 2 years.

Isabel's Language and Literacy Learning

Isabel entered second grade as a late emergent reader and speller who had no independent reading level. Her instructional-level experiences occurred in supported reading activities with the teacher and partners, reading materials with one and two sentences on a page. Isabel was a beginning reader most of this second-grade year. The piece she wrote about her vacation (Figure 5.1) was written in February, when she was a middle beginning reader who had memorized some sight words, reading in level C materials.

Isabel is an English learner whose family came to the United States just before she was born. Her parents stopped by school very occasionally; her father was more interactive than her mother, and he would ask if Isabel had completed her assignments. Isabel's sister, in seventh grade, was the primary contact and an advocate who regularly came by the classroom. Isabel seemed to exhibit a delay in development. There were some questions during a child study team meeting regarding her cognitive and language development. Isabel had been in school since kindergarten and had received assistance from an English language teacher throughout. Her teachers described her language as consisting of short phrases, and this was illustrated in the writing sample that opened this chapter. Isabel's parents said that the rate of her language development in Spanish was not the same as those of their other children. Isabel had extended stays away from school, visiting family in Mexico. Isabel did the vast majority of her reading in school. Her second-grade teachers knew from records and observation that Isabel had not had successful educational experiences in kindergarten and first grade.

Isabel's Orthographic Development over the School Year

Qualitative spelling inventories were administered in this year-round school in July, February, and May, and Isabel's development can be traced through Figure 5.2. In July, Isabel spelled *fan* correctly, and then showed an ability to spell the beginning and sometimes the ending sounds of many words. Her teachers thought that the two correct vowel spellings were accidental and that the first word was spelled correctly because her neighbor told her what letters to write. The slant of development for Isabel showed that she could read some easy words and was consistent in reading the words in familiar rereading activities.

Isabel's instruction focused on learning the letter–sound correspondences in English and developing a COW. Ms. Roberts conducted picture sorts to teach the letter–sound correspondences and to develop Isabel's English vocabulary. Easy-to-memorize short repetitive texts, chants, and rhymes were learned orally and then presented in texts to help Isabel track text as she read aloud the memorized English text. These familiar materials were collected in personal readers. Isabel also dictated in Spanish, one- and two-sentence dictations about her experiences. The dictations, with English translations, were typed in 28-point type and accompanied with a photograph, such as a picture of a favorite pet or a picture drawn by Isabel. A copy was included in her personal reader, one copy was used by Isabel to underline sight words, one copy went home to read with family members, and another was included in the teachers' folders or in a class book.

Between July and February, Isabel made tremendous progress in her reading and spelling. She had successfully achieved a rudimentary COW and was beginning to read some words by sight. Her reading and spelling development in February were discussed in detail earlier in the chapter. At the end of the school year, Isabel had developed a full COW, and Ms. Roberts used reading materials with embedded phrases and some short quotations. She was solidifying her knowledge of short vowel sounds while beginning to study consonant blends and digraphs in her word study. Ms. Roberts taught short vowels in mixed-vowel word sorts (e.g., short ă compared with short ŏ) and introduced consonant digraphs and blends through picture sorts.

We see in Isabel a picture of an English learner who began second grade reading at an emergent level and ended the year reading solidly at a first-grade, beginning reader level. As a beginning reader, Isabel read books with three lines on a page in a word-by-word fashion, without expression. After a few supported rereadings, she was able to read familiar selections accurately and with slight expression. It can be seen across her spelling (Figure 5.2) that Isabel's vowel spellings were more accurate and her errors made more sense. She was still a middle letter-name speller, and it would be another five months before she was proficient in her knowledge of spelling short vowels and most beginning consonant blends and digraphs. She made significant progress but still did not read grade-level materials at an instructional level. To close our look at Isabel, it is noteworthy that by the middle of the following year she learned and generalized long vowel patterns and was a transitional reader, the developmental level of the students discussed in the next section.

Transitional Reading and Within-Word Pattern Spelling

Ignacio is an English learner on or above grade level in second grade. Based on the concordance in Table 5.1, transitional readers' independent reading levels are K and L. Ignacio began the year as an early transitional reader and early within-word pattern speller. In Figure 5.3, the transitional readers are described as the "Wright Brothers of reading." Transitional readers are like the Wright Brothers in three ways: They have not gotten off the ground very high, they don't fly very far, and it does not take much to bring them down. They are not fluent yet, and though they do stop fingerpointing, transitional readers often begin to fingerpoint in slightly more difficult texts. Transitional reading begins with the level J books and easy *I Can Read* series books and ends with easy chapter books such as the *Horrible Harry* series and other beginning chapter books. At the beginning of this stage, students read orally and silently, and by the end of this stage, they are mostly reading silently.

Whereas in word study transitional readers study single-syllable words, by the end of this stage, students read nearly all one- and two-syllable words correctly and may have difficulty pronouncing polysyllabic words such as *religion* and *commotion*. Ignacio, along with the students in the large group in this level in Ms. Roberts and Ms. Husband's classroom, studied long vowel patterns.

Experimentation with long vowels was seen in his initial spelling assessment results in Figure 5.5, which included spelling errors such as WATE/*wait*, COATCH/*coach*, FRITE/*fright*. Ms. Husband began this group's word study instruction with a comparison of short and long vowel sounds and the VCe pattern across vowels. In early February, the spelling errors from Figure 5.5 reveal that Ignacio was still solidly in the within-word pattern stage and reading texts at the late second- to early third-grade level. At the end of the school year, Ignacio was a late within-word pattern speller with errors such as COECH/*coach*, SHAWDED/*shouted*, and CLAPING/*clapping*.

Teachers use this stage to teach English learners more about the

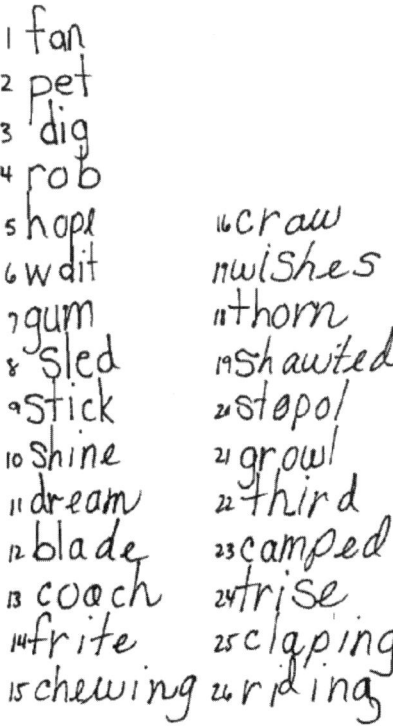

FIGURE 5.5. Ignacio's spelling in February of second grade.

vowel sounds of English. Through picture and word sorts, students obtain a better grasp of the pronunciation of the vowels.

During the transitional stage, English learners may achieve certain skills in reading words but may not comprehend. Reading rates may be slower than for native English-speaking transitional readers, especially when students are held up in processing the language structures of English. For lack of comprehension and verbal planning, some English learners may read with little oral reading expression or prosody. Some students gather the meaning of what they read without reading the text carefully. They read with *partial cues*; using their intelligence, they locate and learn the critical vocabulary to achieve at or above grade level and above their language and literacy skills.

Students in this stage are engaged in fluency and expression activities that include graphing rates of repeated readings and reading for dramatic purposes, as in easy Reader's Theatre activities (Peebles, 2007). They also do a lot of independent-level reading.

Upper-Level Reading and Spelling Development

The last two stages of reading and spelling development are the intermediate reading and syllables and affixes spelling and advanced reading and derivational relations spelling. In many ways, these stages are similar, and the stages are combined here as "upper" level development. Shane Templeton discusses upper-level development in Chapter 10 of this volume and expertly shares ways to use English cognates to expand students' vocabularies.

There are additional reasons to combine the stages here. As can be seen in Figure 5.3, in the upper stages, students' literacy needs are quite similar. In reading, both intermediate and advanced readers read silently. They learn study skills and how to adjust their reading rates depending on the purpose. They learn strategies and ways to comprehend and think their way through textbooks, novels, narratives, and expository materials of all kinds. Vocabulary instruction is linked to morphology and content-area vocabulary study. The depth of vocabulary study of related words and roots will vary by developmental level.

A final reason to combine groups is the need to consider the instruction derivational relations spellers have received. In the intermediate grades, they have not learned information taught during the syllables and affixes stage. For example, in fifth grade, there are excellent readers in the derivational relations stage of spelling who have not learned the principles that underlie consonant doubling, affixation with inflections, accentuation, and the meaning of prefixes and suffixes. Some word study lessons make explicit the meaning connections among interesting words that share roots (e.g., *duct, phobia, psych*, or *arch*); students' orthographic knowledge becomes deeper when what they understand *implicitly* as they read what is understood *explicitly* in word study activities.

The next learner to illustrate a stage of development is Enrique, a fifth grader who in February was an intermediate reader in the middle of the syllables and affixes stage of spelling. Enrique spoke Spanish at home and had been in the same elementary school for five years with good attendance. His oral and written vocabulary and knowledge of language structures were not on a fifth-grade level. Enrique had many interests and enjoyed reading easy novels with approximately 150 words on a page. His silent reading rate in grade-level materials was a little slow at 100 words per minute. Enrique read aloud with little expression even when reading quotations. After reading fifth-grade passages, Enrique scored 50 and 60% answering comprehension questions.

On an upper-level spelling inventory, Enrique spelled 52% of the words correctly, as would be expected of students in the middle of the syllables and affixes stage (see Figure 5.6). It is surprising that Enrique spelled some difficult words correctly (*irresponsible, commotion*) and yet did not spell simpler single- and two-syllable words correctly. Although it is commendable that he spelled difficult words correctly, there are some principles of word structures that will help him learn related words.

Considering the slant of development between reading and spelling, Enrique should be able to read words such as *continental* and *biologist* accurately in context and in word lists. However, if there were many four-syllable and more difficult polysyllabic words, his fluency and comprehension would be strained. In vocabulary instruction in class, content vocabulary was presented. For reading development, he learned the meaning of prefixes and suffixes, from easy to harder ones, and less frequent affixes (e.g., from *un-, re-, dis-, hypo-, hydro-* ...).

This was also a time for Enrique to examine complex vowel patterns in English, such as the *ou* in *pounce*, as well as some of the final consonant sounds (i.e., the *-dge*, in words like *dodge*) and the vowels in words such as *tunnel*, which he spelled TANNEL. There are many ways in which Enrique made meaning connections to content words, and he was able to use his knowledge of the Spanish–English cognates (e.g., *equation* and *ecuación*). Enrique also studied the basics of adding suffixes (e.g., *y* to *i* changes such as *happy* to *happiest*), including a look grammatically at the *-est* suffix).

During this stage, students who read words accurately with limited comprehension may be more visible than in previous stages. Do students look for key vocabulary words and make partial meaning based on par-

Spelling   **Word to Spell**
1. switch   √
2. smuge   smudge
3. trapped   √
4. scrape   √
5. nodded   knotted
6. shaving   √
7. squirt   √
8. pouns   pounce
9. scratches   √
10. creator   crater
11. sailor   √
12. village   √
13. disloyal   √
14. tannel   tunnel
15. humar   humor
16. conffidunce   confidence
17. fortunet   fortunate
18. visible   √
19. circunperence   circumference
20. civiliscation   civilization
21. monarchy   √
22. domenance   dominance
23. correspond   √
24. illeterate   illiterate
25. empasize   emphasize
26. opposition   √
27. chlorine   √
28. commotion   √
29. maddisenal   medicinal
30. irresponsible   √
31. succesion   succession
(erased *t* and wrote second *s*)

16/31 correct, 52% correct, 15 errors

FIGURE 5.6. Enrique's spelling in the seventh month of fifth grade.

tial language cues? There are students who look for the key vocabulary to read around a text. Many bright Spanish speakers who are not proficient in English are able to take key words in a text and think of related words among the 10,000 to 15,000 English and Spanish cognates in order to make good sense and obtain the gist of what they read. Reading with partial cues or just the bare bones does not always yield adequate comprehension. This is a perfect time to study the structures of English morphology and grammar and how changes in spelling and speech signal morphological changes; for example, how the *-ed* inflectional ending changes words to the past tense.

CONCLUSION

We conclude with a few ideas about literacy development to consolidate what has been presented. The activities and ideas that follow support teaching from a developmental perspective. The last two points are paramount and give direction for the integration of development in teaching.

1. Rely on development to focus instruction. English learners follow the same developmental steps, and knowing a stage of literacy development for each student is a first step in planning instruction.

2. Learn how the sounds and structures of students' primary languages interact with English and understand what language and literacy experiences students have in their primary languages.

3. Analyze students' spelling to determine a spelling stage and see how the spelling and reading development relate. The relationships among the levels in the concordance (Table 5.1) can be adjusted and expanded based on norms for schools and districts.

4. Teach students at their instructional and developmental levels. Teaching in developmental groups provides some efficiencies and interactions. Differentiation depends on a variety of instructional groupings, including students learning independently and with partners, and on having time with the teacher in small groups.

5. Meet regularly with colleagues to share and discuss assessments, grouping, and lessons and to share and organize materials.

6. See how students' orthographic and word knowledge relate to their comprehension. If word knowledge outstrips comprehension, it is a clear indication that vocabulary instruction, concept development, and thinking must be taught and engaged. Teaching developmentally makes it easier to concentrate on teaching for comprehension, understanding,

and motivation. See Chapter 9, this volume, for a further discussion of comprehension instruction with English learners.

7. *Explain development to students and families.* During parent–teacher class and individual meetings, show families where students are in their reading, writing, and spelling development. Walk through the developmental model in Figure 5.3 and present examples of the literacy behaviors related to the stages, with artifacts such as instructional and independent-level reading materials, writing samples, and word study activities and games. Showing students development gives them information and a sense of where they are going.

In this chapter, we saw how the language and literacy baskets of English learners such as Isabel are uniquely shaped by their learning ecologies and development. We have explored how teachers may observe the synchrony of development and use this information to plan instruction. To teach in a way that is mindful of students' development will contribute to their baskets for a lifetime of literacy.

REFERENCES

Bear, D. R., Caserta-Henry, C., & Venner, D. (2004). *Personal readers for emergent and beginning readers.* San Diego, CA: Teaching Resource Center.

Bear, D. R., & Helman, L. A. (2004). Word study for vocabulary development in the early stages of literacy learning: Ecological perspectives and learning English. In J. Baumann & E. Kame'enui (Eds.), *Vocabulary instruction: Research to practice* (pp. 139–158). New York: Guilford Press.

Bear, D. R., Helman, L. A., Templeton, S., Invernizzi, M., & Johnston, F. (2007). *Words their way with English learners: Word study for phonics, vocabulary and spelling instruction.* Upper Saddle River, NJ: Pearson/Merrill Prentice Hall.

Bear, D. R., Helman, L., & Woessner, L. (in press). Word study assessment and instruction with English learners in a second grade classroom: Bending with students' growth. In J. Coppola & E. Primas (Eds.), *Teaching and learning in linguistically and culturally diverse classrooms: Bringing theory and research to practice.* Newark, DE: International Reading Association.

Bear, D. R., Invernizzi, M., Templeton, S., & Johnston, F. (2008). *Words their way: Word study for phonics, vocabulary, and spelling instruction* (4th ed.). Upper Saddle River, NJ: Prentice Hall.

Brofenbrenner, U., & Morris. P. A. (1998). The ecology of developmental processes. In R. M. Lerner (Ed.), & W. Damon (Series Ed.), *Handbook of child psychology* (5th ed., Vol. 1, pp. 993–1028). New York: Wiley.

Ehri, L., & McCormick, S. (1998). Phases of word learning: Implications for instruction with delayed and disabled readers. *Reading and Writing Quarterly: Overcoming Learning Difficulties, 14*, 135–164.

Ehri, L. C. (1997). Learning to read and learning to spell are one and the same, almost. In C. A. Perfetti, L. Rieben, & M. Fayol (Eds.), *Learning to spell: Research, theory, and practice across languages* (pp. 237–269). Mahwah, NJ: Erlbaum.

Flanigan, K. (2007). A concept of word in text: A pivotal event in early reading acquisition. *Journal of Literacy Research, 39*(1), 37–70.

Helman, L. (2004). Building on the sound system of Spanish: Insights from the alphabetic spellings of English language learners. *Reading Teacher, 57*, 452–460.

Helman, L. A., & Bear, D. R. (2007). Does an established model of orthographic development hold true for English learners? In D. W. Rowe, R. Jimenez, D. L. Compton, D. K. Dickinson, Y. Kim, K. M. Leander, & V. J. Risko (Eds.), *56th Yearbook of the National Reading Conference* (pp. 266–280). Oak Creek, WI: National Reading Conference.

Helman, L. A., Bear, D. R., Johnston, F., Invernizzi, M., & Templeton, S. (2009). *Sorts with Spanish speakers in the emergent stage.* Boston: Allyn & Bacon.

Henderson, E. H. (1981). *Learning to read and spell: The child's knowledge of words.* DeKalb, IL: Northern Illinois Press.

Henderson, E. H. (1992). The interface of lexical competence and knowledge of written words. In S. Templeton & D. Bear (Eds.), *Development of orthographic knowledge and the foundations of literacy: A memorial Festschrift for Edmund H. Henderson* (pp. 1–30). Hillsdale, NJ: Erlbaum.

Invernizzi, M., Abouzeid, M., & Gill, J. T. (1994). Using students' invented spellings as a guide for spelling instruction that emphasizes word study. *Elementary School Journal, 95*(2), 155–167.

Invernizzi, M., & Hayes, T. (2004). Developmental-spelling research: A systematic imperative. *Reading Research Quarterly, 39*(2), 216–228.

McGee, L. M., & Schickedanz, J. A. (2007). Repeated interactive read-alouds in preschool and kindergarten. *Reading Teacher, 60*(8), 742–751.

Morris, D., Bloodgood, J. W., Lomax, R. G., & Perney, J. (2003). Developmental steps in learning to read: A longitudinal study in kindergarten and first grade. *Reading Research Quarterly, 38*(3), 302–328.

National Reading Panel (NRP). (2000). *Teaching children to read: An evidence-based assessment of the scientific research literature on reading and its implications for reading instruction.* Washington, DC: National Institute of Child Health and Human Development.

Peebles, J. L. (2007). Incorporating movement with fluency instruction: A motivation for struggling readers. *Reading Teacher, 60*(6), 578–581.

Stanovich, K. (2000). *Progress in understanding reading: Scientific foundations and new frontiers.* New York: Guilford Press.

Swan, M., & Smith, B. (2001). *Learner English: A teacher's guide to interfer-*

ence and other problems (2nd ed.). Cambridge, UK: Cambridge University Press.

Templeton, S., & Morris, D. (2000). Spelling. In M. Kamil, P. Mosenthal, P. D. Pearson, & R. Barr (Eds.), *Handbook of reading research* (Vol. 3, pp. 525–543). Mahwah, NJ: Erlbaum.

Wolf, M. (2007). *Proust and the squid: The story and science of the reading brain.* New York: Harper.

CHAPTER 6

Emergent Literacy

Planting the Seeds for Accomplished Reading and Writing

Lori Helman

From a very early age children begin to build the knowledge base that will help them become readers and writers. First, children learn sounds and words and how to communicate with the important people in their lives. Later, children notice the ways people read and write in their daily lives and how they use text in varied ways. Each language or literacy interaction that young children have is like a seed for their emerging literacy understanding. No wonder the name for *kindergarten*, a time of amazing discoveries in emergent literacy, comes from the German for *children's garden*. The oral-language foundation that each student possesses is the soil on which emergent literacy develops. Informal and formal instruction in sounds and letters are like seeds planted that will sprout into understanding the alphabetic code. Emergent learners develop more advanced understandings of print when they have opportunities to tend their garden by practicing language-rich literacy activities at home and school.

English language learners (ELLs) experience the period of emergent literacy in a slightly different way. Students who are learning oral English at the same time they learn its written features are doing double duty—the phonemic and alphabetic seeds in English are being planted just as the soil of the English language is being prepared. Without a foundation of oral language, an understanding of text in that language will not flourish. So learning oral English and the written code become simultaneous goals for ELLs and require concerted planning efforts on the part of curriculum leaders and teachers.

In this chapter I provide an overview of the emergent stage of literacy development for students learning English as a new language. This chapter builds on the developmental framework outlined by Bear and Smith in Chapter 5 of this volume and fills in details, along with specific literacy practices for this early developmental stage. I begin by sharing research relating to emergent literacy skills such as phonemic awareness, alphabet knowledge, reading sight words, and developing a concept of word in print (COW). Next, I highlight similarities and differences for emergent development with English learners. The bulk of this chapter outlines instructional applications that teachers of emergent ELLs will find useful for providing the kinds of language-rich literacy activities mentioned here.

Literacy instruction at all developmental levels may be organized around a set of essential activities: Read To, Read With, Write With, Word Study, and Talk With (RRWWT; Bear, Helman, Templeton, Invernizzi, & Johnston, 2007). In this chapter, I use the RRWWT format to present a variety of instructional activities that support students' emergent language and literacy development, such as developing language using picture books and concept sorts, memorizing poetry to practice sight words and develop COW, hearing sounds in words, and learning the alphabet. The chapter closes with an example week of literacy instruction in an emergent classroom. I share this slice of curriculum to model the ways that language-rich literacy activities exist as both integrated and stand-alone aspects of classroom instruction and to demonstrate how learning skills can be more effective for English learners when meaning and language learning are kept at the center.

EMERGENT LITERACY DEVELOPMENT

Literacy development may be viewed as progress along a continuum beginning with a point of limited print awareness and moving to accomplished reading and writing skills. In Chapter 5 of this book, Donald Bear and Regina Smith laid out this developmental progression and located the emergent stage at the very beginning of the continuum. Emergent learners first imitate reading and writing as they have seen others do it. They are magical thinkers in a certain way; emergent readers pretend read a familiar story and write lists or notes using scribbles or letter-like figures. Figure 6.1 shows the drawing and writing of Chue, a 6-year-old Hmong-speaking student in the emergent stage of development. Chue's sample shows that he can write letters and move from left to right, but his developmental writing is not yet alphabetic. The strings of letters do not relate to the sounds of the words in his story about his family. For

FIGURE 6.1. Chue's writing sample.

students like Chue at the emergent stage of literacy learning, the goals are to develop phonological awareness to isolate aspects of sound in the stream of oral language; to learn the alphabet and begin to attach sounds to the letters; to memorize a core set of high-frequency words that will help them access simple, patterned stories and poems; and to practice using their language and early literacy skills in rereading simple texts to develop one-to-one matching between the oral and printed word (COW). As their emergent skills develop, students are gaining an understanding of the alphabetic principle (Morris, Bloodgood, Lomax, & Perney, 2003). We see growth in their phonemic awareness and the ability to identify individual words in print. Students begin to understand that letters are used to represent the individual sounds we hear in words (Read, 1971). When students are able to segment individual sounds in short words and are representing most of the salient sounds in words they are spelling, they have moved ahead to the stage of beginning reading/letter-name–alphabetic spelling (Bear & Smith, Chapter 5, this volume).

Key Conclusions from the Research

Emergent reading development has been well researched over the past thirty years (cf., Adams, 1990). The report from the Committee on the Prevention of Reading Difficulties in Young Children outlined some foundations that help children learn to read, including normal language skills; early childhood experiences that foster motivation and exposure to literacy use; opportunities to learn letters and the sounds in words and to compare oral language with written language; and to experience effective instruction in schools (Snow, Burns, & Griffin, 1998). They identify three key obstacles to becoming proficient readers: difficulty understanding the alphabetic code, difficulty applying oral-language comprehension skills to work with texts, and lack of motivation to engage in reading (Snow et al., 1998). In a study of kindergartners, Morris and colleagues found four skills that effectively predicted first- and second-grade reading: alphabet recognition, COW, spelling with initial and final consonants, and word recognition (Morris, Bloodgood, & Perney, 2003).

Especially well documented in learning to read and spell is the importance of phonemic awareness, the ability to isolate the individual sounds in words, as a prerequisite to efficient reading and learning the alphabetic code of English (Bradley & Bryant, 1983; National Reading Panel (NRP), 2000). The National Reading Panel found that phonemic awareness instruction helped students apply the skill in their decoding and that instruction that was focused and explicit in one or two aspects of phonemic awareness was most successful (NRP, 2000). The most effective phonemic awareness instruction occurred in small group settings, in short lesson formats, and when letters were used as support materials in activities (NRP, 2000).

Phonics instruction, or the teaching of letter–sound correspondences in English, was also found by the National Reading Panel to improve early reading abilities. Based on their findings, the NRP reported that effective phonics instruction is most effective with kindergarten and first-grade students but that phonics instruction introduced in kindergarten should be foundational and involve learning the alphabet and phonemic awareness (NRP, 2000).

Language development, including but not limited to vocabulary development, is another crucial component of early literacy success (NICHD Early Child Care Research Network, 2005). The exact nature of the role of language development in literacy learning is somewhat complex; language measures are often more associated with reading comprehension than with decoding skills (NICHD Early Child Care Research Network, 2005). Several studies have found strong correlations among language and early literacy skills such as vocabulary, definitional skills, phonological awareness, and print knowledge (Dickinson, McCabe, Anastasopoulos, Peisner-Feinberg, & Poe, 2003; Snow, Tabors, & Nicholson, 1995).

It is clear that alphabetic, phonological, and linguistic skills all come together to help students begin to access print during the period of early literacy development, and researchers have also noted the interrelationships among these skills. For example, Morris, Bloodgood, Lomax, and Perney (2003) noted an interaction between phonemic awareness and COW. Early literacy development involves a complex interaction of language knowledge, hearing sounds in words, learning the alphabetic code, and matching oral to printed words. These varied skills work together to permit students' access to print.

Emergent English Learners

In their review of the research on literacy development with English learners, the National Literacy Panel on Language-Minority Children and Youth reported on a number of studies with English learners at the emergent stage. Although the research base is incomplete in many areas, the panel stated that learning to read in a second language appears to be influenced by the same set of skills as in first-language reading (LeSaux, Koda, Siegel, & Shanahan, 2006). In a longitudinal study of English learners and native English speakers, LeSaux and Siegel (2003) found that the same phonological and alphabetical skills in kindergarten predicted reading performance in second grade. Although ELLs in kindergarten were significantly behind their native-speaking peers, by second grade they had caught up on word-level decoding. This study suggests that instruction in phonological and alphabetic skills in English should begin early and need not wait for ELLs to develop greater proficiency in English (LeSaux & Siegel, 2003).

Research with English learners suggests that being bilingual is not a detriment to literacy development and, in fact, that it may be an asset because students gain metalinguistic skills from negotiating across languages (August & Shanahan, 2006; Bialystock, 2001; Koda, 2005; LeSaux & Siegel, 2003). For example, phonological awareness skills have been shown to transfer from one language to another (Genesee & Geva, 2006). A study of a preschool home reading program using books in the first or second language found that both programs were equally effective in producing gains in English vocabulary (Roberts, 2008). Although the research with English learners suggests that it is not advisable to wait with phonological and alphabet skill instruction while students develop oral English proficiency, it is also clear that vocabulary and language development are crucial to students' reading comprehension (August & Hakuta, 1997; August & Shanahan, 2006). Language development and vocabulary knowledge should be key components of all emergent literacy programs for English learners (August & Shanahan, 2006; Biemiller & Boote, 2006; Helman, 2008). For a detailed overview of language development and instruction with English learners, see Chapter 3 by Dutro and Helman, this volume.

ESSENTIAL LITERACY ACTIVITIES FOR THE EMERGENT STAGE

Based on the research literature, a comprehensive emergent literacy curriculum should include opportunities for English learners to:

- Experience focused, explicit, and short lessons that develop phonological awareness skills such as rhyming, hearing individual sounds in words, and blending.
- Learn the letters of the alphabet and begin to explore the sounds they represent.
- Develop oral language proficiency, including vocabulary knowledge, in English.
- Practice connecting oral language to print.
- Learn to read a core group of important high-frequency words to use in their practice reading.

In this section, I present numerous examples of how these goals can be addressed in typical literacy activities in classrooms with emergent learners. All comprehensive literacy programs, whether commercially produced or locally created, should include the essential literacy activities of RRWWT (Bear et al., 2007). Using the RRWWT format, I outline several ways to incorporate phonological and alphabetical knowledge, language learning, and practice reading and writing into the emergent literacy classroom.

Read To

Reading aloud to students is an excellent way to present new vocabulary, set up small-group conversations, model story structure, teach content knowledge, and motivate students to learn to read. When students listen to material read aloud, they hear the rhythm and flow of English and learn what fluent reading sounds like. Materials for reading aloud to English learners include picture books of many genres, poetry in books and on charts, and stories or nonfiction texts that build on students' background experiences and engage them in interesting topics. The key for English learners is that the content and language of read-aloud material are at their levels of listening comprehension. Students do not need to understand every word that is read, but if too much of the language is over their heads or if it is read too quickly or without visual support, comprehension and new learning will suffer.

For maximum effect, teachers should consider embedding short read-aloud sessions throughout the school day. When working with students with very limited English proficiency, screen the material for its level of linguistic complexity; texts that have fewer words on the page and have simpler syntactical structures may be easier to understand. Less common vocabulary may also create challenges in comprehension for English learners. Take the time to discuss and learn key vocabulary in the content area or read-aloud material that is being used. Structuring informal comprehension questions within group discussions or using other methods of checking for understanding is also critical for selecting appropriate level materials.

When possible, provide opportunities for students to hear the read-aloud material in their home language first. This may be done by finding bilingual editions of books and having them read by a native speaker, by having a bilingual teacher or assistant preview the material in the student's home language, or by using books on tape. Students who have heard the material in their home language will be more prepared to engage with the ideas presented and will gain much more from hearing the text read in English (Bear et al., 2007).

Read With

Read With activities give emergent students an opportunity to read along or reread familiar materials. In these early reading experiences, students begin to notice and remember the shapes of words and letters, to connect the phonological and alphabetic features of words, and to increase their vocabulary and other language skills through rereading simple, memorized texts. At this stage of literacy development, students read predictable or memorized texts such as the simplest leveled books with repetitive patterns, concept books that label objects on the page, or poems that have already been rehearsed several times. As students reread these materials, they begin to recognize key high-frequency words, start recognizing the letters and sounds in the text, and begin to develop the early tracking skills associated with a rudimentary COW.

Read With may occur during shared reading or independent reading activities in the emergent classroom. Students can follow along with enlarged text in big books or charts or in small groups when everyone has a copy of the book. Once the material has been read together enough times so that it is memorized, it can be included in a box of familiar reading materials that the student rereads many times independently. A personal reader can help students reread memorized materials (Bear, Caserta-Henry, & Venner, 2004). Personal readers are collections of the simple poems, language experience stories, or other memorable texts that have been typed onto a single page in a large font size. Students reread the pages in their personal readers and make a tally mark for each rereading. This gives students excellent practice in tracking, using English phrases, and growing their bank of easily recognized sight words. It puts into practice all they are learning in the vocabulary, phonics, and word study components of their literacy curriculum.

Write With

The goal of writing with students at the emergent stage is to help them make connections between spoken words and their representation in print. This takes place in several ways, including shared or modeled writing with students, encouraging students' own writing using developmental spelling, and taking dictations of students' narratives.

Modeled writing happens when teachers write on the board or chart paper. Teachers think aloud about the way they are writing as they put down words so that all the students can see. Teachers also discuss developmentally appropriate concepts about print, such as the sweep from left to right and leaving spaces between words, and encourage students to suggest letters that represent the correct beginning sounds of words. If the teacher or an assistant has literacy skills in students' first languages, modeling writing in that language is very appropriate, too.

Developmental writing occurs when students are asked to write their stories or ideas down "the best they can." This pushes students to use figures, letters, and sounds at the cutting edge of their understanding. All attempts at writing are accepted and praised, and teachers ask students to reread their text while they point at it. Developmental writing is an important informal assessment of emergent students' orthographic knowledge. A teacher can tell whether a student knows letters from other shapes, has an understanding of print concepts such as left-to-right sweep and word boundaries, or is beginning to use sight words or alphabet knowledge in his or her writing. Whether students are using developmental writing in their fantasy play (such as in a pretend restaurant or fire station area of class), in an open-ended writing center in class, in a daily journal, or as they fill in a word on a sentence frame the teacher has created, each student can be encouraged to stretch his or her spelling knowledge. For example, a student who tells a story from a picture alone might be encouraged to "write some words that tell the story." A student who uses letter-like figures to write may be encouraged to look at an alphabet card to see if the figures are there. A student who uses a phonetically appropriate beginning consonant in one word may be encouraged to do that in other words as well. Developmental writing is a great time to provide an individualized phonics and spelling minilesson to each student.

Another way for students to learn about writing and to see oral language written down is to participate in language experience dictations or group experience stories (Nelson & Linek, 1998). This activity is particularly suited to English learners because the teacher learns what vocabulary and language patterns the students know and is assured that the student will later understand the rereading. A language experience activity begins with some kind of activity—a book that has been read, a project completed, a field trip, and so on. Students draw pictures about and dictate a narrative relating to the event and observe as the teacher writes their words down. The teacher and the student reread the text together while pointing to the written words. A group experience story is similar to an individual dictation except that the writing happens in a small group and each student contributes one sentence. Typically, the teacher will write the student's name before the dictation; for example, "Mario says water is cold; Lupe says water is to drink" and so on. Both individual language experience dictations and group experience stories may be typed up in a large font size, printed out, and placed in students' personal readers so they can read them over and over in Read With activities.

Word Study

Sounds, letters, and important words in students' lives are all the focus of word study at the emergent stage. Some of the word study in class may be presented in stand-alone lessons, such as when students practice hearing rhyming words in a rhyming match game or sort pictures of objects by their beginning sounds. Other times, word study components are integrated throughout the curriculum: in the stories, songs, games, content-area studies, and ongoing routines of the emergent classroom. In this section, I discuss several important strands of word study instruction with English learners at the emergent level: alphabet studies, phonological awareness activities, concept sorts for thinking skills and language development, and learning a beginning group of sight words.

Alphabet Studies

Learning the alphabet in English is an important step on the road to understanding the code of phonics. ELLs may not have as many experiences with the alphabet song in English and are not likely to have the breadth of vocabulary knowledge to connect individual words to letters of the English alphabet. For this reason, ELLs entering a classroom in which the literacy curriculum is taught in English will need as much support as possible to learn the letters. An enriched curriculum might include daily chanting and singing the alphabet song, frequent read-alouds with alphabet books, a consistent picture alphabet posted at children's eye level in various parts of the classroom, and vocabulary studies that reinforce the key words used in the alphabet. Some teachers even include a kinesthetic signal to go along with each letter–sound team, such as saying, "B, /b/, /b/, boat" while making the hand motion of a rocking boat. Teachers should create as many meaningful and hands-on ways as possible for students to practice identifying, writing, and talking about the letters, such as by spelling out loud the names of classmates, writing letters to friends and loved ones, playing letter-matching or sorting games, and using alphabet manipulatives to copy important words or names.

Phonological Awareness Activities

The earliest stages of phonological awareness involve helping students distinguish and manipulate chunks within words, such as using words that rhyme, hearing the syllable or *beats* in words, or breaking apart compound words (Helman, Bear, Invernizzi, Templeton, & Johnston, 2009). More advanced phonological skills include isolating the beginning sound in a word and sorting objects or pictures together that start in the same way. As students progress through the emergent stage, their phonemic awareness skills advance; they are able to pull out the most salient sounds in words. Shortly they will enter the fully alphabetic world of the beginning reader/letter-name–alphabetic speller.

A number of instructional activities help emergent readers develop their phonological awareness abilities: listening to rhyming and alliterative books and poems and chanting along on repetitive phrases; doing picture sorts that focus on the phonological properties of words such as rhymes, syllables, and beginning sounds; teacher modeling of blending and segmenting tasks; using developmental writing; and learning to break apart words into sounds in their home languages (Helman et al., 2009). Proficiency in identifying and manipulating the sound aspects of language is enhanced when students have a strong foundation of words to compare. Because the "language baskets" (see Bear & Smith, Chapter 5, this volume) of English learners are not as full as those of native English speakers, vocabulary development will be highly integrated with phonological awareness activities as well. Teachers should present numerous words that represent the features being studied, such as rhyming words or a particular beginning sound, and teach the meaning of each word through pictures or acting out.

Concept Sorts

A critical strand of instruction in word study for emergent learners is to develop vocabulary and thinking skills using concept sorts. Concept sorts can be created using objects or pictures; students are asked to classify the items into categories based on common properties. Because a concept sort may be done before all of the vocabulary relating to a particular topic is known, it also provides an opportunity for students to work with, label, and talk about an expanding number of important words. For example, students may sort buttons in a variety of ways and talk about their colors, shapes, and the numbers of holes they have. Or they may sort pictures of animals and learn and use the labels for each kind of animal, as well as words for features, such as *fur, wings, scales, swim, fly, walk, four-legged*, and so on (Helman et al., 2009). Concept sorts allow students to use higher level thinking skills as they learn new language and teach sorting procedures and important vocabulary at the same time. The picture cards or objects used for concept sorts may also be used in a variety of games and classroom activities that develop language and vocabulary. As students are working with particular content vocabulary, teachers can have students go on picture hunts for related items, play Bingo, act out Charades, or play card games or board games (Bear et al., 2007). Integration, repetition, and application ensure that English learners have the opportunities to fully understand and master the vocabulary and conceptual knowledge being studied in class.

Sight Words

Emergent students are beginning to develop a core group of familiar words that they recognize instantly by sight. These words may include students' names and the names of important people in their lives, as well as words they see frequently in simple reading materials and use in their writing (e.g., *the* and *like*). These sight words form a pool of words that students can use to increase their understanding of letters and sounds over time; in the meantime, knowing some words instantly helps students gain confidence as emergent readers and writers and gives them more access to simple leveled texts.

Teachers can support sight-word learning in a number of ways in the emergent classroom. First, they label important objects and areas in the classroom so students can make the oral–print connection. Next, teachers post key vocabulary and the names of students in the classroom for students to access when they are writing or to use in classroom games or transition activities. In addition, teachers use the Read With materials that students have memorized to have students find key words. For example, a student who has memorized the rhyme "Rain, rain, go away" can review the rhyme and find words such as *rain, go, come*, and *day*. With multiple readings and opportunities to search for and practice individual words in text, students increase their ability to track individual words and automatically recognize more and more high-frequency words.

Talk With

The final essential literacy activity for the emergent classroom is fundamental for the success of English learners: opportunities to engage with others orally in class. Talking With activities do not need to be scheduled as a separate time; they may be embedded into literacy activities throughout the day. For example, during or after a Read To activity, students can share their favorite parts of the story in a small group. In Read With activities, students can read their familiar text to a partner. In word study, sorts can be done or shared in partnerships, and students are asked to explain to the teacher how and why they sorted the way they did. Write With provides numerous opportunities for talking: in sharing and discussing each other's stories and in practicing saying the sentence frames that are used to guide student writing. The teacher's use of small-group and partner structures, open-ended questions, wait time, translation into students' home languages, and structuring a comfortable classroom environment for sharing will encourage students' participation. When students have an opportunity to apply the language they are learning in their literacy activities in meaningful interactions, their new knowledge will be made stronger.

Assessment

Regular assessment of the important aspects of emergent literacy will help teachers identify students who are having difficulty with phonological, alphabet/letter, and language skills. These simple assessments will also inform teachers about which activities are appropriate to teach with certain students at a particular time. Table 6.1 provides a brief summary of the kinds of formal and informal assessments that help identify students at risk for reading and writing difficulties and serve as a guide for curriculum planning as well. An excellent resource for taking the results of assessment and coming up with related instructional activities is available on the Phonolological Awareness Literacy Screening (PALS) website at *pals.virginia.edu/tools-activities.html*.

TABLE 6.1. Emergent Literacy Assessments.

Literacy component	Example assessments
Alphabet knowledge	Assess students' upper- or lower-case letter recognition by presenting the alphabet in a mixed order and asking students to give you the correct name for the letters.
Concepts about print	Assess students' knowledge of print features such as text, word, period, cover, back, title, and so on by having students look for an example feature in a simple book. See Clay (2006) for an example assessment in English and Spanish.
Concept of word (COW)	After helping students memorize a simple four-line poem that includes several multisyllable words, assess their COW in print by having them read and point to the words in the text. Can students fingerpoint to the printed words in memorized text in a one-to-one manner? Next, ask students to identify specific words and note their success in pointing to these words. For an example assessment of COW, see Helman et al. (2009).
Developmental spelling	Assess with a writing sample to see whether students are using scribbles, letter-like figures, or letters. Assess directionality. If letters are used to represent words, are students using alphabetic strategies? See Helman et al. (2009) for an example kindergarten developmental spelling inventory.
Language development and vocabulary	There are many formal and informal assessments of students' language development in English, including commercially developed ones. Investigate what language-development information is available for your ELL students, and go from there. Informal classroom assessments include having individual conferences with students and recording and noting their language skills and confusions. Do regular informal checks of students' knowledge of essential classroom vocabulary. Work with an ELL support teacher to better understand your students' language strengths, including their abilities in the home language.
Phonological awareness	Assess individual phonological awareness skills such as rhyming and beginning sounds by asking students to sort or select individual pictures that match a given key picture. Assess phoneme blending or segmenting by giving students a series of sounds in a single-syllable word and ask students to blend them; or, for segmenting, give students a single-syllable word and ask them to say the sounds they hear. See Invernizzi and Meier (2001) or Yopp (1995) for example assessments.
Sight-word knowledge	Use an agreed-upon list of important, high-frequency words to periodically assess your students' progress in learning the first 10 or 20 of these words. The list may come from your district, state, or a publisher (e.g., Fry's Instant Words; Fry & Kress, 2006).

PUTTING IT TOGETHER: AN EXAMPLE WEEK OF EMERGENT, LANGUAGE-RICH LITERACY ACTIVITIES

A primary goal of the curriculum in emergent classrooms is to support students' literacy skills while building their oral language. Language-rich literacy instruction should occur every day through reading, writing, and talking activities such as those described in this chapter. In this section, I present an example week in a kindergarten classroom to illustrate how skills in phonological awareness, alphabet knowledge, language and vocabulary development, and word learning might come together in meaningful ways using the essential literacy activities. A thematic focus will help students learn a common set of important vocabulary words that may be applied in many parts of the school day. I chose the theme of "making friends at school," because this is a typical early-kindergarten topic and because it reflects a meaningful area of study for ELLs who are learning about schooling in a new language and are anxious to feel connected and understood.

Standard routines for developing an integrated literacy theme may include the following (from Helman et al., 2009):

- Start with a concept sort. A concept sort introduces the theme and key vocabulary words.
- Plan for informal assessment. Consider which emergent literacy or language skills you will focus on during the week (e.g., phonological awareness, alphabet, language, COW, concepts about print or sight words).
- Plan for phonological awareness activities. Depending on the assessed level of your students, plan to work on skills such as rhyming, syllable awareness, beginning sounds, or others.
- Incorporate alphabet and letter–sound learning. This may be done in focused lessons and through daily routines. Your selection here will depend on students' developmental skills.
- Practice concept of word by creating simple texts and rereading familiar materials.
- Connect literature and content-area studies with the week's theme.

With these guidelines in mind, here is a suggested overview of a week's language-rich literacy activities around the theme of "making friends at school." This theme is being planned for Ms. Garcia's kindergarten class near the beginning of the school year and interconnects with other classroom goals, such as developing a classroom community to enhance students' interpersonal relationships. For this example I envision a diverse classroom whose members include English learners from many language backgrounds, as well as native English-speaking students.

Start with a Concept Sort

A good concept sort for the theme this week is "What is at school?" Ms. Garcia collects a set of small pictures of school items (e.g., chairs, tables, books, and pencils), as well as people at school (e.g., teacher, principal, librarian, and students). These can be found in old teaching materials, magazines or calendars, or from commercially produced picture libraries. At the beginning of the week, the teacher guides students to repeat and chant the names of the items. The class plays various games to practice the names of each item, such as Charades, I Spy, and Memory. When students are familiar with the vocabulary, a modeled sort begins in the word study component of the day. Ms. Garcia helps students to sort the pictures into two categories: *things at school* and *people at school*. While sorting, she guides English learners to repeat the sentence frames: A _____ (desk) *is a thing at school*, or A _____ (teacher) *is a person at school*. Over the course of the week, students will get their own copies of the pictures for this sort, and during word study they will have opportunities to sort with partners and on their own. Later in the week, they will think of ways to divide the people and objects into new categories that they have chosen.

Plan for Formal and Informal Assessment

The school year is well under way, and the required fall literacy assessments for kindergarten have been completed. These consisted of upper- and lower-case letter recognition, rhyme identification, and a developmental writing sample, including name writing. For the focus of this week, Ms. Garcia plans to assess whether or not students can identify and compare the beginning sounds /s/ and /f/. These sounds are distinct from each other, they are used in many familiar words, and the /s/ fits with the theme of *school*. Ms. Garcia has a set of picture cards that show things that start with /s/ and /f/, with a picture of a school being one key word and a picture of a family being the other to guide the sort. Throughout the week she conducts small group lessons to assess which students are able to distinguish and categorize the pictures correctly. Students who are unable to do the task in a small group are given the categorization assessment individually. Ms. Garcia learns from the assessment that some students are ready to work with initial consonant sound study and that other students will profit at this time from more directed modeling of picture words with common beginning sounds.

Build in Phonological Awareness Activities

Ms. Garcia has planned two kinds of phonological awareness activities to focus on this week: rhyme awareness and alliteration with /s/. From the district-wide assessment already conducted, she knows that many students are having difficulty with distinguishing rhyming words. She has found two feature books to use throughout the week: *Hello School: A Classroom Full of Poems* (Lillegard, 2003) and *How Do Dinosaurs Go to School?* (Yolen, 2007). She will read these books several times throughout the week, and as the students become familiar with the texts' rhymes and rhythms, she will have students fill in the rhyming words. By the end of the week, students will read more of the text on their own during shared reading, and individual picture and word cards will be placed on the pocket chart so students can identify rhyming words. On a regular basis, Ms. Garcia will also help students sing several rhyming songs about making friends and will point out the rhyming words in them to students.

The sound of /s/ will also be a focus of phonological awareness activities this week. Ms. Garcia will read poems and texts that feature alliteration of the /s/, such as *Silly Sally* (Wood, 1994). She will also sing songs that have the /s/ sound, such as "A Sailor Went to Sea, Sea, Sea" and "Shake Your Sillies Out." Her class will learn how to play Simon Says. Through all of these activities Ms. Garcia will accentuate the /s/ and encourage students to repeat it with her. As students are dismissed to leave the class, she will ask them individually, "Does _____ start with /s/?" When possible, she will show a picture to students when asking the question.

Incorporate Alphabet and Letter–Sound Learning

Every week in her class Ms. Garcia incorporates many alphabet and letter–sound activities. Her classroom is literacy rich; she has a large, easy-to-read alphabet posted at students' eye level, with key pictures that she has reviewed with the students. She has smaller alphabets available in the writing center and plenty of plastic letters, letter tiles, puzzles, and other letter pieces for students to manipulate and use to make words. Each day the alphabet song is chanted and sung in various ways. Students clap, march, and hop as they sing the letters. She is also teaching students a key word for each letter that helps them remember its sound, such as the "/b/, /b/, boat" example.

On a regular basis, Ms. Garcia spells out loud the letters in the names of her students so they have practice identifying letters in meaningful contexts as they learn their classmates' names. She has posted students' names on cards in various locations around the class; there is a bulletin board with photographs and name cards, a graphing center where students make a selection using their name card each day, and sets of name cards in the writing center so students can create letters to each other. Ms. Garcia also focuses on one student each day to be the featured student, and that day the student's name is chanted, written, and spelled by all students.

All of these ongoing alphabet activities will take place this week in Ms. Garcia's classroom. Because of the school theme, she will also focus on the name of her school and provide opportunities for students to find words around the classroom that contain the letter *S*. One activity she has planned is for students to see how many letters are common between their own names and the name of the school. She will also create a homework assignment in which students have an older relative write down the names of family members. When students return their papers, she will help them read the family members' names and have students use the lists for letter hunts.

Practice Concept of Word in Reading and Writing

Activities that develop a COW require a short section of a poem or other text of relevance and interest to students. Because it is early in the school year, Ms. Garcia wants to keep the selected text for this week to two lines. She creates a little ditty to teach the students that reflects the thematic focus and helps them learn interpersonal skills: "There are many kids at school, will you be my friend at school?" After using the rhyme to play a "making friends" game, Ms. Garcia writes the text on cards and puts it in the pocket chart. She reads and chants the ditty with students until it is memorized. Next, she has volunteer students come to the chart and use a pointer to follow along as the group reads. After a few days, Ms. Garcia gives a copy of the ditty to each child so each can point along as he or she reads it. She uses this as an informal assessment of their tracking skills and notices if the word *many* throws students' pointing off. Ms. Garcia then puts the short rhyme in students' personal readers so they can reread the text multiple times to gain sight words and a COW in text.

Connect Literature and Content-Area Studies

Books of all sorts are read in Ms. Garcia's classroom each day. She loves to start the day with a story, use simple books for transition times as students come to the rug, and share interesting information with nonfiction texts in the content-area studies of the class. The theme of the week or month is usually oriented toward a science or social studies topic. This week, the theme "making friends at school" lends itself to many, many children's literature connections—too many to list here. With the help of a children's librarian, Ms. Garcia checks out more than a dozen books to have in class and read throughout the week. Her criteria for selecting the books are: (1) It is aimed at the age and language level of students in her class, (2) it is interesting and worthy of the use of class time, (3) it lends itself to a discussion students can engage in, and (4) it is visually stimulating.

Among the books Ms. Garcia selects for this week are *Froggy Goes to School* (London, 1998), *David Goes to School* (Shannon, 1999), and *School Bus* (Crews, 1993). She plans to use the first two books to share humor, to discuss what happens at school, and to elicit students' ideas about what it is like for them at school. With *School Bus* (Crews, 1993), a wordless book, Ms. Garcia plans to do many Talk With activities in which students talk about the illustrations with a friend sitting near them on the rug.

In addition to literature connections, Ms. Garcia extends the thematic content of the week into as many aspects of classroom life as she can. For example, in writing, students use prompts such as "A good friend _____ (shares with you)." In mathematical studies, students count the letters in classmates' names; in physical education, students work in partnership activities. Through thematic studies, she helps students see the curriculum as cohesive, the vocabulary as transferable to many contexts, and the learning atmosphere as supportive. Each child is expected to participate and use language to the best of his or her ability. Bilingual students support Ms. Garcia in helping all students to understand what is expected and what information is being shared in class. Finally, parents and community members are encouraged to come to school to share the connections they have with the thematic studies of each unit.

FINAL THOUGHTS

Ms. Garcia's classroom represents an intentional *children's garden* where students have opportunities to learn language and to experience focused and explicit literacy activities. The seeds of phonological and alphabetical skills are planted each day within reading, writing, word study, and oral-language activities, and students have numerous opportunities to practice these skills with texts. Vocabulary is taught as an integral part of the curriculum so that students always understand the meaning of the words and texts they are studying.

In this chapter, I have provided an overview of key components of emergent literacy development, such as a strong language foundation, phonological awareness, alphabetical skills, learning a core set of sight words, and developing a COW. English learners need this same foundation to become successful emergent readers and writers. By providing language-rich literacy instruction, teachers help English learners grow and blossom in the emergent classroom. They also ensure that students will be motivated to read and write and are better prepared to understand the complex texts at more advanced levels of literacy development.

REFERENCES

Adams, M. (1990). *Beginning to read: Thinking and learning about print.* Cambridge, MA: MIT Press.

August, D., & Hakuta, K. (Eds.). (1997). *Improving schooling for language minority students: A research agenda.* Washington, DC: National Academy Press.

August, D., & Shanahan, T. (Eds.). (2006). *Developing literacy in second-language learners: Report of the National Literacy Panel on Language-Minority Children and Youth.* Mahwah, NJ: Erlbaum.

Bear, D. R., Caserta-Henry, C., & Venner, D. (2004). *Personal readers for emergent and beginning readers.* San Diego, CA: Teaching Resource Center.

Bear, D. R., Helman, L., Templeton, S., Invernizzi, M., & Johnston, F. (2007). *Words their way with English learners: Word study for phonics, vocabulary, and spelling instruction.* Upper Saddle River, NJ: Pearson/Merrill Prentice Hall.

Biemiller, A., & Boote, C. (2006). An effective method for building meaning vocabulary in primary grades. *Journal of Educational Psychology, 98*(1), 44–62.

Bialystock, E. (2001). *Bilingualism in development: Language, literacy and cognition.* New York: Cambridge University Press.

Bradley, L., & Bryant, P. (1983). Categorizing sounds and learning to read: A causal connection. *Nature, 301,* 419–421.

Clay, M. M. (2006). *An observation survey of early literacy achievement: Revised second edition.* Portsmouth, NH: Heinemann.

Crews, D. (1993). *School bus.* New York: HarperTrophy.

Dickinson, D., McCabe, A., Anastasopoulos, L., Peisner-Feinberg, E., & Poe, M. (2003). The comprehensive language approach to early literacy: The interrelationships among vocabulary, phonological sensitivity, and print knowledge among preschool-aged children. *Journal of Educational Psychology, 95,* 465–481.

Fry, E. B., & Kress, J. E. (2006). *The reading teacher's book of lists* (5th ed.). San Francisco: Jossey-Bass.

Genesee, F., & Geva, E. (2006). Cross-linguistic relationships in working memory, phonological processes, and oral language. In D. August & T. Shanahan (Eds.), *Developing literacy in second-language learners: Report of the National Literacy Panel on Language-Minority Children and Youth* (pp. 175–183). Mahwah, NJ: Erlbaum.

Helman, L. (2008). English words needed: Creating research-based vocabulary instruction for English learners. In A. Farstrup & S. J. Samuels (Eds.), *What research has to say about vocabulary instruction* (pp. 211–237). Newark, DE: International Reading Association.

Helman, L., Bear, D. R., Invernizzi, M., Templeton, S., & Johnston, F. (2009). *Words their way: Emergent sorts for Spanish-speaking English learners.* Boston: Allyn & Bacon.

Invernizzi, M., & Meier, J. (2001). *Phonological awareness literacy screening 2001–2002.* Charlottesville, VA: Rector and the Board of Visitors of the University of Virginia.

Koda, K. (2005). *Insights into second language reading.* New York: Cambridge University Press.

LeSaux, N., Koda, K., Siegel, L., & Shanahan, T. (2006). Development of literacy. In D. August & T. Shanahan (Eds.), *Developing literacy in second-language learners: Report of the National Literacy Panel on Language-Minority Children and Youth* (pp. 75–122). Mahwah, NJ: Erlbaum.

LeSaux, N. K., & Siegel, L. S. (2003). The development of reading in children who speak English as a second language. *Developmental Psychology, 39*(6), 1005–1019.

Lillegard, D. (2003). *Hello school: A classroom full of poems.* New York: Dragonfly Books.

London, J. (1998). *Froggy goes to school.* New York: Puffin Books.

Morris, D., Bloodgood, J. W., Lomax, R. G., & Perney, J. (2003). Developmental steps in learning to read: A longitudinal study in kindergarten and first grade. *Reading Research Quarterly, 38*(3), 302–328.

Morris, D., Bloodgood, J., & Perney, J. (2003). Predictors of first- and second-grade reading achievement. *Elementary School Journal, 104*(2), 93–109.

National Reading Panel. (2000). *Teaching children to read: An evidence-based assessment of the scientific research literature on reading and its implications for reading instruction.* Rockville, MD: National Institute of Child Health and Human Development.

Nelson, O. G., & Linek, W. M. (1998). *Practical classroom applications of language experience: Looking back, looking forward.* Boston: Allyn & Bacon.

NICHD Early Child Care Research Network. (2005). Pathways to reading: The role of oral language in the transition to reading. *Developmental Psychology, 41*(2), 428–442.

Read, C. (1971). Preschool children's knowledge of English phonology. *Harvard Educational Review, 41,* 1–34.

Roberts, T. A. (2008). Home storybook reading in primary or second language with preschool children: Evidence of equal effectiveness for second-language vocabulary acquisition. *Reading Research Quarterly, 42*(2), 103–130.

Shannon, D. (1999). *David goes to school*. New York: Blue Sky Press.
Snow, C. E., Burns, M. S., & Griffin, P. (1998). *Preventing reading difficulties in young children*. Washington, DC: National Academy Press.
Snow, C. E., Tabors, P. O., & Nicholson, P. A. (1995). SHELL: Oral language and early literacy skills in kindergarten and first-grade children. *Journal of Research in Childhood Education, 10,* 37–48.
Wood, A. (1994). *Silly Sally*. Harcourt, Brace.
Yolen, J. (2007). *How do dinosaurs go to school?* New York: Blue Sky Press.
Yopp, H. K. (1995). A test for assessing phonemic awareness in young children. *Reading Teacher, 49*(1), 20–28.

CHAPTER 7

Opening Doors to Texts
Planning Effective Phonics Instruction with English Learners

Lori Helman

Understanding how the written code of English functions is a critical accomplishment for all would-be readers, including students who are learning to speak English at the same time they are learning to read it. Phonics may be likened to a key to how oral language is translated into print; without the key, beginning readers cannot gain access to all of the wonderful texts and useful print information on the other side of the doorway.

Phonics is the set of letter–sound correspondences that assist readers in decoding printed words. In English, phonics knowledge begins as students gain an initial understanding of the alphabetic principle; they discover that the sounds they hear in words can be matched to individual letters in the alphabet. For example, students might attach the /b/ sound they hear in *book* to the letter B. Phonics also encompasses more advanced understandings about the way words are spelled, such as how chunks within words, or *rimes*, represent consistent sound units in English (e.g., *-amp* in *camp, lamp, ramp, stamp*, and *damp*). As students progress along the developmental continuum, phonics knowledge also involves learning more complex spelling patterns, such as long vowel patterns (e.g., *make* or *street*) or other vowel patterns (e.g., *cloud* or *taught*). For an extended discussion of this developmental progression by Bear and Smith, see Chapter 5, this volume.

Despite the essential nature of learning the phonics code in English, the task should not be seen as an end in itself; phonics is a tool that helps readers tackle unknown texts, but the goal of reading is to understand the meaning of those texts. In this chapter, I present research on the importance of phonics with English learners and share information about effective instruction. Following this, I outline a set of building blocks for creating a systematic, explicit, and meaningful phonics program for English learners in classrooms with developing readers.

RESEARCH ON PHONICS WITH ENGLISH LEARNERS

Much research has been done showing the importance of phonics knowledge to learning to read in English and describing effective phonics instruction for native speakers of English. This research shows that students profit from systematic and explicit instruction in the sound–symbol code, including learning letter sounds, as well as onset and rime approaches (Adams, 1990; Ehri, 1991; National Reading Panel, 2000). A summary of findings from the National Reading Panel, *Put Reading First*, describes effective phonics instruction as:

- Helping students relate letters to sounds and to segment and blend words.
- Explaining the purpose of learning sound–letter relationships.
- Applying phonics knowledge to real reading and writing activities.
- Adapting to the needs of individual students based on assessment data.
- A systematic approach that includes alphabetic knowledge, phonemic awareness, and vocabulary development (Center for the Improvement of Early Reading Achievement, 2003).

In a multiyear study, Taylor and her colleagues (Taylor, Pearson, Peterson, & Rodriguez, 2003) found the largest growth in student reading development for students who received phonics instruction at the right time and in the right amount. Students who continued to experience extended phonics skill lessons once they had already mastered the skill did not progress as well as students who moved on to higher level meaning-based instructional activities.

Although research with students learning English as a new language is not as extensive as research with native speakers, available studies conclude that word recognition development for native speakers and English learners appears to develop in a similar way (Chiappe & Siegel, 2006; LeSaux, Koda, Siegel, & Shanahan, 2006). Chiappe and Siegel (2006) found that patterns of growth were similar for native speakers and English learners on word recognition and phonological processing. LeSaux and Siegel (2003) found that the same variables identified struggling beginning readers in both native-speaking and English-learning groups.

Although a limited number of studies have examined effective instructional methods for phonemic awareness and phonics with English learners, members of the National Literacy Panel on Language-Minority Children and Youth suggest that the available results support the findings of the National Reading Panel for use with English learners (Shanahan & Beck, 2006). It is important to note, however, that most of the studies on phonics development with English learners did not measure students' ability to comprehend the material. In their analysis of effective teaching practices for English learners, Baker, Gersten, Haager, and Dingle (2006) describe quality performance as including: systematic and explicit instruction in letter–sound correspondence and decoding, checking for student comprehension through questioning, and engaging students in meaningful interactions about text. Until the research field has collected further data on English learners' development of phonics knowledge and the methods that most effectively produce this learning, we can cautiously say that learning the code of written English is equally as important for the reading development of English learners as it is for native speakers (Birch, 2002).

THE BUILDING BLOCKS OF EFFECTIVE PHONICS INSTRUCTION WITH ENGLISH LEARNERS

What implications may be drawn from the research literature on phonics instruction with English learners? How can teachers adapt their classroom practices to best meet the needs of students who are learning oral English while also learning the sound–symbol relationships of the language? How can teachers ensure that phonics instruction does not become a rote activity, disconnected from comprehension and meaning making? In this section, I outline eight key ideas for tailoring phonics instruction to the strengths and learning needs of English learners. I share each idea, describe one scenario that highlights the principle, and then sketch an example of an effective instructional practice in a linguistically diverse classroom.

Work with Students at Their Developmental Levels

Students' understandings of the English writing system grow as they engage with print and make connections between oral and written language. A student's developmental level will begin with emergent concepts of print, progress to developing an understanding of the alphabetic principle, and expand to clustering letters into pattern groups that represent particular sounds (Ehri, 1997). At each step along the developmental continuum, it is important that the phonics instruction that students receive matches their current understanding of the orthography (see Bear & Smith, Chapter 5, this volume, for an in-depth discussion). By focusing on students' instructional levels, teachers ensure that the content is accessible to students and builds on their understanding of print.

Jessica is a Spanish-speaking student in the spring of her second-grade school year. She has memorized about a hundred of the most frequent high-utility words but struggles to decode text if it does not have lots of picture clues or does not contain the words she has memorized, even if the words are easily decodable with simple phonics principles. Jessica's teacher wonders if the second-grade phonics curriculum is sinking in; Jessica does not seem to be able to use any of the ideas that have been presented in class in her own reading and writing. The teacher decides to assess Jessica's literacy development to see whether there is a mismatch between her current understanding and the level of classroom instruction. She asks Jessica to spell a list of progressively more difficult words on a qualitative spelling inventory (Bear, Invernizzi, Templeton, & Johnston, 2008) to give her a better idea of Jessica's orthographic understanding.

From the assessment, Jessica's teacher discovers that the material being presented in class is over Jessica's head. Jessica is operating at an alphabetic level, attempting to represent each sound she hears in a word with a single letter. The phonics and word study lessons in class are not making sense to Jessica, so she has done her best to memorize each new word she learns without a cohesive strategy. Unfortunately, this line of attack does not serve her well in decoding new texts or in spelling words with more advanced patterns.

By assessing Jessica, her teacher has taken the first step in carrying out effective phonics instruction. The next step involves matching the instruction to her learning level. Jessica's teacher can build a word study program based on the features in words that the student struggles with—in Jessica's case that would likely involve the study of simple word families. As classroom instruction becomes more closely aligned to Jessica's developmental understandings, she will be able to make sense of the phonics features and will not need to rely so heavily on rote memorization of whole words.

Build on Students' Home-Language and Literacy Skills

Students come to school with a variety of language and literacy skills: Some bring a strong home language that they use to communicate with family and friends; others bring bilingual skills; all bring some level of awareness of a writing system, whether it be English or the home language. The language and literacy strengths that students already have may be seen as a foundation for teachers to add to. Especially when students bring reading and writing skills in a home language, teachers have the opportunity to make connections with students to facilitate their learning of English phonics.

Before teachers can build on students' language and literacy skills in a home language, they need to know what those are. A variety of formal and informal assessments can help with this. First of all, teachers can review any enrollment information pertaining to a student. What information was included on the home language survey? What language does the student speak at home? What level of oral proficiency does the student have in English? If any assessments were done in the home language, what do they show about other literacy strengths? Once this information has been reviewed, teachers can collect their own informal assessment data, such as observational notes about the student's use of English and the home language. How does the student do in informal situations with English? In more academic contexts? When does the student use the home language?

One assessment that will help teachers understand the background language and literacy strengths of their students is to take a writing sample in the home language. This activity will tell teachers whether students bring literacy experiences from another language to school and to what degree. Teachers can seek out the advice of a community liaison at the school or a community member who speaks that particular language to help analyze the level of literacy demonstrated by the student. Once teachers have a sense of the language and literacy strengths that students bring to the classroom, they can investigate the relationships between oral and written characteristics of the home language and English and use that information to help students transfer what they know to learning the code of English.

Mr. Kelly teaches a first–second combination class with many English learners. He frequently gets immigrant students who join his classroom as their first experience in a U.S. school. His district collects some data on new students, but it is often a week or more before Mr. Kelly sees that information. So, when Mr. Kelly gets a new student, he does several things:

1. He has a brief conversation with the student in English to estimate his or her oral skills.
2. He ascertains, if possible, what home language the student speaks and, if there is another student who speaks the same language,

holds a three-way conversation to estimate language skills in the primary language.
3. He asks the new student to draw and write a short story using any literacy skills the student has. If the student writes in English, Mr. Kelly uses that information as a way to see what the student understands about the written code. Mr. Kelly also asks the student to write in the home language if he or she can. When Mr. Kelly gets a writing sample from another language, he calls on the resources of his school or district office to find a proficient speaker to help him better understand the student's literacy strengths. This is not always possible, because the district has students from more than a hundred different language backgrounds, yet they do have many resources and are improving all the time.
4. Mr. Kelly informally observes and takes notes about the student's language and literacy habits over the course of the first week at school. He finds that these informal observations help him tailor instruction that is comprehensible to the student and allows him to use what the student knows to bridge to new learning in English.

Once teachers such as Mr. Kelly have an understanding of the background language and literacy experiences of their students, they can use this knowledge to plan differentiated instruction for their English-learning students. Mr. Kelly has many Chinese-speaking students in his class. To educate himself, he went on the Internet to find out about the Chinese language and investigated the sounds that would be difficult for students to distinguish and pronounce. Now, when he teaches those sound–symbol relationships in English, he knows to contrast very distinctive sounds first. He also knows that certain sound features of English will be especially difficult for Chinese speakers, such as the vowel sounds; the contrasts between /p/ and /b/, /t/ and /d/, and /k/ and /g/; and certain sounds such as /v/ and /th/ (Swan & Smith, 2001). Although he can't research each of the many home languages of his students, Mr. Kelly is enjoying becoming a better teacher by developing his background knowledge one step at a time.

Follow a Systematic Sequence of Phonics Instruction

English learners have not had the same immersion in letters, words, and print materials in English as have native-speaking students who have grown up listening to books and seeing print written in English on a more regular basis. In addition, finding sound–spelling connections in the written language is more difficult when students have a limited oral language to match to printed words. For example, if a student has not heard and used words such as *queen, quarter,* and *quilt,* learning the sound of the letter *q* will be more difficult than for a student who brings many experiences with these words from children's books, oral language, and the artifacts of literate adults nearby. It would also be unlikely that an English learner would be able to make sense of a word in the print environment if he or she does not know what the word means. Because learning the building blocks of written language will need extra support and direction for English learners, it is critical to present the alphabetic code in a systematic format, building on the simplest features and extending to more complex patterns.

What makes a phonics feature simple or complex? When we are talking about comparing sounds, the simplest features will be the ones that are easy to distinguish and that contrast easily with other sounds. For example, the sound of the letter *m*, /m/, is easy to express and hear, and one can even notice visually what is happening in the mouth. Comparing the sounds of the letters *m* and *s* is very straightforward; the two sounds are quite distinct and easy to contrast. A phonics program that begins by comparing distinct sounds that are easy to produce and discriminate is easiest for students to understand.

Another factor that influences the complexity of phonics features is the background language experiences of students. Students bring an ability to discriminate sounds from their home languages; if the languages they bring to the classroom do not identify the same distinct sounds as those used in English, this may complicate the identification of sounds in English. For example, Spanish-speaking students may have difficulty discriminating the sounds of /s/ and /z/ in English because the /z/ sound is not present in Spanish (Helman, 2004). The sounds of many of the short vowels in English do not exist in a good number of languages in the world; thus they will be more difficult for students to learn. In order to provide systematic instruction in phonics that moves from simple to complex features, teachers need to have an understanding of how the sounds within students' home languages relate to the sounds of English; where there are differences between languages, there may be extra obstacles to students' learning.

Phonics features that match one sound to one letter are simpler than those that require more than one letter. For example, learning the sound of /t/ is easier than /th/. Short vowel sounds follow a one-letter-to-one-sound code (e.g., *mat*) and so are easier than long vowel patterns that often require the use of a silent letter or a particular spelling pattern (e.g., *mate*).

Many established phonics programs have clear scope and sequences that build from letter–sound knowledge to short vowel words to long vowel patterns and into more complex vowel patterns. Systematic phonics programs move step by step from simple to complex features, and this progression is organized and comprehensive. Phonics features build on previous understandings, and the scope and sequence is not haphazard. For example, students who are ready to study short vowels will do well to study a number of words with the short *a* sound; when this vowel sound is secure, introducing a second short vowel that clearly contrasts to the short *a* (such as the short *o*) will be a good next step. Flitting from vowel sound to vowel sound without cohesion or mastery would not be a systematic approach.

Ms. Walker is a new first-grade teacher, and she has many English learners in her classroom. She has noticed that a good number of her students are having difficulty discriminating and writing the short vowel sounds in words, such as the sounds in *bat, bet, bit*, and *but*. They often insert the wrong vowel sound in the words they write. Whenever she tries to clarify this confusion for students, Ms. Walker ends up feeling like she is going around in circles and isn't sure the students are learning from her direction.

Ms. Walker considers what it will take to provide more effective instruction. She realizes that learning so many new and different vowel sounds is confusing to her English-learning students. She decides to take a step back, focusing on one vowel at a time, and chooses a vowel that seems to be easiest for students. She will work with this vowel in depth with her students until they are secure in discriminating it and using it in their writing. Then she will introduce a second short vowel that contrasts easily and provide plenty of opportunities for students to compare the two sounds and spellings in hands-on activities. In this way, she will systematically work through the short vowel sounds, simplifying the tasks for students and providing extra support as needed.

Make Phonics Instruction Clear and Explicit

Anyone who has been immersed in a foreign-language experience knows that learning is challenging when you are working hard to understand what is being communicated. Think of what might have helped you learn in the context of an unfamiliar language: A graphic aid? Written text that you could try to understand? A translator? Young students also learn more effectively when the material is clear and easy to understand. For this reason, teachers should incorporate explicit instructional strategies such as the following (Bear, Helman, Templeton, Invernizzi, & Johnston, 2007):

- Model activities to show students your expectations.
- Bring in real objects and activities to help demonstrate the context of skill-based lessons.

- Use metacognition to think out loud about the skill being learned.
- Modify your language so that it is streamlined and simple.
- Have visual support materials readily available for student reference.

For a further discussion on the use of explicit instructional strategies with English learners, see Chapter 12, this volume.

Vang is a Hmong-speaking student in kindergarten who seems a bit overwhelmed by the barrage of letter–sound instruction heading his way in the classroom. He is confused by the shapes and sounds of the various graphemes and as yet is not able to associate lower- and upper-case letter matches or to connect a letter to the sound it represents. Vang's teacher, Ms. Sikowsky, believes in a print-rich environment, but her phonics instruction—teaching individual letters, listening to and discussing ABC books, chanting the ABC song, and doing worksheets—does not seem to be enough for him. She wonders what she can do to make her alphabet instruction more understandable and meaningful for Vang.

After attending a workshop on how to support English learners, Ms. Sikowsky comes away with several ideas to apply in her classroom. First of all, she realizes that although she has studied individual letters with her class and has a large alphabet strip posted above the chalkboard, her students haven't had access to student-sized reference materials with the letters. She finds a set of alphabet strips that have the upper-case and lower-case letters, along with simple pictures of objects that go with each letter sound. She posts these small alphabets throughout the classroom and in the writing area. Ms. Sikowsky also takes the time to teach each of the picture words on the alphabet strip and plays guessing games with her students to make sure they have learned the words (e.g., "What picture is next to the letter *t*? *Turtle*, you are right!") Now, when Vang seems confused about a letter, the first thing Ms. Sikowsky does is ask him to find it on his alphabet strip and guides him to use the picture as a clue when he has trouble.

Providing visual support through the use of alphabet strips was just a first step for Ms. Sikowsky. As she thought more about how much help it was for her students to have easy access to visual reference materials, she brainstormed several more ideas: She had students create their own picture dictionaries in which they could paste pictures and write letters and words. She labeled photos of the students and objects in the classroom to provide an oral-to-written-language scaffold for learning. She created charts with photos and simplified directions for the steps in common classroom tasks, such as "how to use writing center materials." Ms. Sikowsky knew that these simple materials were helping her English learners when she saw them consistently reviewing the charts and labels as they completed their jobs in class. Vang, in particular, seemed to show more and more confidence every day.

Use Active Learning Strategies to Teach and Practice Skills

All students are at risk of experiencing phonics instruction as a rote task that may become disconnected from active thinking, such as when students copy spelling words for a test. Perhaps you have seen students do this task by copying words one letter at a time—the first letter ten times, the second letter ten times, and so on. Clearly, when phonics becomes busy work, it is not useful for better understanding the written code of English. English learners who are already challenged to make sense of oral and written language are in particular danger of experiencing phonics as a repetitive or meaningless activity. To counteract this problem, engage students in learning and practicing phonics skills through purposeful and active lessons such as in hands-on sorts and games, using their bodies and voices, creating products, and interacting with fellow students (Bear et al., 2007).

Mr. Jensen is a first-grade teacher who has made a goal for the new school year: He wants to try word sorting with his class. In his first couple of years of teaching, Mr. Jensen noticed that the phonics worksheets he asked students to complete quickly became boring and laborious. He was always prodding students to "just finish up the last two lines." For all the effort and expenditure of paper, it was unclear whether students even got much practice out of filling in the blanks on the pages.

Mr. Jensen observed another first-grade teacher at his school as he used picture and word sorts to help students learn beginning sounds, word families, and vowel sounds in words. During word study time, he observed students manipulating small cards into two or three categories, such as beginning consonant picture sorts with /t/, /p/, and /c/. Students had to recognize the picture in English, connect the beginning sound to the correct header card, and sort the items accordingly (Bear et al., 2007). If a mistake was made, students could simply rearrange the picture card. After completing a sort, students shared them with the teacher or a partner and reflected on what made each category distinct. The sort could be repeated several times until students gained fluency in identifying and categorizing the items. It gave the teacher an opportunity to work with students on learning and practicing new vocabulary, searching for other words that had the same phonic feature, playing related sound and spelling games, or even sending the sort home to practice with family members (Helman, Bear, Invernizzi, Templeton, & Johnston, 2009). When students were finished with the unit under study, the pictures or words they were studying were sorted one last time and glued down to create a completed sheet. Mr. Jensen liked seeing students so enthusiastic and actively involved. He liked the freedom to use the pictures over and over in a variety of activities, and he felt good about the idea of cutting back on the overuse of paper in his classroom.

Integrate Vocabulary Study into Phonics Instruction

A recurring theme throughout this chapter is the need to make phonics instruction understandable and meaningful for English learners. If words are presented in isolation and no attempt is made to define or use them in context, students will come to assume that learning the sound–letter code of English is an abstract task—a puzzle with unclear application to real life. One way to counter these impressions is to make sure that students know the meanings of words they study in their phonics lessons. Consider for a moment a first-grade student studying the short vowel patterns in words such as *bag, rag, wag, nag, tag,* and *sag*. Or a second-grade student studying long vowel patterns in words such as *male, sale,* and *tale,* along with homophones *mail, sail,* and *tail*. These students may be able to decode the words in their phonics lessons but not move forward in their language and literacy learning because they do not understand the meanings of the words. Taking the time to clarify words reinforces the principle that the goal of learning about how letters, sounds, and words are structured is to access meaningful print. If meaning is set to the side, this message is invalidated.

Bear et al. (2007) offer a set of suggestions that can help teachers plan modifications to their phonics and word study lessons to make sure that English learners understand the vocabulary associated with each activity and don't engage in phonics in isolation of meaning. These considerations for word study with English learners include the following:

- Students read the pictures and words before they begin a sort or lesson.
- They set aside unknown words or pictures.
- A few words and pictures can be pretaught.
- Teachers use pictures or actions to illustrate the vocabulary of unknown phonics words.
- Sorts or lessons are discussed to give students practice hearing and using the words in context.
- Teachers should reconsider a sort or lesson if too many words or pictures are unknown.

When teachers do find that too many words or pictures are unknown, they suggest the following:

- Turn to an easier sort or lesson.
- Add easier words to the activity.
- Delete a difficult pattern to simplify the sort or lesson.
- Plan more time for instruction and practice.
- Practice vocabulary through concept sorts and using related words (Bear et al., 2007).

Mai Kia is one of a small group of second-grade students working with her teacher on a word study lesson to examine the phonograms *-et*, *-eg*, and *-en*. The group, including Mai Kia and other English learners, has no problem looking at the words and sorting them into categories by phonogram. The students are also able to decode and pronounce the words fairly easily. When asked what the words mean, however, Mai Kia does not know about half of the words, including *net, vet, hen, den, peg, beg*, and *keg*. Mai Kia is completing her phonics task as requested and feels that she is being successful. Unfortunately, she is treating the task as an abstract assignment in which the words she manipulates do not connect to meaningful concepts in her world.

To help Mai Kia and others like her, the teacher can supplement the lesson as described by Bear and his colleagues (2007). The teacher can remind students to set aside words they don't understand and use these words for vocabulary instruction. The teacher can show pictures of the words, act them out, and have students use them in sentences. If the phonics activity contains too many unknown words, the teacher can simplify the task by reducing the number of new words, by including pictures as well as words in lessons, and by planning more time for instruction and practice. See Chapter 3, this volume, for additional ideas on how to structure language practice into literacy lessons with students. With this insistence on making phonics comprehensible, Mai Kia's literacy learning will be moving ahead with all cylinders running.

Connect Phonics Instruction to Meaningful Texts

Phonics is not an end in itself; it is a tool to help students access print in meaningful ways in their world. Students who see the connection between skills and real reading are more motivated to learn the code of written English. When students use what they are learning in phonics and word study to read texts such as books, rhymes, signs, mail, and so on, they solidify their phonics skills and become better readers at the same time. If phonics is the *key*, then practice reading might be thought of as the *unlocking*.

Depending on students' developmental stage, different kinds of materials provide opportunities to practice what they are learning in phonics. Students at the emergent level, who are studying the alphabet and letter–sound correspondences, can practice reading with patterned or predictable little books and memorized texts of familiar rhymes or dictations. With repeated readings, students make associations between each word they are reading and its beginning letter, enhancing their learning of the phonics code (see Chapter 6, this volume, for additional examples). Students who are beginning readers are becoming fully alphabetic; they use information about all of the letters in a word to decode it. Beginning readers will transition away from memorized texts to ones that include words that they can decode based on sound–symbol relationships, as well as on their knowledge of high-frequency words. These leveled books systematically build on the early decoding skills of students and their expanding collection of automatic sight words. It is important for teachers to provide opportunities for students to put their phonics knowledge into practice while at the same time avoiding unnatural language patterns that will be hard for English learners to understand and connect to their oral language. For example, although *Nan can fan* does provide an opportunity to read *-an* words, the phrase doesn't make very much sense. On the other hand, a text that blends decodable words and high-frequency words that students have learned to read by sight allows even beginning readers to practice reading some meaningful sentences such as, *The man ran and ran to catch the bus*. Step by step, as phonics skills and a larger bank of automatic sight words develop, students practice in more difficult, but still leveled, books. By the time students have reached the end of the beginning reading stage, they practice their advanced phonics skills in longer and less constrained reading materials from the bookstore, the library, and the community that have not been intentionally simplified to accommodate their decoding skills.

Ms. Martinez has been working on the short vowel sounds with her beginning-of-the-year first graders. Students have done word sorts, have practiced writing words on small white boards, and have constructed words using small letter tiles. Although all of these activities are helpful to her students, Ms. Martinez knows that it is only by reading these words in real texts that students will come to internalize the spelling–sound relationships and become automatic readers. She considers the kinds of reading materials she could use with students to help them practice what they are learning in their phonics program.

Ms. Martinez makes up her mind that each phonics lesson will start and end by reading and noticing the words or features being studied within a piece of connected text. She decides that each lesson will begin with a short poem or story that has several examples of the phonics feature embedded within. First, she reads the poem or story and students chant along on repeated readings. Next, students search for words that have the feature under study (such as the phonogram -*an*). She thinks this will be a very explicit way for students to see that the words and features they are studying are a part of the stories and poems they read and have direct application to real reading. Ms. Martinez comes up with a list of materials for students to read after the phonics lesson as well. These simple materials will at times be a poem that has been written on chart paper, a pocket chart story, a leveled book that uses the focus feature, or a book from students' familiar reading boxes. Ms. Martinez knows that the more students practice reading text that includes the phonics they are using, the more automatic they will become, and the more connected her instruction will be to authentic reading tasks.

Check for Understanding and Use Frequent Informal Assessments

Even using the best instructional strategies in the world does not ensure that students are learning what is being taught. A wise teacher once said that what matters is not how well we think we are teaching but, rather, how much is being learned. Teachers can assess student learning through summative formal assessments at the end of a unit, but more important, they can use ongoing informal assessments and checks for understanding.

Every lesson is an opportunity to gauge students' understanding of written words and the reading and writing processes. Most of these assessments and checks for understanding are quick and unobtrusive and do not require special forms. Some examples of these informal "checks" include:

- Keeping a notepad nearby to take informal notes about what students are doing during small- and large-group phonics lessons.
- Moving around the room and taking observational notes while students are sorting and playing word study games.
- Having students "read" their sorts and share their reflections orally or in writing.
- Instead of calling on an individual student, asking all students to show a "thumbs up" sign or other physical signal to demonstrate a yes answer to a teacher question or a "thumbs down" for no.

- Having students do mini-spell checks or quizzes on small white boards on a regular basis, especially before completing a phonics unit.
- Periodically asking students to "turn to a partner and share" about the current feature under study. For example, "Tell your partner as many words as you can that start with *s*."

In addition to these regular checks for understanding, one instructional activity doubles as an informal assessment: encouraging developmental spelling. Developmental spelling means that teachers ask students to spell "the best you can; write down all the sounds you feel and hear" (Bear et al., 2007, p. 217). If developmental spelling procedures are used on a regular basis in the classroom, teachers have an ongoing fountain of informal assessment information. For example, a student who is spelling *home* as H is showing knowledge of the sound of the letter *h*, as well as awareness of the beginning sound of the word. A student who spells it as HM is showing an understanding of beginning and ending sounds, as well as knowledge of the consonant sounds /h/ and /m/. A student who spells *home* as HOM is demonstrating phonemic awareness and fully alphabetic spelling strategies. Finally, a student who spells the word correctly, HOME, is showing knowledge of long vowel spelling patterns by adding the silent e marker. Thus students' developmental spellings are a continuous source of informal assessment data with which teachers can better understand students' orthographic knowledge.

Ms. Bradley is a recent college graduate whose first full-time teaching position was as a mid-year substitute in a second-grade classroom. She was aware from her college course work that developmental spelling was not only an effective learning tool but also allowed her to better understand her students' spelling and phonics knowledge (National Reading Panel, 2000). There was only one problem: Her new students would not write what they were insecure about spelling. She was constantly confronted with questions about how to spell individual words and found that students used very simple sentences in their writing because they were afraid to be incorrect.

Ms. Bradley decided that in order to reap the benefits of using developmental spelling, she would have to take a "tough love" approach. She told her students that during their writing time she would not be spelling words for them. In fact, she would rather they listened to the sounds they could hear in words and try to spell them the best they could. She modeled a lesson for the whole class in which she used a think-aloud procedure to write a sentence using a developmental spelling approach. She showed several variations of how such a sentence might be spelled and said that all of the approaches were "good tries." When the writing workshop began, Ms. Bradley held to her rule of not spelling words for students. After seeing that she would be firm in her procedures and that she would not penalize them for misspelling a word, the students soon became much freer at using developmental spelling attempts. In addition to the practice this gave them in applying their phonics knowledge, the approach had the added benefit of encouraging students to use any word in their writing, not just the words that they knew how to spell. Of course, for certain projects that would be shared publicly, Ms. Bradley helped her students work through editing and correcting their spelling to create a finalized product.

CONCLUSION

Phonics, the knowledge of the letter–sound relationships in English, is an essential component of literacy learning. At the beginning stage of reading, phonics is key to literacy learning for both native speakers and English-learning students. This chapter has outlined the importance of phonics in learning to read and has described eight instructional guidelines to support English learners in acquiring the written code:

1. Work with students at their developmental level.
2. Build on students' home language and literacy skills.
3. Follow a systematic sequence of phonics instruction.
4. Make phonics instruction clear and explicit.
5. Use active learning strategies to teach and practice skills.
6. Integrate vocabulary study into phonics instruction.
7. Connect phonics instruction to meaningful texts.
8. Check for understanding and use frequent informal assessments.

English learners need to learn the code of written language to be successful, but decoding is not the only goal in reading development. This chapter has highlighted how skills are integrated into meaningful activities and how the meaning of words is always taught in tandem with decoding processes. A simple-to-complex approach to learning letter–sound relationships in English allows English learners to experience success without becoming overwhelmed. And, when teachers understand the linguistic challenges for students, such as difficult sound contrasts between their home languages and English, instruction can be differentiated to build on their literacy strengths and needs.

A strong foundation in phonics is a key for students to open doors to a wealth of texts and other literacy opportunities in their lives. Effective instruction with English learners is an important step in supporting them to unlock the doors to meaningful reading and writing experiences.

REFERENCES

Adams, M. J. (1990). *Beginning to read: Thinking and learning about print.* Cambridge, MA: MIT Press.

Baker, S. K., Gersten, R., Haager, D., & Dingle, M. (2006). Teaching practice and the reading growth of first-grade English learners: Validation of an observation instrument. *Elementary School Journal, 107*(2), 199–219.

Bear, D. R., Helman, L., Templeton, S., Invernizzi, M., & Johnston, F. (2007). *Words their way with English learners: Word study for phonics, vocabulary, and spelling instruction.* Upper Saddle River, NJ: Pearson/Merrill Prentice Hall.

Bear, D.R., Invernizzi, M., Templeton, S., & Johnston, F. (2008). *Words their way: Word study for phonics, vocabulary, and spelling instruction* (4th ed.). Upper Saddle River, NJ: Prentice Hall.

Birch, B. M. (2002). *English L2 reading: Getting to the bottom.* Mahwah, NJ: Erlbaum.

Center for the Improvement of Early Reading Achievement. (2003). *Put reading first: The research building blocks for teaching children to read* (OERI Publication No. R305R70004). Washington, DC: U.S. Department of Education.

Chiappe, P., & Siegel, L. S. (2006). A longitudinal study of reading development of Canadian children from diverse linguistic backgrounds. *Elementary School Journal, 107*(2), 135–152.

Ehri, L. (1991). Development of the ability to read words. *Handbook of Reading Research* (Vol. 2, pp. 383–417). New York: Longman.

Ehri, L. C. (1997). Learning to read and learning to spell are one and the same, almost. In C. A. Perfetti, L. Rieben, & M. Fayol (Eds.), *Learning to spell: Research, theory, and practice across languages* (pp. 237–269). Mahwah, NJ: Erlbaum.

Helman, L., Bear, D. R., Invernizzi, M., Templeton, S., & Johnston, F. (2009). *Words their way: Letter name–alphabetic sorts for Spanish-speaking English learners.* Boston: Allyn & Bacon/Pearson.

Helman, L. A. (2004). Building on the sound system of Spanish: Insights from the alphabetic spellings of English language learners. *Reading Teacher, 57*, 452–460.

LeSaux, N., Koda, K., Siegel, L., & Shanahan, T. (2006). Development of literacy. In D. August & T. Shanahan (Eds.), *Developing literacy in second-language learners: Report of the National Literacy Panel on Language-Minority Children and Youth* (pp. 75–122). Mahwah, NJ: Erlbaum.

LeSaux, N. K., & Siegel, L. S. (2003). The development of reading in children who speak English as a second language. *Developmental Psychology, 39*(6), 1005–1019.

National Reading Panel. (2000). *Teaching children to read: An evidence-based assessment of the scientific research literature on reading and its implica-*

tions for reading instruction. Rockville, MD: National Institute of Child Health and Human Development.

Shanahan, T., & Beck, I. L. (2006). Effective literacy teaching for English language learners. In D. August & T. Shanahan (Eds.), *Developing literacy in second-language learners: Report of the National Literacy Panel on Language-Minority Children and Youth* (pp. 415–488). Mahwah, NJ: Erlbaum.

Swan, M., & Smith, B. (2001). *Learner English.* New York: Cambridge University Press.

Taylor, B. M., Pearson, P. D., Peterson, D. S., & Rodriguez, M. C. (2003). Reading growth in high-poverty classrooms: The influence of teacher practices that encourage cognitive engagement in literacy learning. *Elementary School Journal, 104,* 3–28.

CHAPTER 8

English Language Learners and Fluency Development
More Than Speed and Accuracy

M. Kristiina Montero
Melanie R. Kuhn

Some 90% of public school teachers in the United States are members of the dominant-language (English), ethnic (White/Caucasian), and religious (Christian) majority, a statistic that has remained relatively stable for the past 35 years (National Education Association, 2003); similar statistics regarding the teaching population exist in Canada (Carr, 1995) as well. The linguistic, cultural, ethnic, and religious composition of children in today's pre-K to grade 12 classrooms, however, is far more varied in countries in which English is the language of currency. Countries such as Australia, Canada, and the United States are experiencing the largest waves of immigration in each country's respective history, and, as long as these immigration patterns continue as projected, educators will continue to witness substantial changes in their classroom demographics. Teachers will see—if they haven't already—that traditional homogeneous classrooms, which closely resemble the characteristics of the dominant culture, are beginning to reflect these larger demographic changes.

To better understand the rapid changes that are being seen in classroom demographics, we need only examine the recent statistics of foreign-born immigrants. The most recent census data indicated that an estimated 22% of the Australian population was born outside of the country and that over 18% of the total Canadian population was also estimated to be foreign born (Statistics Canada, 2003). Similarly, in the United States, the estimated number of foreign-born immigrants was close to 12% as of 2004 (U.S. Census Bureau, 2004). These figures are significant because a substantial percentage of students labeled "limited English proficient" (LEP) are either foreign born themselves or are the children of foreign-born immigrants; in the United States, this is the case for over 90% of the LEP population (Morse, 2005). Given the number of children born to immigrant parents, one can easily see how, in the 2000–2001 academic year, the number of English language learners (ELLs) enrolled in U.S. schools was close to 5 million (approximately 10% of the student population), with the most common home languages being Spanish (79.2%), Vietnamese (2%), Hmong (1.6%), Cantonese (1%), and Korean (1%; Kindler, 2002). In Canada, of the immigrants who arrived in the 1990s, 17% were school-age children (Statistics Canada, 2003). Additionally, a range of national linguistic and cultural minorities—for example, Native American (United States) and people of the First Nations (Canada), Aborigines (Australia), and Native Hawaiian (United States)—who bring with them varying degrees of bilingualism and cultural, ethnic, and religious diversity may also be categorized as ELLs.

A large and persistent achievement gap exists between ELLs and native English speakers, as is indicated by national assessments conducted in the United States (August, Carlo, Dressler, & Snow, 2005; Carlo et al., 2004). For example, according to the 2005 National Assessment of Educational Progress (NAEP), only 29% of ELLs in the eighth grade scored at or above the basic achievement level, significantly lower than the 73% of non-ELL eighth graders who scored at the same level (National Center for Education Statistics, 2005). One problem lies in teacher preparation; many general education teachers perceived themselves to be ill prepared to adequately meet the needs of ELLs (Darling-Hammond, Chung, & Frelow, 2002; Karabenick & Noda, 2004). Yet the changes in student composition that are being seen in many classrooms mean that teachers and teacher education programs need to address the full range of students' respective learning needs through evolving pedagogies that are informed and evidence-based and that hold the best interest of each child at the forefront.

The purpose of this chapter is twofold. First, we provide an overview of fluency's role in literacy development, followed by a series of issues related to fluency development and ELLs that need to be considered in research venues. Second, we present a series of considerations that teachers need to bear in mind when instructing students who are learning to read and write in English when it is not their first language. Because there are many questions regarding fluency development and instruction for ELLs and little research specifically conducted on fluency development with this general population of students, our chapter focuses primarily on research-based strategies that promote fluent reading for English-dominant learners and notes specific adaptations that can be made specifically to support the various learning needs of ELLs.

CONSIDERING FLUENCY DEVELOPMENT IN ENGLISH-DOMINANT PRIMARY SCHOOL-AGE CHILDREN

According to Jay Samuels, a pioneer in fluency research, "the most important characteristic of the fluent reader is the ability to decode and to comprehend text at the same time" (Samuels, 2006, p. 9). Fluency is critical to reading success in English, or in any alphabetic language, because the ability to determine meaning from print depends on a reader's ability to develop accurate, automatic word recognition and the appropriate use of prosody[1] (Snow, Burns, & Griffin, 1998). We would argue that fluency is important because it contributes to students' reading comprehension in two ways. First, when students establish automatic word recognition, they are able to shift their focus away from the decoding of words and toward constructing meaning from what has been written. Second, by integrating appropriate prosody, students are able to determine shades of meaning, developing nuanced understandings as a result. Although the exact relationship between comprehension and prosody is unclear (e.g., reciprocal, leading from prosody to comprehension, or leading from comprehension to prosody), few doubt that a relationship does exist.

Strategies that support fluency include repeated reading, scaffolded wide reading, and other guided oral reading procedures in school (National Institute of Child Health and Human Development [NICHD], 2000), as well as independent reading outside of school (Anderson, Wilson, & Fielding, 1988). However, it is important to remember that the superficial features of fluent reading, such as automaticity and expression, are not the end goal of reading instruction; rather, the end goal is the comprehension of and transaction with printed material. Additionally, students making the transition to fluency will also benefit from instruction in a range of comprehension strategies, including prediction, the use of graphic organizers, and developing the ability to access the meaning of words through the use of context clues. If we accept that fluency is vital to reading success (and, as authors of this chapter, we do), we

---

[1] Those elements such as expression and appropriate phrasing that, taken together, make oral reading sound like speech.

should also consider it critical to the literacy curriculum and well deserving of a teacher's limited instructional time.

Interestingly, for most English-dominant students learning to read and write in English, their mother tongue, the emphasis on fluency instruction occurs during the second or third grades (e.g., Chall, 1996; Kuhn & Stahl, 2003). Developmentally, this makes sense. By this time, students should have an established receptive and productive oral-language vocabulary, on established understanding of the concepts of print (e.g., directionality, the understanding that print carries a message), the ability to hear and manipulate sounds in words (phonemic awareness), a basic sight-word vocabulary (i.e., any word the learner can recognize immediately and without decoding; Ehri, 1995), and a growing understanding of how words work within the larger grammatical structures of language (syntax). Prepared with these skills, students can begin to develop automatic word recognition, or automaticity (see also Chapter 5, this volume, for a discussion of development by Bear and Smith).

As readers become fluent, their word recognition, which was likely accurate but laborious, should become effortless. Further, because students no longer have to focus significant amounts of attention on word recognition, they are better able to consider phrasing and the use of appropriate expression in oral reading. Taken together, these elements allow readers to deal with the meaning of text rather than simply concentrating on the surface features. And although comprehension should be stressed throughout the school years, fluent readers will have an advantage over their disfluent peers because they are able to determine the meaning of a text as they read, rather than having to figure out the words before they can concentrate on the meaning or having to rely on someone else, for example, the teacher, to read the text to them.

A focus on fluency in the later primary grades allows English-dominant students to consolidate their word-recognition and written-vocabulary knowledge, as the vast majority of words they encounter in primary texts fall within their oral vocabulary. This consolidation occurs through the reading of significant amounts of connected text using both assisted and unassisted reading strategies. Similarly, many concepts—for example, family, friendship, and community—presented in these primary-level texts fall within learners' existing knowledge base. However, students can also continue to strengthen their productive vocabulary through exposure to a wide range of reading materials, because, even in the primary grades, texts present words that are outside the day-to-day vocabulary of these English-dominant readers (Beck, McKeown, & Kucan, 2002). Repeated exposure to known vocabulary words and related concepts serves to deepen and refine the learner's knowledge of these concepts, and exposure to previously unknown words and concepts help learners broaden their knowledge bases and prepares them for more challenging material (Stanovich, 1986). By developing their ability to automatically decode words, readers are able to access the meaning of the text at least at a basic level, to strengthen productive and receptive oral and written language, and to develop their understanding of text structure. Provided English-dominant students have adequate opportunities to read and are given sufficient support as part of their instructional environment—and these are two critical assumptions—their fluency development will likely proceed without too much difficulty.

CONSIDERING ELLs

The issue of fluency development for ELLs is significantly more complex. As discussed in Chapters 6, 7, and 9 of this volume, instruction in the key components of reading (National Reading Panel [National Institute of Child Health and Human Development, 2000])—phonemic awareness, phonics, fluency, vocabulary, and text comprehension—have clear benefits for language-minority students (August & Shanahan, 2006). However, ELLs have specific linguistic needs that may compound the type of instruction needed to advance their development and acquisition of English language literacy. Therefore, before trying to understand how to best provide ELLs with fluency instruction, we feel it is important to discuss the term *English language learner* and demonstrate that it is not a one-size-fits-all term. In fact, the literacy instructional strengths and needs of ELLS are diverse and varied, requiring differing levels of support throughout the literacy curriculum.

Valdés, Bunch, Snow, Carol, and Matos (2005) grouped ELLs into three categories based on their active and receptive oral- and written-language proficiencies: incipient bilingual, ascendant bilingual, and fully functional bilingual. In other words, the criteria for these categories are based on individuals' ability to comprehend and to produce oral and written English. In order to make these notions more concrete, we describe three ELLs who are illustrative of these categories and the typical difficulties, as identified by Valdés and her colleagues (2005), that these learners may experience in an English-dominant school.

Incipient Bilingual

Marisol is 8 years old and has recently arrived in Toronto, Canada, with her mother and grandmother from the Republic of El Salvador. She attended public school in a rural area of the country but often missed months of classes because she helped her mother harvest sugar cane.

Marisol has rudimentary Spanish-language reading and writing abilities but has not had much opportunity to develop them. Her mother has minimal literacy skills, and her grandmother does not know how to read and write. Marisol is an example of an incipient bilingual; upon arrival to Canada, Marisol was placed in a second-grade classroom and began to receive pull out English as a second language (ESL) services. Her teachers immediately realized that her comprehension levels of oral and written English were extremely low, and her teachers noted high levels of frustration when she was asked to produce oral and written English.

Ascendant Bilingual

Ming-Tai moved from Taiwan to Sydney, Australia, with her parents and younger brother when she was 10 years old. Her parents were entrepreneurs and went to Australia to open up a sister company of the one already established in Taiwan. At home, Ming-Tai always spoke Mandarin Chinese with her father and Min-nan, the southern Fujianese dialect, with her mother. She is reading and writing on grade level in Mandarin and has an excellent oral-language proficiency in Min-nan. In Taiwan, Ming-Tai attended a private school where students were taught English as a foreign language for 60 minutes per day, and, as a result, Ming-Tai developed some degree of oral- and written-language proficiency in English. Upon arrival in Sydney, Ming-Tai was placed in a fourth-grade classroom. Her teachers note that she generally understands oral English but has difficulty understanding explanations of unfamiliar topics. She also has difficulty understanding written English as presented in textbooks and other school-based text. She experiences difficulty expressing opinions, explaining statements, or challenging others because of the influence her mother tongue vocabulary and/or syntax has on her production of oral language in English, causing a breakdown in communication. She also struggles with writing in English—it is laborious and time-consuming. She produces texts that contain many errors, making it difficult for the reader to focus on the ideas that she intends to communicate.

Fully Functional Bilingual

Luis is 12 years old. His parents were born in Mexico and immigrated to the United States to work in its service industry. Luis was born in the United States and used Spanish in the home up until the time he went to kindergarten at the Oyster School, a two-way bilingual school in Washington, DC. He attended the school until the sixth grade, at which time his family decided to move to central New York. Luis was using Spanish and English interchangeably, both in written and spoken domains. He loved reading the *Harry Potter* series in Spanish and graphic novels in English. In central New York, Luis was enrolled in the seventh grade in a school that offered only free-standing ESL services, so two-way bilingual education was no longer an option for him. Luis is a fully functional bilingual; he has native-like oral-language proficiency, both in oral comprehension and production, in Spanish and English. He is able to comprehend written academic texts with little difficulty given typical classroom instruction, and his written production resembles that of his monolingual peers.

These three examples are intended to provide you with an idea of the types of students who can be generally categorized as ELLs; these examples are not meant to be representative of all types of ELLs. It is important to remember that ELLs who fall into these categories are not restricted by age; in other words, a 5-year-old can be a fully functional bilingual, whereas a 16-year-old can be an incipient bilingual; students in any of these categories may be present in K–12 classrooms. Given the three categories described by Valdés and her colleagues (2005), the use of ELL as an umbrella term to describe students with a wide range of abilities and needs becomes apparent.

CONSIDERING FLUENCY DEVELOPMENT FOR ELLs ENROLLED IN ELEMENTARY SCHOOLS

The most effective and efficient way to teach language-minority students to read and write in English is to take advantage of their oral proficiency in their home languages, along with the varying degrees of literacy that exist in their mother tongue (August & Shanahan, 2006). However, this is not always possible because of legislative restrictions (e.g., English-only legislation passed in the name of national unity: Proposition 227 in California and Proposition 223 in Arizona) or restrictions in available resources—both personnel and material. For example, two-way bilingual programs, or programs that emphasize bilingualism and biliteracy in English and Spanish, are rare in the United States (Freeman, 1996). Students who participate in such programs have the opportunity to become fully functional adult bilinguals. Transitional bilingual programs, on the other hand, aim to mainstream students by the end of first or second grade (early-exit) or to work with the students through to the end of sixth grade (late-exit); unfortunately, bilingualism and biliteracy are not the goals of such programs (Ramírez, Yuen, & Ramey, 1991). Transitional bilingual programs may be offered in school districts with a critical mass of students with the same home language (in many U.S. states, the critical number is 20). If the critical mass of students is not attained, ELLs are limited to free-standing ESL services (pull-out, push-in, or self-contained ESL programming). Students receiving ESL services may only have instruction for a small portion of the day (normally less than an hour); as a result, the remainder of their day is spent in the general education classroom with a teacher who may or may not have had adequate training and experience to meet the needs of his or her ELLs.

Given the information we have outlined regarding both ELLs and the programs that provide them services, we argue that the fluency development of incipient and ascendant bilinguals is more complicated than is the fluency development of their monolingual and/or fully functional bilingual peers. This results from a range of factors, including the incipient and ascendant bilinguals' lower levels of linguistic control (e.g., vocabulary) and limited oral-language proficiency.

Linguistic Control

Exposing ELLs to a range of concepts and English language vocabulary in both speech and text is critical to their oral-language and literacy development, because vocabulary acquisition is positively correlated with the ability to comprehend grade-level texts (Nagy, 1988; Stahl, 1999). It is also the case that the typical ELL knows far fewer words in English than does his or her monolingual peer; in fact, on average, students for whom English is their primary language will have learned approximately 5,200 root words by the end of second grade, increasing to 8,400 root words by the end of eighth grade, as determined by oral-language testing (Biemiller & Slonim, 2001). This implies that the student knows a word's literal meaning, as well as some of its derived meanings; how the word is used in syntax; and how the word can be changed through morphemes (e.g., adding *-ed* to *look* to make the past tense *looked*) and that he or she has a basic understanding of how other words, such as synonyms and antonyms, relate to it (Nagy & Scott, 2000). Biemiller and Slonim (2001) also found that those students with depressed vocabularies at the end of second grade never reached the higher end of the spectrum of learned root words by fifth grade. Although it is essential that all students be exposed to oral language, it is especially important for students who are likely to be at risk in their literacy learning (e.g., ELLs and students from homes with low literacy levels; see, e.g., Baron, Schwanenflugel, & Collins-Block, 2007). This can best be done through conversations, read-alouds, and reading and discussing texts.

Oral-Language Proficiency

Oral-language proficiency encompasses knowledge of phonology, vocabulary, morphology, grammar, discourse features, and pragmatic skills that enable a person to have fluent receptive and expressive oral language (Lesaux & Geva, 2006). A limited knowledge of oral English can create difficulties both at the level of word identification and in terms of the reader's ability to access multiple word meanings (Bear, Invernizzi, Templeton, & Johnston, 2008). To begin with, decoding can be problematic for students who are not familiar with English phonemes. For this reason, it is recommended that your instruction for ELLs focus more on the phonemes and combinations of phonemes that exist in English but that are not present in the students' mother tongues (August & Shanahan, 2006; see also Chapter 5, this volume, for similar work by Bear and Smith). At the level of pronunciation, if students have difficulty mapping a series of sounds to their corresponding letters, they will have trouble correctly identifying the word in print. (This said, ELLs may read and speak English with an accent and still be able to read fluently; the two should not be confounded.) Similarly, if a word is to be identified as an instant word (words such as *and, the,* and *of*),[2] it is essential that the learners know both how to recognize it as a unit and what the word means. Finally, it may be that a student will be able to correctly sound out a word and have no idea what that word means. Although this happens to all readers on occasion, it is less likely to happen to beginning readers who are English-dominant because most of the words they encounter in text will be words that already exist in their sight vocabulary, once decoded.

Given the differences between early-English-dominant readers and ELLs, we feel it is essential that any fluency work done with early readers who are simultaneously learning English be complemented with work in oral-language and comprehension development. According to a number of researchers (e.g., Baron et al., 2007; Shanahan, 2005), one of the most important things teachers can do for young monolingual learners (preschool, kindergarten, and grade 1) is to ensure that they have access to and use complex oral language. The same is true for bilingual learners. Although attention to fluency-promoting strategies is necessary for ELLs, it is not sufficient; oral proficiency in English is critical but unfortunately often overlooked as an element of literacy instruction (August & Shanahan, 2006; see also Chapter 3, this volume, for a discussion by Dutro and Helman).

Attending to oral-language development does not mean simply talking to your students, either in terms of presenting directions or

---

[2] We use the term *instant word* for high-frequency, irregular words, that is, words that should not be decoded but learned as units; we differentiate them from sight words, preferring Ehri's (1995) definition of *sight word* as any word within a reader's sight vocabulary.

through the typical initiation (teacher poses a question)–response (child responds to the question)–evaluation (teacher evaluates the response) exchange that dominates traditional classroom discourse (e.g., Cazden, 2001). Instead, it involves creating meaningful, student-centered dialogues with the children, ensuring that they have a chance to be involved in daily conversations with the teacher or more knowledgeable others, for example, a teacher's aide, a family member, or another student, perhaps in a higher grade. This is especially important for students who have limited experiences with English. It is essential that students have access to as much comprehensible input, or opportunities to listen to speech, as possible (Krashen, 1989), as well as venues for output, or opportunities to engage in talk (Cummins, 1994). Luckily, because most fluency work involves oral reading and incorporates either repetition of a single text or the wide reading of a range of texts, it lends itself to developing word recognition, oral and written vocabulary, and a range of concepts that may or may not be part of the students' knowledge base.

WHAT WE NEED TO KNOW

We began this chapter with a definition of fluency as the ability to decode and comprehend text at the same time (Samuels, 2006). We have also made the argument that this process has an added level of complication for ELLs. Before presenting strategies that we feel may be effective, we want to stress that, although we have anecdotal evidence that these work, as a field we are sorely lacking any research to confirm this belief. It is critical that research in this area be undertaken to expand our understanding of what we as educators can do to assist ELLs in becoming fluent readers. We also have several questions regarding this area of potential research that we feel can help to open up a dialogue. Though we by no means consider this to be a comprehensive list, we feel it is important to present a series of possible directions in which future research can be undertaken.

- There are indications that reading fluency is best taught to English-dominant learners after they have established a given level of comfort with text (e.g., they have established basic phonemic awareness, concepts of print, a sight word vocabulary, etc. (Kuhn et al., 2006; Stahl & Heubach, 2005). Is this the same for ELLs, or would a different amount of early literacy instruction be preferable (e.g, more intensive phonemic awareness work or establishing a larger sight vocabulary) or, on the other hand, would it be better to develop this in unison with their reading fluency?

- To what degree do oral-language discussions on a particular topic (e.g., the desert) help to build the reading fluency of ELLS on that topic?
- How effective are repeated readings as a strategy for the fluency of ELLs with a particular text? Do repeated readings lead to improved fluency, or do they lead to rote memorization without the corresponding understanding that is central to fluent reading?
- Would the reading of multiple texts on the same subject be an effective alternative to repetition, helping to increase word knowledge at the meaning and decoding levels, along with general comprehension, or would this be less effective than seeing the same text multiple times?
- It is worth noting that a number of research studies have indicated that English-dominant learners learn to recognize a word better when it is seen in multiple contexts (Kuhn & Stahl, 2003; Mostow & Beck, 2005). Is this the same for ELLs?
- What role does prosody play in the fluency development of ELLs? For example, does misplaced stress interfere with understanding, or is it more of a superficial aspect of written English for these learners?
- How valuable is fluency with written text in a learner's primary language in the subsequent development of fluency with English texts?
- We know that sustained attention must be given to the vocabulary development of ELLs because levels of vocabulary are shown to influence reading fluency and because little experimental research has been conducted to examine the development of vocabulary in ELLs (August et al., 2005). We also know that explicit vocabulary instruction (e.g., morphemic and context analysis; Baumann et al., 2002) may enable students to infer the meanings of untaught words. What we know less about is, will explicit vocabulary teaching help ELLs acquire greater levels of oral-language proficiency that will serve to improve reading fluency?
- Garton and Pratt (1989) suggested that oral-language proficiency can be facilitated by learning to read. Understanding that oral-language proficiency in English is fundamental to literacy acquisition, the question that begs to be asked is: Do assisted and unassisted repeated readings with ELLs facilitate oral-language proficiency in English in a way that advances their progressive success in acquiring academic language proficiency?

As we stated, we are not suggesting that these questions cover the entire range of research for fluency and ELLs, but we feel they can help move the discussion forward by opening a dialogue that needs to begin to take place.

STRATEGIES THAT PROMOTE READING FLUENCY

In the following section we briefly describe some of the strategies that promote fluency, with specific attention given to ways in which these strategies can be adapted to meet the specific linguistic, cognitive, and academic needs of ELLs. As noted earlier, many of the approaches that are used with English-dominant students can be used with ELLs; however, adaptations need to be made to have maximum benefit (August & Shanahan, 2006). It is, however, insufficient to simply implement a well-known, research-based strategy; instead, it is important to think through your specific goals and make sure that the strategy can help to meet the goals established for the individual student.

When we think about literacy acquisition and development on a sociocultural level, we understand that it is critical to teach in culturally responsive ways by using students' "cultural knowledge, prior experiences, frames of reference, and performance styles of ethnically [and we would add linguistically] diverse students to make learning encounters more relevant to and effective for them" (Gay, 2000, p. 29; Au, Chapter 2, this volume). ELLs come to our classrooms with many social, cultural, linguistic, and cognitive competencies; they are not blank slates. Therefore, we must take advantage of the knowledge and experiences they bring to the instructional forum and be prepared to learn from them, as much as guide them, on their academic journey. We know that to guide our students' fluency development teachers need to support the word recognition skills and abilities, the oral reading expression (prosody), and the text comprehension in English of ELLs. In order to facilitate literacy development in English, we need to find ways to increase the active and receptive oral proficiency in English of ELLs, to develop their vocabulary and concept base in English, and, whenever possible, to take advantage of students' oral proficiency and literacy in their home languages. Each of the strategies mentioned can only be enriched by the use of trade books that speak to a child's ethnic, linguistic, and cultural background(s) or strategies that validate a child's home language and culture. Table 8.1 lists each of the strategies mentioned in this chapter, highlighting the emphasized elements that may help increase students' fluency development.

Language Experience Approach, Modified with Digital Photography and/or Bilingual Text

The language experience approach (LEA) has been documented as an instructional strategy as early as 1908 but was brought to mainstream education during the whole language movement of the 1960s (Davidson, 1999). Generally speaking, the LEA emphasizes children's own produc-

TABLE 8.1. Recommended Strategies for Developing Fluency in ELLs

	Strategy				
	LEA, modified	Repeated reading	Reading while listening	Cross-age reading	Independent reading
Culturally responsive teaching	x	x (depending on the text being used)	x (depending on the text being used)	x (depending on the text being used)	
Word recognition	x	x	x	x	x
Prosody/expression	x	x	x	x	
Oral-language proficiency in English	x	x	x	x	
Oral-language proficiency in home language	x (dual-language texts)	x	x	x	x
Vocabulary and concept knowledge base development in English	x	x	x		x
Vocabulary and concept knowledge base development in home language	x (dual-language texts)				x (if chosen text is written in the home language)

tion of language, based in personal experiences, to help create a natural bridge between oral and written language (Stahl & Miller, 1989), and it was traditionally used to support reading development, although it has much value supporting all of the language arts. The LEA, along with its various modifications, can be used to support oral-language as well as written-language development (see also Chapter 6, this volume). It is one of our recommended strategies because the LEA has the potential to validate the child's home language and culture while at the same time supporting elements (e.g., word recognition and prosody) that characterize a fluent reader.

The LEA is a shared experience between adult and child in which an activity is designed and implemented, resulting in the creation of an LEA text. This text can then be used to help a learner to clarify the functions of reading. For example, it can be used to demonstrate the relationship between spoken and written words, to present phonemic combinations that are specific to the English language (e.g., *-tion*, *-ought*, *-ight*), to develop recognition of words in print that already exist in the child's expressive oral language, to refine the child's conceptual knowledge base, and to model and practice what a fluent reader sounds like. The LEA activity can be as simple as having a shared storybook reading experience and creating a child-dictated text from this event, or it can be increasingly complex. The activity can also incorporate digital photography and use readily available and widely supported software such as Microsoft PowerPoint or KidPix to record and present the written text (Labbo, Eakle, & Montero, 2002). Digital or film photography can also be used to enhance the shared literacy experience; for example, some preservice and inservice teachers we know of successfully fused photography and literacy, inspired by Ewald's work in *American Alphabets* (2005) and *The Best Part of Me* (2002). Some of these teachers and teacher candidates took photographs in their students' community to create bilingual alphabet books, whereas others used photography to spark students' creative free-verse poetry about their best body parts; some students wrote about their eyes, hair, and teeth. A larger scaled project was conducted in the Syracuse City School District, engaging students in equally meaningful ways (Meighan & Mahan, 2006).

Another exemplary project using a modified LEA is the dual-language book project, which was pioneered at Thornwood Public School in Toronto, Canada. Students who attend Thornwood School speak more than 40 different home languages, with no one language dominating (Cummins et al., 2005). (The dual-language books that were created at Thornwood Public School can be viewed at the website *thornwood. peelschools.org/Dual/about.htm.*) In order to take advantage of students' home cultural and linguistic knowledge and to engage the students academically, teachers at the school created dual-language "identity texts" with the goal of creating opportunities for students to make positive statements about themselves. These dual-language identity texts could be written, spoken, visual, musical, dramatic, or any multimodal combination. To create these texts, students were encouraged to choose their own topics and write their first drafts in whichever language they chose; normally, texts were written in the child's most dominant language. Then the texts were translated to either English or the child's home language (depending on the language of first draft) by a teacher, class member, or community member from the same language background whose English language abilities were more fluent. Dual-language books have the potential to validate each student's home culture and language; to offer students an opportunity to communicate their thoughts and feelings in two languages; to create learning opportunities rooted in a child's interests, experiences, and knowledge; and to offer the students opportunities to see the connections between oral language and printed text in both the home language and English. These texts also offer instructional opportunities for fluent reading in two languages. For example, the student-generated texts can be used during guided reading, shared reading, and read-alouds; as readers' theatre scripts; for partner reading; and as independent reading—all strategies that help students become fluent readers.

Repeated Readings

Repeatedly reading texts is probably the best known and most commonly implemented method for developing fluency (Kuhn & Stahl, 2003). The basic process involves rereading a short passage (anywhere from 50 to 200 words) several times (generally three to five repetitions). This allows learners to develop comfort with the selection and develop their automaticity with the words they are repeatedly encountering, a process that helps turn these words into sight words (Ehri, 1995). Additionally, their increased word recognition has been shown to transfer to previously unread texts (Dowhower, 1989). In other words, if students learn the word *forgive* as part of their repeated-readings passage, they are likely to recognize *forgive* when they read it a different text. We feel that a myriad of repeated-readings strategies can be employed with ELLs but suggest that a special emphasis on phonology, vocabulary development, and oral-language proficiency be implemented along with this procedure in order to prevent the process from becoming one of rote memorization with little or no corresponding comprehension. We also have one caveat regarding the material you select for these strategies. We would typically recommend that you use challenging texts for such approaches; the reason is that struggling readers' comprehension skills are often stronger than their word-recognition skills (Kuhn & Schwanenflugel, 2006). As a result, it is likely that they will be able to understand such texts once they have identified the words that compose it. This is not necessarily the case when ELLs are reading English texts, as both vocabulary and word identification may be a challenge for them. As such, we suggest that you take language knowledge, as well as word recognition, into account when selecting appropriate texts for these students. Although we feel many repeated readings of texts would be effective for ELLs, we present two strategies, reading while listening and cross-age reading, that we feel will be of particular value for your students.

Reading-While-Listening

Carol Chomsky (1976, 1978) designed the reading-while-listening approach for third graders who were skilled at decoding but who were having trouble developing their automaticity and prosody. As a result, the learners were reading 1 to 2 years below grade level. In order to assist these students with the transition to fluent reading, Chomsky felt it was necessary that they have greater access to connected text. Because it was difficult to carve out consistent opportunities for the teacher to work with these students, either independently or in a small group, Chomsky felt that it might be beneficial to provide the learners with a model of a skilled reader narrating a range of texts. In order to do so, she recorded two dozen books that were considered challenging for the students (the material she selected ranged in reading level from second to fifth grade). The students were expected to listen repeatedly to the recordings while reading along with the text until they were able to read the material fluently on their own. Because the students had extensive opportunities to read along with a fluent model, their own fluency improved, and they became more engaged readers as a result. In order to implement this procedure in your own classroom, you need to ensure that your students have access to recordings of a number of books at a reasonable challenge level. Because your learners are working on developing their fluency and not just their oral language, it is critical that the tapes are accompanied by the texts themselves. In order to gain maximum benefit for your ELLs, you should gear these texts to concepts you have covered in your classroom. What may be of particular value to these learners is the fact that this approach provides repeated access to oral language while simultaneously exposing learners to written text. Further, given the range of complex picture books that are now available in content areas (e.g., weather) and the use of illustrations in many textbooks, you may be able to provide your students with visual aids as well. And, of course, given the advances in technology, creating a digital version that can be used on an MP3 player may also increase the likelihood that your students will be willing to listen and read along!

Cross-Age Reading

In their work with older struggling readers (fourth grade and beyond), Linda Labbo and Bill Teale (1990) noticed that these students often expressed a reluctance to read books that were at their instructional reading level because such texts were usually written for much younger learners (first and second graders in many cases). However, the authors felt that these students could clearly benefit from reading such texts and that they would likely benefit from reading them repeatedly. They developed cross-age reading as a means of encouraging learners to read books at their instructional level by providing them with a reason to do so: reading the books aloud to the audience for whom the texts were intended. In order to determine the effectiveness of the approach, several fifth graders were invited to participate in a project that involved reading a particular storybook for a kindergartner. The authors explained to the older readers that they would have to practice reading their stories in such a way that the younger students would enjoy listening. In other words, their rendering would need to be fluent; they would need to read the text smoothly, with few hesitations or miscues, and in an expressive manner. The students took on the challenge and found that they were up to the task, improving their own reading in the process. As was the case for the struggling readers in this study, many ELLs could benefit from developing their word recognition in texts that are written for much younger students. Additionally, these students could also benefit from developing the English vocabulary for the concepts presented in these books. We feel this approach has the potential to be particularly effective for ELLs.

Independent Reading

The Report of the National Reading Panel (NICHD, 2000) did not find any appreciable benefits of classroom-based independent reading programs (e.g., sustained silent reading, Drop Everything and Read). However, this does not mean that independent reading should not be encouraged in the classroom, and, certainly, independent reading should be encouraged in home and community contexts to help readers find a love for reading and learning through printed texts (Anderson et al., 1988). Further, Krashen (2003) noted that free voluntary reading, regardless of genre, is a powerful tool for improving reading comprehension, vocabulary, grammar, and writing among second-language learners. He further argued that free voluntary reading may help with the transition from proficiency in interpersonal communicative abilities to proficiency in academic language abilities; the school achievement of ELLS depends on their being proficient in the language of classroom instruction and textbooks (Wilkinson & Silliman, 2008). Depending on the child's proficiency in his or her home language, independent reading may be encouraged in the home language, as well as in English. Unfortunately, students who do not have a high comfort level with texts (i.e., ELLs and struggling readers) tend to spend independent reading time avoiding reading as much as possible (e.g., flipping through books, going to the bathroom, etc.). We suggest that, rather than eliminate independent reading in its entirety, you expand your options regarding what qualifies as "independent reading." By including reading-while-listening, partner reading, repeated readings, and whisper reading as options, you can help to increase your students' engagement with text and provide a level of accountability as well.

CONCLUSION

We can't stress enough how important fluency is to learners' access to literacy-rich opportunities. Vocabulary development and conceptual sophistication are both achieved through extensive reading (Stanovich, 2000). If students do not read fluently, then they are unlikely to spend significant amounts of time reading; those students who read fluently, on the other hand, are likely to read and thus to reap the benefits of reading as a result. As educators, we are responsible for finding ways to motivate all students in the classroom to read independently, regardless of the text's perceived social value (e.g., comic strips, romance novels, certain magazines). We are also responsible for finding approaches that provide all students, but particularly those learning English, with access to texts that develop their fluency. We believe the approaches presented in this chapter can help to begin this process. We also feel that the questions we posed help advance the dialogue that needs to occur for educators to understand what makes for effective fluency instruction with ELLs.

REFERENCES

Anderson, R. C., Wilson, P. T., & Fielding, L. G. (1988). Growth in reading and how children spend their time outside of school. *Reading Research Quarterly, 23*, 285–303.

August, D., Carlo, M., Dressler, M., & Snow, C. E. (2005). The critical role of vocabulary development for English language learners. *Learning Disabilities Research and Practice, 20*(1), 50–57.

August, D., & Shanahan, T. (2006). *Executive summary: Developing literacy in second-language learners: Report of the National Literacy Panel on Literacy-Minority Children and Youth*. Mahwah, NJ: Erlbaum.

Baron, D., Schwanenflugel, P., & Collins-Block, C. (2007, May). *Promising practices in early literacy*. Paper presented at the International Reading Association Preconference Institute, Toronto, Ontario, Canada.

Baumann, J. F., Edwards, E. C., Font, G., Tershinksi, C. A., Kame'enui, E. J., & Olejnik, S. (2002). Teaching morphemic and contextual analysis to fifth-grade students. *Reading Research Quarterly, 37*(2), 150–176.

Bear, D. R., Invernizzi, M., Templeton, S., & Johnston, F. (2008). *Words their way: Word study for phonics, vocabulary, and spelling instruction* (4th ed.). Upper Saddle River, NJ: Prentice Hall.

Beck, I. L., McKeown, M. G., & Kucan, L. (2002). *Bringing words to life: Robust vocabulary instruction*. New York: Guilford Press.

Biemiller, A., & Slonim, N. (2001). Estimating root word vocabulary growth in normative and advantaged populations: Evidence for a common sequence of vocabulary acquisition. *Journal of Educational Psychology, 93*(3), 498–520.

Carlo, M., August, D., McLaughlin, B., Snow, C., Dressler, C., Lippman, D., et al. (2004). Closing the gap: Addressing the vocabulary needs of English language learners in bilingual and mainstream classrooms. *Reading Research Quarterly, 39*, 188–215.

Carr, P. R. (1995). Employment equity for racial minorities in the teaching profession. *Multicultural Education Journal, 13*(1), 28–42.

Cazden, C. (2001). *Classroom discourse: The language of teaching and learning* (2nd ed.). Portsmouth, NH: Heinemann.

Chall, J. (1996). *Stages of reading development* (2nd ed.). Fort Worth, TX: Harcourt-Brace.

Chomsky, C. (1976). After decoding: What? *Language Arts, 53*, 288–296.

Chomsky, C. (1978). When you still can't read in third grade? After decoding, what? In S. J. Samuels (Ed.), *What research has to say about reading instruction* (pp. 13–30). Newark, DE: International Reading Association.

Cummins, J. (1994). The acquisition of English as a second language. In K. Spangenberg-Urbschat & R. Pritchard (Eds.), *Kids come in all languages: Reading instruction for ESL students* (pp. 36–62). Clevedon, UK: Multilingual Matters.

Cummins, J., Bismilla, V., Chow, P., Cohen, S., Giampapa, F., Leoni, L., et al. (2005). Affirming identity in multilingual classrooms. *Educational Leadership. 63*(1), 38–43.

Darling-Hammond, L., Chung, R., & Frelow, F. (2002). Variation in teacher preparation: How well do different pathways prepare teachers to teach? *Journal of Teacher Education, 53*, 286–302.

Davidson, J. L. (1999). The history of language experience: A U.S. perspective. In O. G. Nelson & W. M. Linek (Eds.), *Practical classroom applications of language experience: Looking back, looking forward* (pp. 25–36). Needham Heights, MA: Allyn & Bacon.

Dowhower, S. L. (1989). Repeated reading: Theory into practice. *Reading Teacher, 42*, 502–507.

Ehri, L. C. (1995). Phases of development in learning to read words by sight. *Journal of Research in Reading, 18*, 116–125.

Ewald, W. (2005). *American alphabets.* Zurich, Switzerland: Scalo.

Ewald, W., & Tingley, M. (2002). *The best part of me: Children talk about their bodies in pictures.* New York: Little, Brown and Company for Young Readers.

Freeman, R. (1996). Dual-language planning at Oyster bilingual school: "It's much more than language." *TESOL Quarterly, 30*(3), 557–582.

Garton, A., & Pratt, C. (1989). *Learning to be literate: The development of spoken and written language.* Oxford, UK: Blackwell.

Gay, G. (2000). *Culturally responsive teaching: Theory, research, and practice.* New York: Teachers College Press.

Karabenick, S. A., & Noda, P. A. C. (2004). Professional development implications of teachers' beliefs and attitudes toward English language learners. *Bilingual Research Journal, 28*(1), 55–75.

Kindler, A. L. (2002). *Survey of the states' limited English proficient students and available educational programs and services: 2000–2001 summary report.* Washington, DC: National Clearinghouse for English Language Acquisition and Language Instruction Educational Programs.

Krashen, S. (1989). *Language acquisition and language education.* Englewood Cliffs, NJ: Prentice Hall.

Krashen, S. (2003). *Explorations in language acquisition and use: The Taipei lectures.* Portsmouth, NH: Heinemann.

Kuhn, M. R., & Schwanenflugel, P. J. (2006). All oral reading practice is not equal (or how can I integrate fluency instruction into my classrooms?). *Literacy Teaching and Learning, 11*, 1–20.

Kuhn, M. R., Schwanenflugel, P. J., Morris, R. D., Morrow, L. M., Woo, D. G., Meisinger, E. B., et al. (2006). Teaching children to become fluent and automatic readers. *Journal of Literacy Research, 38*(4), 357–387.

Kuhn, M. R., & Stahl, S. A. (2003). Fluency: A review of developmental and remedial practices. *Journal of Educational Psychology, 95*(1), 3–21.

Labbo, L., & Teale, W. H. (1990). Cross-age reading: A strategy for helping poor readers. *Reading Teacher, 43*, 363–369.

Labbo, L. D., Eakle, A. J., & Montero, M. K. (2002). *Digital language experience approach: Using digital photographs and software as a language experience approach innovation* [Electronic version]. Retrieved December 7, 2008, from *http://www.readingonline.org/electronic/elec_index.asp?HREF=labbo2/index.html.*

Lesaux, N., & Geva, E. (2006). Synthesis: Development of literacy in language-minority students. In D. August & T. Shanahan (Eds.), *Developing literacy in second-language learners: Report of the National Literacy Panel on Language-Minority Children and Youth* (pp. 53–74). Mahwah, NJ: Erlbaum.

Meighan, J., & Mahan, S. (2006). *Literacy through photography: The Partnership for a Better Education between the Syracuse City School District (SCSD) and Syracuse University Visual Arts Infusion.* Retrieved June 5, 2007, from *http://partnership.syr.edu/Partnership/display.cfm?content_ID=%23%281%23%2B%0A.*

Morse, A. (2005). *A look at immigrant youth: Prospects and promising practices.* Washington, DC: National Conference of State Legislatures Children's Policy Initiative.

Mostow, J., & Beck, J. (2005, June). *Micro-analysis of fluency gains in a reading tutor that listens.* Paper presented at the Society for the Scientific Study of Reading, Toronto, Ontario, Canada.

Nagy, W. E. (1988). *Teaching vocabulary to improve reading comprehension.* Urbana, IL: National Council of Teachers of English/International Reading Association.

Nagy, W. E., & Scott, J. (2000). Vocabulary processes. In M. L. Kamil, P. Mosenthal, P. D. Pearson, & R. Barr (Eds.), *Handbook of reading research* (Vol. 3, pp. 187–219). Mahwah, NJ: Erlbaum.

National Center for Education Statistics. (2005). *The nation's report card: Reading 2005.* Washington, DC: U.S. Department of Education.

National Education Association. (2003). *Status of the American public school teacher 2000–2001.* Retrieved December 2, 2004, from http://www.nea.org/edstats/images/status.pdf.

National Institute of Child Health and Human Development. (2000). *Report of the National Reading Panel. Teaching children to read: An evidence-based assessment of the scientific research literature on reading and its implications for reading instruction* (No. 00-4769). Washington, DC: U.S. Government Printing Office.

Ramírez, D. J., Yuen, S. D., & Ramey, D. R. (1991). *Executive summary of the final report: Longitudinal study of structured English immersion strategy, early-exit, and late-exit transitional bilingual education programs for language minority children.* Retrieved December 7, 2008, from http://www.nabe.org/documents/research/Ramirez.pdf.

Samuels, J. (2006). Reading fluency: Its past, present, and future. In T. Rasinski, C. Balachowicz, & K. Lems (Eds.), *Fluency instruction: Research-based best practices* (pp. 7–20). New York: Guilford Press.

Shanahan, T. (2005, May). *Improving instruction for young children: Making sense of the National Literacy Panel.* Paper presented at the International Reading Association Preconference Institute, San Antonio, TX.

Snow, C. E., Burns, M. S., & Griffin, P. (Eds.). (1998). *Preventing reading difficulties in young children.* Washington, DC: National Academy Press.

Stahl, S. A. (1999). *Vocabulary development.* Cambridge, MA: Brookline Books.

Stahl, S. A., & Heubach, K. (2005). Fluency-oriented reading instruction. *Journal of Literacy Research, 37,* 25–60.

Stahl, S. A., & Miller, P. A. (1989). Whole language and language experience approaches for beginning reading: A quantitative research synthesis. *Review of Educational Research, 59*(1), 87–116.

Stanovich, K. E. (1986). Matthew effects in reading: Some consequences of individual differences in the acquisition of literacy. *Reading Research Quarterly, 21,* 360–407.

Stanovich, K. E. (2000). *Progress in understanding reading: Scientific foundations and new frontiers.* New York: Guilford Press.

Statistics Canada. (2003). *Canada's ethnocultural portrait: The changing mosaic.* Ottawa, Ontario: Minister of Industry.

U.S. Census Bureau. (2004). *The foreign-born population in the United States: 2003.* Retrieved December 7, 2008, from http://www.census.gov/prod/2004pubs/p20-551.pdf.

Valdés, G., Bunch, G., Snow, C., Carol, L., & Matos, L. (2005). Enhancing the development of students' language(s). In L. Darling-Hammond & J. Bransford (Eds.), *Preparing teachers for a changing world* (pp. 126–168). San Francisco: Jossey-Bass.

Wilkinson, L. C., & Silliman, E. R. (2008). Academic language proficiency and literacy instruction in urban settings. In L. C. Wilkinson, L. M. Morrow, & V. Chou (Eds.), *Improving literacy achievement in urban schools: Critical elements in teacher preparation* (pp. 121–142). Mahwah, NJ: International Reading Association.

CHAPTER 9

The Case of Ying

The Members of a Teacher Study Group Learn about Fostering the Reading Comprehension of English Learners

CYNTHIA BROCK
SUZETTE YOUNGS
ELENI OIKONOMIDOY
DIANE LAPP

SETTING THE CONTEXT: SUSAN, ELENA, AND SANDY EXPLORE WAYS TO IMPROVE LITERACY INSTRUCTION

Susan, Elena, and Sandy are three fifth-grade teachers who teach in White Pine School District (pseudonym). White Pine School District is situated in White Pine, a moderate-sized community in the west. Susan and Sandy are white monolingual English-speaking women. They were born and raised in White Pine and have taught only in the White Pine School District. Elena has been a teacher in White Pine School District for 10 years. She was born in Greece, and Greek is her first language; she speaks and writes fluently in both Greek and English.

In the past, most of the children in White Pine School District (i.e., almost 90%) were white and monolingual. Increasingly, over the past decade, the numbers of children who speak a language other than English as their first language (hereafter referred to as English language learners, ELLs) have risen dramatically. For example, 70–80% of the children in some schools in White Pine School District are ELLs. Additionally, many of the rest of the schools in the district are serving large and growing numbers of ELLs. There are no bilingual education programs in White Pine School District. The district does provide some English as a second language (ESL) support, but it is limited. Approximately 40% of the children at Evergreen Elementary (pseudonym), where Susan, Sandy, and Elena teach, are ELLs. The teachers, like many teachers throughout the United States, find that over the past few years they are teaching increasing numbers of ELLs (Gándara, 2007; Morse, 2005; National Center for Educational Statistics, 2003).

Given the limited district support available for their ELLs, the trio decided to create its own study group to learn to more effectively foster the literacy development of their ELLs. They decided to take turns having Thursday evening dinner meetings at one another's homes.

INITIAL THURSDAY COLLABORATIVE STUDY MEETINGS: FOCUSING ON YING'S LITERACY LEARNING

During their first study group conversation, these teachers decided that they wanted to employ a two-pronged approach to improve their instruction for ELLs. Their first goal was to collaboratively study the effectiveness of their instructional practices for their ELLs. Realizing that they could not focus on all of the ELLs in their respective classrooms, they decided to select one or two representative students as their focus. They also decided that Sandy would focus on her classroom during their first meeting. She told her colleagues that she wanted to select an ELL named Ying in her classroom. Ying was a Hmong[1] child who had been in the United States for almost 2 years. Sandy explained that Ying could read aloud the English words in many texts, but, when asked about his reading, he often had no idea what he had read. Additionally, Sandy said that Ying never voluntarily spoke in class. She wanted to try to determine how to work with Ying to improve his English reading comprehension. Because Ying's strengths and needs were similar to those of many ELLs in all three teachers' classrooms, the team agreed that they would begin their work focusing on ways to foster Ying's English comprehension.

---

[1]Like many Hmong who have come to the United States over the past decades, Ying and his family were originally from Laos. Many Hmong families left Laos after the Vietnam War to avoid mistreatment by the communist Lao government. Also, like many other Hmong families, Ying and his family lived in Thai refugee camps for many, many years before coming to the United States.

Second, they decided to read and discuss professional literature on effective instructional practices for ELLs. In particular, their professional reading included literature on facilitating the English comprehension of ELLs, second-language acquisition, and the impact of sociocultural factors on second-language learning. They decided to use their reading and discussions about their classroom practices to design and implement new instructional practices in their classrooms. In short, they would draw on professional literature as one means to evaluate how they taught literacy in general and comprehension in particular.[2]

The teachers met once a week on Thursday evenings. During the first meeting they created a reading list and a reading plan and began reading according to their established deadlines. (Appendix 9.1 contains their reading list.) Each week, one teacher was to bring a videotaped lesson segment of a portion of a literacy lesson from her classroom. Thus each teacher shared a video segment from her teaching approximately once every 3 weeks. (Note that the teachers kept their plans open enough to focus on the same lesson segment for several weeks if it made sense to do so.)

After watching the video clip, the teachers critiqued the video segment, drawing on their own backgrounds and experiences, as well as related professional readings. During one of the first weeks, Sandy brought a video clip of a lesson segment that occurred as she, Ying, and her class read and discussed the book *Maniac Magee* (Spinelli, 1990). *Maniac Magee* (which is part fantasy and part realistic fiction) is about a little white boy (nicknamed Maniac) who lost his parents at the age of 4, moved in with his feuding aunt and uncle, and then ran away from their home at the age of 12 to a town called Two Mills, Pennsylvania—a town that was half black and half white. The first family Maniac encountered in the town—the Beales, an African American family—invited him to live with them when they found out that Maniac was homeless. Overall, in Two Mills, Pennsylvania, Maniac is exposed to issues of prejudice, racism, and homelessness. Sandy addressed the issues that Maniac encountered in the story with her students as the class read the text of *Maniac Magee* together. Sandy did want everyone in her class to read and discuss this engaging text, but not all of her children were reading at the fifth-grade level. Consequently, during reading time, she had all of her students sit in a semicircle around her with a copy of the text. She read much of the text aloud to the students as they followed along in their own texts.

---

[2]Note that these teachers had engaged in professional reading circles prior to the formation of this particular study group. So, some of the readings we mention in this chapter occurred prior to the formation of this particular study group, which was designed specifically to explore issues pertaining to English learners and comprehension.

She also chose various students to take turns reading small excerpts of text aloud in a round-robin fashion. This would, she believed, allow all children to hear and discuss the story even if all of them couldn't read the story on their own.[3]

The following excerpt, which Sandy shared with her colleagues, is taken from the final 6-minute portion of a whole-group lesson, when Sandy's class was in the process of constructing two charts together. On one chart the students identified the *conflicts* that had occurred in the story to that point, and on the other chart they identified different *contrasts* in the story.[4] Sandy led the discussion and wrote the children's suggestions on the charts during the discussion. The students had just mentioned that the author contrasted *black* and *white*. Sandy wrote "black versus white" on the chart, and the discussion proceeded as follows:

SANDY: I don't know why I put *versus*. I guess because one opposes the other or one is on the opposite end of the other. What else did we see contrasted in the story? What was he [Maniac] without for so long?

SALLY: House.

BILL: *(laughing)* Chicken pox.

Bill's comment had nothing to do with the ongoing conversation and was largely ignored by everyone, including the teacher. The teacher followed up on Sally's comment.

SANDY: *Homes versus*—what's the opposite of having a home?

UNISON RESPONSE: Homeless, *homelessness*.

DAN: He was without parents for a while.

SANDY: OK.

---

[3] Although Sandy was not aware of the many instructional problems with round-robin reading, her two fellow study group members were. Throughout their discussions together, Elena and Susan taught Sandy about the many drawbacks of round-robin reading. See Worthy, Broaddus, and Ivy (2001) for a complete discussion of round-robin reading as a poor instructional practice.

[4] During typical whole-group lessons, all 22 of Sandy's students sat in a semicircle around her. Each child had a copy of *Maniac Magee*. Sandy took many turns modeling fluent reading as she read portions of the text aloud and discussed those portions of the text with her students. She also chose different children to take turns reading one or two paragraphs of text at a time. After each student read a portion of the text, the whole class stopped to discuss what had just been read.

SALLY: Still, I mean they're [referring to the Beale family] still not his real parents but ...

DAN: But they're [i.e., Mr. and Mrs. Beale] like parents.

SANDY: So we could have *parents*.

CHRIS: Legal, not legal, but guardians.

SANDY: *And none*. What are some of the other contrasts that you saw in the story? Let's start bringing some of these out. This story is a combination of two types of genres. (modified from Raphael, Brock, & Wallace, 1997, pp. 196, 201)

After watching the brief 6-minute lesson segment with her colleagues, Susan asked if they could watch the segment again to see what else they might discern from rewatching it. So the triad watched the segment again and took notes about what they noticed as they watched it. The following discussion ensued between Sandy, Susan, and Elena:

ELENA: Did you notice that three Anglo children[5] in your class [i.e., Sally, Dan, and Chris] and you, Sandy, did all of the speaking during the filmed segment?

SANDY: Hmmm ... actually, I didn't notice that until you mentioned it, Elena. As I think about it, however, I think that may be a common occurrence in my classroom. I'll have to watch for that more as I teach. Clearly, if only a few of the white children are talking, I'm not providing a space for everyone's voice to be heard. I have African American children, Latino children, and Asian American children in my classroom in addition to Anglo-American children. All of the children need to have opportunities to share their thoughts and ideas.

SUSAN: You know, another thing that I noticed was that when you asked questions, Sandy, you seemed to ask questions to the student audience in general rather than addressing your questions to any particular child; thus the conversational floor was seemingly open to anyone who might like to respond. Additionally, no one raised his or her hand to be called on by you; instead, Sally, Dan, and Chris took turns making and building on one another's comments. And, frankly, their comments revealed a quite sophisticated understanding

---

[5]The racial makeup of Sandy's class was as follows: 50% white, 25% black, 25% Latino and Asian American.

of the story. They knew, for example, the difference between legal guardians and guardians—like the Beales, who were just informally looking after Maniac.

ELENA: Yes, I agree that the comments made by the three children revealed a sophisticated understanding of the story. I'd like to return to your comment about turn taking, Susan. While I think that it is important to acknowledge the benefits of allowing children the opportunity to decide whether or not they want to speak, I have to tell you that as an immigrant and English learner, myself, there are plenty of times I'd never enter a conversation in English unless someone made it a point to invite me into a conversation—maybe by asking my opinion or posing a question of some sort to me. It can be very intimidating to learn a new language and a different culture, and sometimes a gentle nudge to join the conversation is all an English learner needs.

SANDY: You know, Elena, your comments remind me of one of the readings we did for this week. Li [2004] pointed out that teachers must be aware of the fact that students from different cultures can be socialized to "do school" in very different ways. For example, the "norm" for doing school in Thailand, where Ying attended school, may have been to sit quietly in rows, do your work, and only speak when spoken to. If that happened to be the case for Ying, he would likely never speak in class unless I invited him to do so. Come to think of it, I don't recall Ying ever voluntarily speaking in class. I'll have to pay closer attention to this and make sure to gently invite him into the class conversation from time to time.

SUSAN: You know, ladies, it strikes me that we have no way of assessing Ying's comprehension of that part of the reading lesson since he didn't talk at all during that segment of the lesson. Sandy, do you have any writing or work samples at all that we can look at to try to get a sense of Ying's comprehension?

SANDY: Good question, Susan. Actually, no, I don't. In general, we're mostly reading aloud and discussing this particular book. While I do have the children write in their journals sometimes, I mostly rely on discussion to get a sense of the children's evolving understandings of the story. Clearly, with over 20 children in the class, it is hard to get a handle on what each child understands on an ongoing basis. Also, based on the video segment we just watched, it is also becoming clear to me that a lot of the children in class aren't even talking. Consequently, I really don't have a handle on how most of the children in the class are interpreting the story when I don't have any data (in the form of discussion comments or written work) to draw on.[6]

ELENA: Sandy, I really agree with you that it would be important to try to figure out additional ways to get a sense of how each child is understanding the story. It does strike me that it would be especially helpful to try get a handle on Ying's understanding of the story, in particular, since he is one of our focus students for this project.

SANDY: Well, one thing I might try in order to assess Ying's comprehension is to ask him to rewatch this segment of the lesson to see what he understands from the lesson. I could give him the opportunity to speak in Hmong or English and then have another, more fluent Hmong student in my class, named Dong, translate, if necessary.

ELENA: I think that is a great idea!

SUSAN: Me, too! Let's focus on Ying again next week when we meet. Also, let's continue with our readings pertaining to comprehension and English learners.

SANDY MEETS WITH YING AND DONG AT SCHOOL

Early the next week at school, Sandy enlisted the help of Dong. Ying, Dong, and Sandy sat down during lunch to watch and discuss the 6-minute videotape of the literacy lesson that Sandy had taken to her teacher study group. Sandy decided that she would videotape their conversation so that she could show the videotaped conversation to her colleagues at their next Thursday evening meeting. As a brief recap, Sandy had begun the lesson in question with an introduction to the words *contrast* and *conflict*. Further, the class had discussed contrasts and conflicts in this final portion of the lesson as they constructed large contrast-and-conflict charts together. They had already identified and discussed the contrast between Maniac's inside name

---

[6]Although Sandy initially spent quite a bit of time engaging in whole-group reading instruction, which included round-robin reading and oral discussion, across time she came to learn that this was not effective literacy instruction for her students in general and her ELLs in particular. Susan and Elena taught Sandy to provide meaningful daily reading instruction to small groups of children who were grouped according to their appropriate instructional reading levels.

at the Beales' house (Jeffrey) and his outside name in the community (Maniac), and they had identified and discussed contrasts between black and white.

During the lunchtime meeting, when Ying, Dong, and Sandy met to watch the 6-minute video clip of the lesson, Sandy told Ying that as they watched the lesson segment together Ying could stop the tape any time he'd like to make comments and ask questions. Ying stopped the videotape of the lesson slightly *before* the conversational segment described earlier in this chapter and *after* the class had already generated the name and color contrasts Sandy had listed on the chart. Ying asked, "What are they say?" Sandy responded that she was not sure what he was referring to and asked if he would like her to rewind the tape so that she could try to discern what he was asking. They rewound the tape to Sandy's original words during the lesson, "Are there any other contrasts that we've run across?" Then the following discussion ensued between Ying, Dong, and Sandy:

SANDY: Oh, contrasts? (*to Ying*) Do you know what contrasts are?

DONG: Contractions or contrasts?

SANDY: (*carefully enunciating*) Contrast. (*looking at Ying*) Do you, do you know what a contrast is?

YING: (*Speaks in Hmong to Dong.*)

DONG: He said, he said, like a race or something?

SANDY: (*confused*) Like a race?

DONG: Yeah.

SANDY: You mean like trying to run fast or something? Oh, oh, oh, *contests*!

YING: Yeah. (*begins talking in Hmong to Dong.*)

DONG: Not contests, contrasts.

SANDY: (*to Ying*) You thought she said contests?

YING: Yeah.

SANDY: Oh, OK. (*modified from Raphael et al., 1997, pp. 196, 201*)

Ying then asked if a *contrast* is something you "sign your name to." Sandy said that she suspected he was referring to a *contract*. They talked about the definition of *contract*, and Sandy mentioned that the word *contract* is different from *contrast*. Then they discussed the definition of the word *contrast* and talked about how Sandy used the word in class.

FOLLOWING THURSDAY EVENING MEETING BETWEEN SANDY, SUSAN, AND ELENA

That Thursday, Sandy took the videotape of the conversation between Sandy, Ying, and Dong to her meeting. After the trio watched the videotaped conversation between Sandy, Ying, and Dong, the following discussion ensued:

SUSAN: Wow, I'm so glad that you followed up by talking with Ying and Dong, Sandy. That was so informative!

SANDY: No kidding. Before that conversation with Ying and Dong, I had absolutely no idea how confused Ying was about central ideas we were discussing in the lesson that day. For example, in our class discussion of the story, we were talking about conflicts and contrasts—for example, black–white, having a home–homelessness, parents–guardians–legal guardians, and so forth). Clearly, Ying had no understanding of the central concept, *contrast*. In fact, he thought that we were talking about *contests* (as in races) or possibly *contracts* (as in legal documents).

SUSAN: Yes, I, too, am so glad that you got that additional information, Sandy. It raises two sets of issues that would be helpful for me to explore relative to working with the English learners in my classroom. First, I'd like to examine research-related considerations I should take into account as I design literacy lessons to foster the comprehension of my English learners. Second, I want to explore how I can design my literacy lessons more effectively so that my English learners comprehend the concepts and ideas I want to teach them. And, I think I need to build into my lesson design ways to gauge my English learners' confusions on an ongoing basis during every lesson.

ELENA: Yes, I'm interested in sorting out both of these issues, too. I think that some of the readings we have been doing can be helpful in this regard. For example, regarding the first issue you raise, Susan, as the study we read by Avalos [2003] suggests, fostering English learners' comprehension is a complex undertaking. We, as teachers, have to pay attention to text-based features (such as vocabulary and syntax) and reader-based features (such as students' backgrounds and their cultural knowledge) when we are designing literacy lessons for our students.

SANDY: So, applying these ideas to the case of Ying, it would be important for me to not just assume that Ying knows what the words *conflict* and *contrast* mean. Rather, I should design my lessons to explicitly teach the central vocabulary words in my lessons. This should be helpful to all students, and especially the English learners. As we learned from reading the text *Robust Vocabulary Instruction: Bringing Words to Life* [Beck, McKeown, & Kucan, 2002], students may or may not have conceptually deep understandings of vocabulary words. Explicit instruction over key vocabulary, then, is crucial to help all students, including English learners, to develop deeper levels of understanding of these key words.

SUSAN: Yes, and we know that quality vocabulary instruction impacts children's comprehension. Recall that Carlo and her colleagues [2004] explored relationships between improvement in vocabulary and improvement in reading comprehension. They found that improvement in vocabulary did, in fact, improve students' reading comprehension.

ELENA: I think that it is also important to point out that the nature and structure of a child's first language can also impact his or her ability to learn and comprehend in English. For example, Loizou and Stuart [2003] found that children whose first language was English and whose second language was Greek outperformed students whose first language was Greek and second language was English. While this initially struck me as strange, their explanation was that English-to-Greek students outperformed Greek-to-English students because Greek is more orthographically regular than English, and it is harder to move from a language that is more phonetically regular to one that is more complex orthographically than the other way around.

SANDY: While I will admit that I know little about languages other than English, I can see that the nature of the child's first language really matters. Realistically, I can't learn all of the languages my children speak, but I can start to learn a little bit about them to help me have a sense of how they are related to English and how I might use this information to design literacy lessons. For example, most speakers of Asian or African languages may have difficulty with *a* and *the* because most languages on those continents do not use articles. Also, sometimes sounds in one language may not exist in another language. It is important for us as teachers to know that when sound variations do not exist in a speaker's native language, it is very difficult for students to produce them in the early stages of acquiring English [Lapp, Flood, Brock, & Fisher, 2007; see also Chapter 5, this volume, for similar work by Bear and Smith].

SUSAN: I want to return to one of the central points you identified this evening as important to consider when working with English learners. You suggested that we need to structure lessons in ways to foster comprehension and, in the process, explore ways to constantly monitor our English learners' understandings during our lessons. I think that the work of Saunders and Goldenberg (1999) raises important points in this regard. They studied various aspects of using literature-based instruction with English learners. They found that the combined use of instructional conversations and literature logs improved the factual and interpretive story comprehension for all students in their study; however, the extent of the combined effects depended on the language proficiency of the English learners—that is, students in the early stages of learning English appeared to benefit more from the combined use of literature logs and instructional conversations than students at other levels of English proficiency. In short, I think that this work illustrates that our English learners need plenty of opportunities to write—such as in their literature logs—and engage in meaningful, scaffolded conversations—such as instructional conversations—during our lessons.

SANDY: Yes, I can see that just *talking about* definitions of words and central concepts in stories is especially problematic for English learners. They need to see words and ideas in print, they also need to see pictures and realia, and they need plenty of opportunities to write to express their evolving understandings of stories. You know, at this point, I'd appreciate drawing on the ideas we have been discussing to explore some specific lessons we might design to more effectively foster the comprehension of our English learners.

SUSAN: If you two wouldn't mind indulging me, I've been thinking about this over our last few meetings, as well as tonight. I'd like to share some thoughts with you.

ELENA: Of course! We're anxious to hear your ideas, Susan!

DESIGNING AN EFFECTIVE LESSON FOR ELLs: SUSAN'S IDEAS

I recently read a book by Fitzgerald and Graves (2004) that focused on providing quality literacy instruction for English learners. Fitzgerald and Graves (2004) emphasized the importance of providing prereading, during-reading, and after-reading instruction for English learners. So, in thinking about how I'd restructure a lesson for Ying and other English learners, I would set the lesson up based on their ideas. I think that Ying could really benefit from explicit instruction, in which he is taught key concepts in a small group prior to focusing on them in the larger group. In this way Ying would be taught the important background knowledge he needed to be able to participate in the whole group. This approach would serve at least two functions. First, covering them twice would deepen his understanding of ideas related to the text. Second, prior preparation on key whole-group lesson concepts would enable him to participate in the whole-group community and thus to become a contributing participant in the broader classroom community.

Prereading Instruction

Before the whole-class lesson, I would provide some scaffolded instruction in a small-group setting. During this small-group lesson, I would preteach the concept of *contrasts* and *conflicts*. To begin, I would help Ying and the other students in the group who need language support to understand the concept of *conflict*. If we are going to discuss this as a whole group and use this concept to engage with the *Maniac McGee* text, it will be important for Ying to fully understand the word in a variety of contexts. I would help Ying and the other children in his small group to create a web and place the word *conflict* in the center. I would have the students put words around the central word *conflict* that define, describe, or serve as examples of *conflict*. I could treat this web much like a pretest and see what understandings each student brought to the lesson. After I assessed each web, I would make some instructional decisions. It would then be necessary to describe *conflict* in our own local contexts and ask such questions as: Have you had any conflicts at home? Do you and any siblings argue? What about? How do you resolve these conflicts? Do you ever have conflicts at school? Why do you think these conflicts occur?

After we discussed answers to these questions, I would then ask each child to create an individual web in his or her *Maniac McGee personal journal*. In this journal, the students in this particular language support group would include key vocabulary terms with definitions, as well as pictures, to illustrate their understanding of the vocabulary and key concepts.

Once the small group seemed to have a good understanding of the term *conflict*, I would read aloud some or all of the chapter that we would be reading in the next day's whole-group lesson. In this manner, the students would be prepared and able to fully participate in the whole-group lesson rather than hearing and sorting out key concepts for the first time in the whole group. Students in this small group would read and discuss important conceptual ideas relative to the story in a safe environment, one in which they will feel comfortable asking for clarification on any aspect of the chapter. As we read, I would highlight and invite the small group to find places in the text that related to the word *conflict*. I would give each student a small pack of sticky notes and, as we read the chapter, have them place sticky notes on places they wanted to discuss or clarify ideas.

As the discussion continued, I would make sure that the members of the small group had an understanding of the book as a whole, and we would discuss any other concepts or vocabulary unfamiliar to them and have them record these words in their personal journals. As the discussion of the chapter came to a close, I would help this group prepare for the whole-class discussion that will take place the next day by giving them a sticky note of another color and having them mark places where they could potentially contribute to the whole class's understanding of *conflict*. Students in this small group would then mark two or three different places or passages in the text that they feel are good examples of *conflict*. I would even encourage them to share their personal examples of *conflict*; they could first practice with a partner and then share their ideas with the rest of the class, so that all class members could understand the concept at a deeper level.

Whole-Class Read-Aloud of *Maniac McGee* and Concept Lesson

The next day in the whole-class lesson, I would put the word *conflict* up on the white board and put it in the middle of a web. Then I would ask students to share ideas they had about *conflict*—what they know about it from their own personal and literary experiences. I would chart out answers and then read aloud the first few pages of the chapter and ask students to think about how Maniac deals with conflict in the text. Also, I would ask what *conflicts* the students notice in the story. In the previous day's lesson I would have helped Ying to prepare for this specific discussion, and so I would call on him first, as I would have prompted him to participate.

I would model to the whole class how to complete a T chart. On the left we will record the page number, and on the right we record our thoughts on *conflict*. (On another day we could look at the concept of *contrasts* and the impact this concept has in the story.) I would ask all students to place a sticky note on at least one part that highlights their interpretation of the term *conflict*. I would circulate around the room and check in with Ying, who already would have two or three examples, and encourage him to share his ideas with his partner and to look for additional ideas to share.

Then I would ask the students to partner read the rest of the chapter, looking for evidence to support their notions of *conflict* in the text. I would be careful to make sure that the dyads were constructed carefully according to reading ability. Students should place sticky notes in their books, as well as mark pages and interpretations in their personal journals, and then we would come back together as a whole group and discuss the concepts even further. After reuniting as a whole group, I would choose Ying to participate so he could share the sticky notes we prepared the previous day. Throughout this lesson on *conflict*, the students and I would include examples from the text, as well as from our personal and literary experiences.

After Whole-Group Reading Lesson

After the whole-group lesson concluded, I would meet with a series of small groups. First, I would meet with Ying's group and discuss the whole-group lesson that just took place to check for comprehension. I would ask what questions they may still have and what interpretations and connections they made to the chapter. I would then go to the next chapter to prepare Ying and his group for the next day's reading of *Maniac McGee*. Having read the chapter previously, I would have marked some places that might pose some problems for Ying and other English learners for preteaching. Additionally, I would leave the discussion open to allow Ying to share his own insights and to stop at any place in our small-group work where comprehension was lost. I would ask Ying to record key terms in his personal journal that he found confusing and use examples as well as pictures to help him come to a better understanding of the chapter and the book as a whole.

CONCLUDING COMMENTS: WHAT WE LEARNED ABOUT COMPREHENSION INSTRUCTION FROM YING, ONE ANOTHER, AND OUR PROFESSIONAL READING

As a result of the collaborative study-group conversations that involved analysis of instruction shared through videotaped clips of lessons conducted by us (i.e., Sandy, Susan, and Elena) and a discussion of the insights we were gaining from our professional readings, we conclude that our best comprehension instruction for all of our students occurs when:

1. We explicitly teach comprehension-related strategies by modeling, explaining, and thinking aloud about them before inviting our students to try them (Duffy, 2003).
2. We do not assume that our ELLs already understand key concepts

and/or vocabulary without double-checking to make sure that they actually understand them (Fitzgerald & Graves, 2004).
3. We provide explicit, meaningful instruction pertaining to key vocabulary and concepts that all students need to know to understand the stories we are reading by using pictures, diagrams, realia, actions, and so forth (Fitzgerald & Graves, 2002; McLaughlin & Allen, 2002).
4. We provide myriad daily opportunities for our students to talk with us (individually, in small groups, and in whole groups) and their peers and to write informally (usually in journals) about their evolving understandings in literacy (and content subjects) so we can get ongoing insights into our children's thinking and learning and base our instruction on our students' instructional needs (Collins Block & Pressley, 2002).
5. We provide daily, explicit, meaningful reading instruction in small reading groups that are composed of students grouped according to their appropriate reading instructional levels[7] (Lapp et al., 2007).
6. We make sure that our reading lessons are structured in terms of prereading activities, during-reading activities, and after-reading activities in order to provide appropriate scaffolding and support to our English learners (Fitzgerald & Graves, 2004).
7. We support our students in all of their literacy attempts (Pressley, 2000).
8. We remain learners who continue to work in study groups with colleagues and engage in meaningful inservice classes so that we can continually learn new ways to meet the literacy learning needs of our students (Florio-Ruane, 2001).

REFERENCES

Avalos, M. A. (2003). Effective second-language reading transition: From learner-specific to generic instructional models. *Bilingual Research Journal, 27*(2), 171–206.

Beck, I., McKeown, M., & Kucan, L. (2002). *Bringing words to life: Robust vocabulary instruction.* New York: Guilford Press.

Carlo, M. S., August, D., McLaughlin, B., Snow, C. D., Dressler, D., Lippman, D. N., et al. (2004). Closing the gap: Addressing the vocabulary needs of

---

[7]Sandy, Susan, and Elena agreed that their small groups should be flexible, not static. By regularly assessing their students' strengths and needs, these teachers grouped and regrouped students as their instructional needs changed.

English language learners in bilingual and mainstream classrooms. *Reading Research Quarterly, 39*(2), 188–215.

Collins Block, C., & Pressley, M. (Eds.). (2002). *Comprehension instruction: Research-based best practices.* New York: Guilford Press.

Duffy, G. G. (2003). *Explaining reading: A resource for teaching concepts, skills, and strategies.* New York: Guilford Press.

Fitzgerald, J., & Graves, M. (2004). *Scaffolding reading experiences for English language learners.* Norwood, MA: Christopher-Gordon.

Florio-Ruane, S. (2001). *Teacher education and the cultural imagination: Autobiography, conversation, and narrative.* Mahwah, NJ: Erlbaum.

Gándara, P. (2007, February 13). *Multiple pathways for immigrant and English learner students.* Los Angeles: University of California Institute for Democracy, Education, and Access. (Paper No. mp-rr003-0207). Retrieved May 10, 2007, from *repositories.cdlib.org/idea/mp/mp=rr003=02078.*

Lapp, D., Flood, J., Brock, C., & Fisher, D. (2007). *Teaching reading to every child* (4th ed.). Mahwah, NJ: Erlbaum.

Li, G. (2004). Perspectives on struggling English language learners: Case studies of two Chinese-Canadian children. *Journal of Literacy Research, 36*(1), 31–72.

Loizou, M., & Stuart, M. (2003). Phonological awareness in monolingual and bilingual English and Greek five-year-olds. *Journal of Research in Reading, 26*(1), 3–18.

McLaughlin, M., & Allen, M. (2002). *Guided comprehension: A teaching model for grades 3–8.* Newark, DE: International Reading Association.

Morse, A. (2005). *A look at immigrant youth: Prospects and promising practices.* Washington, DC: National Conference of State Legislatures.

National Center for Education Statistics. (2003). *The nation's report card.* Available at *nces.ed.gov/nationsreportcard/reading/results2003.*

Pressley, M. (2000). What should comprehension instruction be the instruction of ? In M. L. Kamil, P. B. Mosenthal, P. D. Pearson, & R. Barr (Eds.), *Handbook of reading research* (Vol. 3, pp. 541–561). Mahwah, NJ: Erlbaum.

Raphael, T., Brock, C., & Wallace, S. (1997) Encouraging quality peer talk with diverse students in mainstream classrooms: Learning from and with teachers. In J. Paratore & R. McCormack (Eds.), *Peer talk in the classroom: Learning from research* (pp. 176–206). Newark, DE: International Reading Association.

Saunders, W. M., & Goldenberg, C. (1999). Effects of instructional conversations and literature logs on limited- and fluent-English-proficient students' story comprehension and thematic understanding. *Elementary School Journal, 99*(4), 277–301.

Spinelli, J. (1990). *Maniac Magee.* New York: Harper Trophy.

Worthy, J., Broaddus, K., & Ivey, G. (2001). *Pathways to independence: Reading, writing, and learning in grades k–8.* New York: Guilford Press.

APPENDIX 9.1. Suggested Professional Reading List

Resources for Learning about Language, Culture, and Teaching

Banks, J. A., & McGee Banks, C. A. (Eds.). (2007). *Multicultural education: Issues and perspectives.* Hoboken, NJ: Wiley.
Delpit, L. (1995). *Other people's children: Cultural conflict in the classroom.* New York: New Press.
Gay, G. (2000). *Culturally responsive teaching: Theory, research, and practice.* New York: Teachers College Press.
Howard, G. R. (1999). *We can't teach what we don't know: White teachers, multiracial schools.* New York: Teachers College.
Ladson-Billings, G. (1995). Toward a theory of culturally relevant pedagogy. *American Educational Research Journal, 32*(3), 441–465.
Listen, D., & Zeichner, K. (1996). *Culture and teaching.* Mahwah, NJ: Erlbaum.
Minami, M., & Kennedy, B. (1991). *Language issues in literacy and bilingual/multicultural education.* Cambridge, MA: Harvard Educational Review.
Nieto, S. (2002). *Language, culture, and teaching: Critical perspectives for a new century.* Mahwah, NJ: Erlbaum.
Philips, S. (1983). *The invisible culture: Communication in classroom and community on the Warm Springs Indian Reservation.* Prospect Heights, IL: Waveland Press.

Resources for Teachers of English Learners

Cary, S. (2000). *Working with second-language learners: Answers to teachers' top ten questions.* Portsmouth, NH: Heinemann.
Diaz-Rico, L., & Weed, K. (2005). *The crosscultural, language, and academic development handbook: A complete K–12 reference guide* (3rd ed.). Boston: Allyn & Bacon.
Ovando, C. J., & Collier, V. P. (1998). *Bilingual and ESL classrooms: Teaching in multicultural contexts.* New York: McGraw Hill.
Spangenberg-Urbschat, K., & Pritchard, R. (Eds.). (1994). *Kids come in all languages: Reading instruction for ESL students.* Newark, DE: International Reading Association.
Suarez-Orosco, M., & Suarez-Orosco, C. (2001). *Children of immigration.* Cambridge, MA: Harvard University Press.
Tran, M. T. (1998). Behind the smiles: The true heart of Southeast Asian American children. In V. O. Pang & L. L. Cheng (Eds.), *Struggling to be heard: The unmet needs of Asian Pacific American children* (pp. 45–60). Albany, NY: State University of New York press.

Resources on Understanding the Second-Language Learning Process

Cook, V. (2001). *Second language learning and language teaching.* New York: Oxford University Press.

Crawford, L. W. (1993). *Language and literacy learning in multicultural classrooms.* Boston: Allyn & Bacon.

Harklau, L. (2000). From the "good kids to the 'worst'": Representations of English language learners across educational settings. *TESOL Quarterly, 34,* 35–39.

Krashen, S. (1982). *Principles and practices in second language acquisition.* Oxford, UK: Pergamon Press.

McKay, S. L., & Wong, S. L. (1996). Multiple discourses, multiple identities: Investment and agency in second-language learning among Chinese adolescent immigrant students. *Harvard Educational Review, 66,* 577–608.

Peirce, B. N. (1995). Social identity, investment, and language learning. *TESOL Quarterly, 29,* 9–31.

CHAPTER 10

Spelling–Meaning Relationships among Languages

Exploring Cognates and Their Possibilities

SHANE TEMPLETON

During her math block, fifth-grade teacher Sandra Matera writes the following words on the overhead:

polygon   *hexágono*
quadrilateral   *triangle*
pentagon   *cuadrilátero*
triángulo   *polígono*
pentágono   *hexagon*

Pairing the students, she asks them to match up the words they believe go together: to put the English words in one column and the other words that match in a second column. She anticipates that their finished sort will look like the following:

polygon   *polígono*
quadrilateral   *cuadrilatero*
pentagon   *pentágono*
triangle   *triángulo*
hexagon   *hexágono*

When the sort is completed, Sandra asks the students to discuss with each other what they notice about the matched words, addressing questions such as how the words are alike, different, and how they are spelled and pronounced. Most students notice how similar in appearance and spelling a number of the pairs are but that they are pronounced differently. They also decide that the words have the same meaning in the different languages, and a number of the students point out that the words that were not English were from the language they spoke at home.

One-third of the students in this classroom come from Spanish-language backgrounds and a handful from Korean-language backgrounds; the remainder are native English speakers. Most of the students from Spanish- and Korean-language backgrounds have good competence with conversational English, and their reading levels in English range from second to seventh grade; native English-speaking students' reading levels range from third through ninth grade. These students are exploring *cognates*—words that have the same or similar meanings in different languages and that are spelled the same or similarly.

The term *cognate* comes from Latin and originally meant "born together." Many cognates in different languages, and the word parts from which they were created, were indeed "born together" in a common language spoken thousands of years ago. Students who become aware of, explore, and understand cognates acquire an invaluable tool that helps to bridge their heritage language to the language they are acquiring (August & Shanahan, 2006; Bear, Helman, Templeton, Invernizzi, & Johnston, 2007; Bravo, Hiebert, & Pearson, 2005; Diamond & Gutlohn, 2007; Hancin-Bhatt & Nagy, 1994; Jiménez, García, & Pearson, 1996). Notably, in recent years, textbook publishers for the elementary grades have increasingly included attention to cognates, primarily English–Spanish. This inclusion has come in response to state-mandated content standards and curriculum frameworks (e.g., California State Board of Education, 2008; Texas Education Agency, 2008).

In presenting the foundation for teaching about cognates, this chapter explores (1) the spelling–meaning connection in English; (2) how Latin and Greek word roots provide a context for exploring cognates; and (3) a two-phase approach to cognate instruction, including the category of "false" cognates. As I discuss, instruction involving cognates extends beyond pointing them out and cataloguing them across languages. Effective instruction involves talking and thinking about language and about words in ways that are significantly different from what most of us have experienced as learners. For this reason, the chapter concludes with suggested resources to support this new way of talking and thinking. Most examples in this chapter involve English and Spanish, although the approach applies to most Western languages that share cognates with English. Bear and colleagues (2007) address a number of Asian and Pacific Rim languages, as well.

THE SECRET OF ENGLISH SPELLING: IT'S MORE LOGICAL THAN WE MAY THINK

In order to realize the full potential of cognate instruction for students at the intermediate grade levels, we need to begin with the ways in which the spelling system of English represents the language. Students will learn that English spelling is far more logical than they may think only if their teachers point this out. This is why it is important that we begin with an examination of the *spelling–meaning connection* in English (Templeton, 1983, 2004). To illustrate this connection, let's pretend for a moment that the spelling of the following fairly common English words was changed to reflect a closer match between letters and sounds:

dufiyn
defunishun
defunut
dufinutiv

Now examine the conventional spelling of these words:

<u>defi</u>ne
<u>defi</u>nition
<u>defi</u>nite
<u>defi</u>nitive

Thinking about spelling in this way may help to illustrate the fundamental relationship between spelling and meaning in English: Words that are related in meaning are often related in spelling as well, despite changes in sound (Templeton, 2003). In these examples, as the underlined letters indicate, the spelling of the base—*define*—is retained in the spelling of the words that are derived from the base by the addition of suffixes. Although adding these suffixes changes the pronunciation of the base, it does not change significantly the *spelling* of the base. In short, words that are similar in meaning *look* similar, and that is the trade-off in English spelling: We do not spell most words in English strictly in accordance with letter–sound "rules," because if we did we would lose the *visual* similarity among words that are similar in meaning. For readers and their developing vocabularies, knowledge of this relationship between spelling and meaning can be a powerful tool—for both native English speakers and students learning English as a new language.

Linguists have long noted this relationship between spelling and meaning (e.g. Bradley, 1919; Chomsky & Halle, 1968; Venezky, 1970). Most linguists use the term *morphology* to refer to aspects of language that have to do with how the structure and form of a language reflect meaning, but I have chosen to use the more specific term *spelling–meaning connection* because it captures *what* morphology does when English is written down. The balance of this chapter explores how the spelling–meaning connection operates not only in English but between English and many other languages as well.

Most educators are not aware of this relationship between spelling and meaning. It is probably not coincidental, therefore, that most students do not notice these relationships, either. This is the reason that it is necessary to present words related in spelling and in meaning *together* in pairs and in small groups. What about, however, the alphabetic and pattern aspects of English spelling? Chapters 5, 6, and 7 in this volume have discussed these aspects and have pointed out the significant challenge for English language learners with the alphabetic or letter-to-sound features and the pattern-to-sound features. Although these letter-to-sound and pattern-to-sound relationships are more logical than we often believe (Templeton & Morris, 2000; Venezky, 1999), it still requires concentrated, systematic, and sustained exploration in order to learn how to decode and to spell them (Bear et al., 2007; Bear, Templeton, Helman, & Baren, 2003). For English learners who are reading on at least the intermediate level in their home languages, however, learning these letter-to-sound correspondences, although important, is not a prerequisite for exploring spelling-to-meaning relationships. For the majority of words in English, older English learners need to learn that they should look for groups of letters within words that may represent chunks of *meaning* rather than chunks of *sound*. It is not as productive to invest a lot of time in trying to decode unfamiliar words into sound if the words appear unfamiliar; for the most part, these words are not part of the students' speaking–listening vocabularies, anyway, so even a correct pronunciation would not cue the meaning of the word. This strategy is not just for English learners; this applies to native English speakers as well. For students whose home languages are written with a significant logographic or meaning-based component (e.g., Chinese), this awareness may allow them to scaffold their approach to learning and reading English words in a way that is similar to their approach to reading the writing system of their home languages.

Although we introduce the spelling and meaning connection with words that are clearly and transparently related—words such as *resign/resignation*, *muscle/muscular*, and *compose/composition*—we should extend this exploration to words that, at first glance, appear *not* to be related. These are words such as *cave* and *cavity*, *author* and *authority*. Upon closer inspection, students realize that such words most often *are* related at a more general conceptual level. These relationships often explain the "exceptions" to reliable spelling rules that English learners are attempting to learn. For example, the spelling rule that states "in two-syllable words, double the consonant after the first syllable if it contains a short vowel" appears to be violated in the word *finish*. To explain the reason that this occurs, a teacher may write the following words on an overhead, underlining the letters *fin* in each:

fi̲n̲ish
fi̲n̲al
fi̲n̲ite
infi̲n̲ite

The teacher explains that, when a word doesn't seem to follow a sound-to-spelling rule, the reason usually is that the word is related in meaning to other words and that this meaning relationship has to be preserved in the word's spelling. Pointing to both *finish* and *final*, she or he asks the students if they are similar at all in meaning. When the students realize that they *are* similar, the teacher then reminds them of the connection between spelling and meaning: "Words that are related in meaning are often related in spelling as well, even though sounds within them may change." She or he goes on to explain how this similarity in meaning occurs in the words *finite* and *infinite* ("not" finite). Students will not notice, much less understand, these more subtle yet productive relationships unless teachers point them out. Importantly, when teachers do point out these relationships they also provide opportunities for students to expand their vocabularies: Students who know *finish* and *final* but are not as familiar with *finite* and *infinite* will, as a consequence of this teacher's explanation, probably add these two additional words to their vocabularies.

THE CONTEXT FOR COGNATES: EXPLORING LATIN AND GREEK ROOTS

Cognates provide a two-way bridge for negotiating the meaning between many heritage languages and English, as well as vice versa. As students read, talk about, and explore cognates, they are learning much more than the meanings of particular words in a new language; they are learning processes of thinking about language in general and the discourses, large and small, that scaffold meaning systems in the new language (Corson, 1997; Gee, 2005). It is important to note that, along with cognate instruction, teachers should walk students through processes of word formation in English, from the combination of basic prefixes and suffixes with base words to the exploration of Greek and Latin roots (see Templeton, Bear, Johnston, & Invernizzi, 2000, for a comprehensive scope and sequence of this word study curriculum). Although it is not necessary to begin to explore Latin and Greek roots before pointing out cognates, most students in the intermediate grades are conceptually ready to begin exploration of both roots and cognates at the same time. The primary value of learning about Greek and Latin word roots is that they build *generative* vocabulary knowledge (Stahl & Nagy, 2006; Templeton, 2004): Understanding what roots are and how they work will support students' learning and remembering literally thousands of words independently. The Latin roots *rupt* (break) and *struc* (build), for example, generate hundreds of related forms, such as *interrupt, bankrupt, abrupt, corruption,* and *structure, construct, destruct,* and *obstruct.*

Teachers should begin the exploration of word roots by pointing out to students, first, that a lot of words in English have come from Latin and Greek, two languages that were spoken over 2,000 years ago; and, second, that a great many more words have been created over the last few hundred years by combining Greek and Latin word parts. Most of the prefixes they have already learned came from Latin or Greek. Now they are going to explore word *roots*, other word parts that came from Latin and Greek. A root usually cannot stand by itself as a word, but it is a very important part of a word. We tell students they've probably found a root in a word when, after taking off all of the prefixes and suffixes, what's left doesn't look like a word anymore. We may illustrate this by comparing and contrasting words such as *unbreakable* and *invisible*. We point out that with *unbreakable*, they can take off the prefix *un-* and the suffix *-able*, and the word *break* remains. In contrast, with *invisible*, after removing the prefix *in-* and the suffix *-ible*, *-vis-* remains—definitely not a word. They've found the *root*. The two illustrations that follow describe the ways in which teachers may introduce and walk students through an awareness and understanding of word roots; the first focuses on Latin roots, the second on Greek roots.

Latin Roots

In this example, the teacher reminds the students of their previous discussion concerning the difference between a base word and a word root—*break* in *unbreakable* versus *-vis-* in *invisible*. She or he then elaborates on the concept of a word root:

> "Roots usually have the same meanings they had back when people spoke Latin and Greek. In ancient Rome, where they spoke Latin, *vis* meant 'to see.' Let's look at *invisible* again: We know what the

prefix *in-* means, don't we? Right! 'Not.' So, if something is 'not visible,' what does that mean? [Students respond.]

"Now let's look at this word:

predictable

"If something is *predictable*, what does that mean? [Students respond.] If we take the suffix *-able* off, what's left? Right, *predict*. Do you see a prefix in *predict*? Yes, there's *pre-*. What does *pre-* mean? Right, 'before.' If we take *pre-* off, we're left with *dict-*, which is not a word. So, *-dict-* is the root of *predictable*. It comes from a Latin word that meant 'to say or speak.' To 'predict' that something will happen literally means to 'say before.'"

Next, the teacher writes the words *vision* and *revision* on the board and continues:

"*Vision* has to do with seeing, right? What about *revision*? We use this word when talking about writing, don't we? Turn to a partner, and talk about what you think *revision* has to do with 'seeing' as it applies to writing. When you 'revise' something that you've written, what does that mean?"

This discussion should help students understand that *revision* literally means "to see their writing again."

On the next day, the words from Day 1 are displayed, and the teacher again asks the students about the definition of the root *-vis-*. She or he then writes the following words on the overhead:

visit	*dictate*
visor	*dictionary*
visibility	*contradict*
supervise	

"Talk with a partner about how the meaning of each root contributes to the meaning of the word in which it appears. For example, how does the meaning of 'say' or 'speak' contribute to the meaning of *contradict*? When you *contradict* someone, what does that mean? Then, with your partner, compose a sentence for *visor* or *supervise* and for *dictate* or *contradict*."

Students then write their sentences in their vocabulary notebooks (Templeton, Bear, Johnston, & Invernizzi, 2010), a composition book in which interesting words, spelling–meaning families, and other interesting aspects of words are recorded. Students may be surprised to realize that *visit* literally means to "go see" someone. A number of individual, paired, and small-group independent activities occur throughout the balance of the week (Bear, Invernizzi, Templeton, & Johnston, 2008). For example, the students may share their sentences, followed by the teacher posting a "golden sentences" chart or charts on which students may write their favorite sentences, with the word containing the root underlined. Students may create words with previously studied prefixes and suffixes; words that do not yet exist in English but that *could* are definitely encouraged (e.g., one student coined *postdictability*). Students then write the word in their vocabulary notebooks, write a definition for it, and—if the word can be illustrated—include the illustration, too. Students will later share their new words, and the words may be entered into the class "dictionary of possible words" (Templeton, 1997).

Greek Roots

The following week, the Greek roots *micro-* (small), *phon-* (sound), *scop-* (look at), *tele-* (distant), and *photo-* (light) may be introduced. Here is how that lesson might proceed:

The teacher reminds the students that the previous week they began looking at roots that come from Latin. This week, they are going to be looking at a handful of roots that come from Greek. Most often these roots do not occur by themselves as words, though on occasion some of them may do so. The teacher reminds the students that learning the meaning of a number of these roots and understanding how they combine to create words will be extremely helpful to them in figuring out and learning new vocabulary.

The teacher writes the following two words on the overhead:

microscope
microscopic

If some of the students come from Spanish-language backgrounds, the teacher asks them if they know of a word in their home language that is like *microscope* (*microscopio*). He or she then discusses with the students how these two words are related, or alike. After students discuss this, the teacher points to *microscope* and says:

"We know these words, but let's look at the Greek roots that make them up: *Scope* comes from a Greek word that means 'to look at,' and *micro* means 'small,' so when we put them together we literally get the meaning 'to look at something small.' A *microscope* is an instrument for looking at very small or tiny things, and if we say that something is *microscopic*, what does that mean?"

The teacher writes the following words:

telescope
telescopic
periscope

"We know these first two words, but let's look at their Greek parts. We already know what *scope* means, but what do you suppose *tele-* means?"

The students will probably get close to the meaning of "far off" or "distant"; if not, however, the teacher tells them explicitly that *tele-* comes from Greek and means "distant." A *telescope* is an instrument for looking at distant objects.

If students are not certain about *periscope*, the teacher writes *perimeter* and reminds them that it means "to measure around." So, a *periscope* is an instrument on a submarine used to look around—quite literally, all the way around.

Next the teacher has the students turn to a partner and talk about how the Greek roots combine to create the meaning of each of the following words:

television
telephone

The teacher follows up by asking the students if they talked about how a television delivers vision from a distance. She or he asks them what they think *phone* means. If no students have an idea after their partner talk, she or he tells them that *phone* comes from a Greek word that means "sound." So *telephone* is "sound that comes from a distance." They then discuss the word *microphone*. The teacher comments:

"When we put the roots together, we literally get the meaning 'small sound.' Of course, a *microphone* is not literally a small sound, but it picks up sounds that would otherwise not be heard very well."

She or he then asks the students to write their words just as she or he has done, one underneath the other, because that will help them remember how the words are alike in meaning and what their roots mean.

The next day, the teacher writes the following words on the overhead:

telecommunications
telemetry
telephoto

"What type of communication might be involved in *telecommunications*? With a partner, talk about what *telemetry* and *telephoto* might mean. Because you know what *tele-* means, how does it combine with the rest of each word?"

If necessary, the teacher discusses the word *telephoto* with the students; they may have heard the word in the context of a telephoto lens but not thought about the meaning. She or he tells them that *photo* means "light," and this may lead to a productive discussion about the literal meaning of *telephoto*—"light from a distance." The teacher asks the students if that makes sense when they think of a "telephoto lens."

This type of explicit walk-through and discussion of how word roots function within words is critical for guiding students to an awareness, understanding, and appreciation of the value of understanding word roots. Some students require quite a bit of this explicit guidance, while others are ready to move out on their own after a few walk-throughs. Regardless, there will often be serendipitous moments when a particular word is so intriguing that it lends itself to whole-class analysis and discussion. This type of attention to words also helps students develop, more broadly, a curiosity and inquisitiveness about words that will be a powerful engine driving their vocabulary knowledge forward.

EXPLORING COGNATES: PHASE I

The types of examples at the beginning of this chapter—*polygon/polígono* and *triangle/triángulo*—illustrate phase 1 instruction in cognates: Our focus is on words in different languages whose spelling is the same or almost identical and that represent the same concepts. The concepts that the words in the math example represent are related—shapes, sides, angles—and the correspondence between the English and Spanish forms is direct and straightforward.

The following cognates, although not related by content area, are also examples of cognates whose spelling and meaning relationships are straightforward:

*office   oficina
important   importante
exasperated   exasperado
calmness   calma
gymnasium   gimnasio
initial   inicial
solve   solver*

The next step is to present students with cognates that are similar but not identical. The following example, modeled on Johnston (2007), illustrates this:

*study   estampa   space   esquí
espectador   school   style   estudiar
escuela   spectator   estado   beast
chaqueta   espacio   stamp   state
estilo   bestia   ski   jacket
legend   estadio   leyenda   stadium*

For classrooms in which all students are native English speakers, have them match English words with Spanish words, discuss the possible meaning of the Spanish words, then discuss what they can discover about Spanish spelling. They may notice—or you may ask about—the beginnings of the words, which letters stay the same in related words and which change, and possibly *why* they change. For classrooms with both Spanish and English speakers—as well as, perhaps, students who speak other languages—the discussions may be considerably enriched, and the reasons for different spellings across words may be more powerfully explored. And words such as *chaqueta* and *jacket*, although not visually as similar, are similar enough in pronunciation to prompt interesting discussion. Students may add other words from their respective languages and explore their hypotheses about what underlies the spelling changes.

Teachers may also guide students' examination of the similarities among specific meaningful parts of cognates; after matching the following cognates, they discuss how the endings, or *suffixes*, are alike and different and discuss the possible meaning of each:

*abreviación—abbreviation   creación—creation
anticipación—anticipation   imitación—imitation
declaración—declaration   vegetación—vegetation
elevación—elevation   vocación—vocation*

In cognates such as *capacity—capacidad* and *probability—probabilidad*, students would be asked if they think the suffixes in English and Spanish have the same meaning, despite a significant change in spelling.

Cognates may also be explored in the context of phrases or words that refer to a specific concept. The following examples are from the intermediate-level math curriculum:

bar graph   *compatible numbers*   *valor de posición*
gráfica de barras *números compatibles*   *place value*

congruent figures   *equivalent fractions*
figuras congruentes *fracciones equivalentes*

When students explore this variation in word order, teachers may ask questions that often lead to a discussion about parts of speech: for example, do Spanish adjectives show number? Do English adjectives?

EXPLORING COGNATES: PHASE 2

Traditionally, instruction involving cognates has not gone beyond the basics of phase 1—exploring words that mean the same or similar things in different languages and that are also virtual mirror images of one another. Pedagogically, that is, of course, where our instruction should begin. The next phase in cognate instruction, however, applies this awareness in more breadth and depth, exploring words that represent the same concept but that are *not* cognates. Key to this exploration, however, is the realization that the written and spoken language that surrounds the use of these words often *does* contain cognates. This exploration works particularly well in the contexts of thematically related content units (Carlo et al., 2004; Echevarria, Vogt, & Short, 2004). While same and similar meanings are explored, the types of classroom discourse in which this exploration is embedded scaffolds English learners' acquisition of vocabulary and deepens understanding (August & Shanahan, 2006; Bear et al., 2007; Corson, 1997; Bravo et al., 2005).

For example, in science the terms *decomposer* in English and *desintegrador* in Spanish represent the same concept, as do the terms *array* and *arreglo*, and *outcome* and *resultado* in math. Such words, however, are still part of a semantic or conceptual neighborhood that *can* be discussed using cognates. Students of different heritage languages benefit from this type of exploration. To illustrate, when native Spanish and native English speakers in a fifth-grade class turn to the glossary in their science textbook to check the definitions for the equivalent terms *desintegrador* and *decomposer*, the Spanish definition is *Ser vivo que descompone los restos de los organismos muertos* (Badders et al., 2007, p. H25). *Descompone*, the verb in this definition, is certainly a cognate of the English word *decomposer*, and *desintegrador* is similar to *disintegrate*. Exploring these relationships should involve students in thinking more precisely about the features of the concepts that underlie terms such as *decompose–descompone–disintegrate–desintegrador*, exploring how they are alike and how they are different. In science, a *decomposer* is a living thing that breaks down or decomposes the remains of dead organisms. The corresponding term in Spanish is *desintegrador*; although Spanish also has the cognate *descomponador*, the term *desintegrador* is more precise in Spanish. This is an excellent opportunity to point out the English word *disintegrate* and to talk about the same "core" meaning that underlies *decompose–desintegrador–disintegrate*.

Over time, teachers can help students get a sense of different nuances of meaning between languages, as well as how a cognate in one language may have a more specific, more general, or more nuanced meaning than its counterpart in another language. Examples from an earth science unit, for example, could include the following: The English word that means "slow movement of land along a fault" is *creep*, and the Spanish word is *arrastre*. In English, the similar form *arrest* means not only what often happens to suspected criminals but also to slow and stop the movement of something. This is not the same meaning as "creep" but *is* similar in terms of the core concept of "to slow, stop" in both English and Spanish.

In other words, even when cognates exist, the *use* of the cognate in each respective language may be somewhat different. For students learning the academic vocabulary of an additional language, it is important to be aware of this fact. A native Spanish speaker who encounters the word *decomposer* while reading a science textbook in English and who tries to think of a similar Spanish word will be "close enough" to the appropriate meaning; similarly, a native English speaker encountering the word *desintegrador* in Spanish who tries to think of a similar English word will also be "close enough" to the appropriate meaning.

Following are some examples that illustrate the types of possibilities for exploration and questioning:

addition—suma   *ancient—antiguo*   *library—biblioteca*

- For *addition* and *suma*, teachers may point out how these terms both represent the same process or *operation* in math. The English cognate of *suma*, *sum*, refers more specifically to the *result* of that operation, but it is "close enough" for Spanish-heritage speakers to learn this more specific meaning of *sum*. The Spanish cognate of *sum*, *suma*, is close enough for English heritage speakers to learn the more general meaning of *suma*.

• For the adjectives *ancient* and *antiguo*, teachers may ask native English speakers if there is a word in English that looks similar to *antiguo* (*antique*). Spanish-heritage speakers may think of words in Spanish similar to *ancient* (*anciano*).

• *Library* and *biblioteca* both have to do with books. In this case, however, there is an excellent opportunity to point out to students that roots with the same or similar meanings come from both Greek and Latin. The Greek root meaning "book" is *bibli-*; the Latin root is *libr-*. What are some English words that have *-biblio-* in them? What are some Spanish words that have *-libr-* in them?

WHAT ABOUT "FALSE" COGNATES?

A small percentage of English–Spanish and, more broadly, English–Romance cognates are "false"; that is, although they are spelled similarly, they do not have the same or similar meanings. Spanish *largo* and *embarazada* and English *large* and *embarrass* are examples. In Spanish, *largo* means "length," and in English, *large* means "big"; *embarazada* means "pregnant" in Spanish, and *embarrass* means to feel self-conscious or ill at ease in English. If we dismiss "false" cognates and go no further, however, we are missing an excellent opportunity for analysis and insight that extends well beyond the meaning of the individual words. When students explore them, they will probably notice that the words for "large" in English and Spanish *are* semantically quite similar. Does the word for "large" in Spanish, *grande*, remind them of an English word (*grand*)? In English, if we say that something is "grand," can that also mean "large"? Both of these terms are describing the dimensions of objects or ideas, and they are the same part of speech. As for *embarazada* and *embarrass*, older students may explore the possible connections between these two.

Because of shared etymological roots, it is rarely the case that two "false" cognates are truly unrelated. Although false cognates may not stand for the same *literal* referent, they often *do* belong to the same conceptual network. By exploring the possible connections, students are thinking more deeply about words in the same way that we encourage them, with English, to think more deeply about relationships between words such as *cave* and *cavity*, *author* and *authority*.

FINAL THOUGHTS

By exploring cognates across languages, students (and their teachers!) not only learn a new language; we grow and significantly enrich the concepts underlying the vocabulary of our own native language. In doing so, we expand the concepts underlying our knowledge of the world in general. The approach described in this chapter emphasizes a different way of talking about, and therefore *thinking* about, words and the relationships among words. Even if we have studied a language other than our own, many of us are not in the habit of thinking about words this way. If we had a teacher who was excited about words and shared that excitement with us, however, we may have glimpsed the possibilities of these types of explorations into words and their related meanings within and across languages. Where do we, as teachers, begin to develop the foundational knowledge about words that supports our guidance of the types of students' explorations illustrated in this chapter? Where do we begin to develop the teaching activities and ways of organizing words for exploration? Taken together, the suggested resources at the end of this chapter should be very helpful in providing the foundation and examples for exploring spelling–meaning relationships among words, cognates, Latin/Greek word roots, and word histories. Using information from such sources, you may begin to explore the types of examples shared in this chapter with your students; remember, so much of this exploration involves *your* learning right along with them!

REFERENCES

August, D., & Shanahan, T. (2006). *Developing literacy in second-language learners: Report of the National Literacy Panel on Language-Minority Children and Youth*. New York: Taylor and Francis.

Badders, W., Carnine, D., Feliciani, J., Jeanpierre, B., Sumners, C., & Valentino, C. (2007). *Houghton Mifflin California science*. Boston: Houghton Mifflin.

Bear, D., Helman, L., Templeton, S., Invernizzi, M., & Johnston, F. (2007). *Words their way with English learners*. Upper Saddle River, NJ: Merrill/Prentice Hall.

Bear, D. R., Invernizzi, M., Templeton, S., & Johnston, F. (2008). *Words their way: Word study for phonics, vocabulary, and spelling instruction* (4th ed.). Upper Saddle River, NJ: Merrill/Prentice Hall.

Bear, D. R., Templeton, S., Helman, L., & Baren, T. (2003). Orthographic development and learning to read in different languages. In G. Garcia (Ed.), *English learners: Reaching the highest level of English literacy* (pp. 71–95). Newark, DE: International Reading Association.

Bradley, H. (1919). *On the relations between spoken and written language*. Oxford, UK: Clarendon Press.

Bravo, M. A., Hiebert, E. H., & Pearson, P. D. (2005). *Tapping the linguistic resources of Spanish/English bilinguals: The role of cognates in science*. Berkeley: Lawrence Hall of Science, University of California.

California State Board of Education. (2008). *Standards and frameworks*. Retrieved July 5, 2008, from *http://www.cde.ca.gov/be/st/*.

Carlo, M. S., August, D., McLaughlin, B., Snow, C. E., Dressler, C., Lippman, D. N., et al. (2004). Closing the gap: Addressing the vocabulary needs of English language learners in bilingual and mainstream classrooms. *Reading Research Quarterly, 39*(2), 188–215.

Chomsky, N., & Halle, M. (1968). *The sound pattern of English*. New York: Harper & Row.

Corson, D. (1997). The learning and use of academic English words. *Language Learning, 47*, 671–718.

Diamond, L., & Gutlohn, L. (2007). *Vocabulary handbook*. Baltimore: Brookes.

Echevarria, J., Vogt, M., & Short, D. (2004). *Making content comprehensible for English learners*. Boston: Pearson/Allyn & Bacon.

Gee, J. P. (2005). *An introduction to discourse analysis: Theory and method* (2nd ed.). New York: Routledge.

Hancin-Bhatt, B., & Nagy, W. (1994). Lexical transfer and second language morphological development. *Applied Psycholinguistics, 15*(3), 289–310.

Jiménez, R. T., García, G. E., & Pearson, P. D. (1996). The reading strategies of bilingual Latina/o students who are successful English readers: Opportunities and obstacles. *Reading Research Quarterly, 31*(1), 90–112.

Johnston, F. (2007, April). *Word sorting with cognates*. Paper presented at the George Graham Memorial Lecture, University of Virginia.

Stahl, S. A., & Nagy, W. (2006). *Teaching word meanings*. Mahwah, NJ: Erlbaum.

Templeton, S. (1983). Using the spelling/meaning connection to develop word knowledge in older students. *Journal of Reading, 27*(1), 8–14.

Templeton, S. (1997). *Teaching the integrated language arts* (2nd ed.). Boston: Houghton Mifflin.

Templeton, S. (2003). Spelling. In J. Flood, D. Lapp, J. R. Squire, & J. M. Jensen (Eds.), *Handbook of research on teaching the English language arts* (2nd ed., pp. 738–751). Mahwah, NJ: Erlbaum.

Templeton, S. (2004). The vocabulary–spelling connection: Orthographic development and morphological knowledge at the intermediate grades and beyond. In J. F. Baumann & E. J. Kame'enui (Eds.), *Vocabulary instruction: Research to practice* (pp. 118–138). New York: Guilford Press.

Templeton, S., Bear, D. R., Johnston, F., & Invernizzi, M. (2010). *Vocabulary their way: Word study with middle and secondary students*. Boston: Prentice Hall/Allyn & Bacon.

Templeton, S., & Morris, D. (2000). Spelling. In M. Kamil, P. Mosenthal, P. D. Pearson, & R. Barr (Eds.), *Handbook of reading research* (Vol. 3, pp. 525–543). Mahwah, NJ: Erlbaum.

Texas Education Agency. (2008). *Texas essential knowledge and skills.* Retrieved July 5, 2008, from *http://www.tea.state.tx.us/teks/index.html.*

Venezky, R. L. (1970). *The structure of English orthography.* The Hague: Mouton.

Venezky, R. L. (1999). *The American way of spelling: The structure and origins of American English orthography.* New York: Guilford Press.

SUGGESTED RESOURCES

Ayers, D. M. (1986). *English words from Latin and Greek elements* (2nd ed.; rev. by T. Worthen). Tucson, AZ: University of Arizona Press.

Ayto, J. (1990). *Dictionary of word origins.* New York: Arcade.

Bear, D., Helman, L., Templeton, S., Invernizzi, M., & Johnston, F. (2007). *Words their way with English learners.* Upper Saddle River, NJ: Merrill/Prentice Hall.

Claiborne, R. (1989). *The roots of English: A reader's handbook of word origins.* New York: Times Books.

Crystal, D. (2006). *Words, words, words.* Oxford, UK: Oxford University Press.

Crutchfield, R. (1997). *English vocabulary quick reference: A comprehensive dictionary arranged by word roots.* Leesburg, VA: LexaDyne.

Kennedy, J. (1996). *Word stems: A dictionary.* New York: Soho Press.

Merriam Webster New Book of Word Histories. (1991). Springfield, MA: Merriam-Webster.

Moore, B., & Moore, M. (1997). *NTC's dictionary of Latin and Greek origins: A comprehensive guide to the classical origins of English words.* Chicago: NTC.

Nash, R. (1997). *NTC's dictionary of Spanish cognates: Thematically organized.* Chicago: NTC.

Templeton, S., Johnston, F., Bear, D., & Invernizzi, M. (2009). *Word sorts for derivational relations spellers* (2nd ed.). Upper Saddle River, NJ: Merrill/Prentice Hall.

www.onelook.com. This website provides opportunities to explore definitions and word histories.

CHAPTER 11

Examining Teacher Dispositions toward Linguistically and Culturally Diverse Students

JULIE L. PENNINGTON
RACHEL G. SALAS

The 2001 reauthorization of the Elementary and Secondary Education Act (ESEA), commonly known as No Child Left Behind (NCLB), demonstrated a shift from promoting bilingualism to a focus on English-only instruction by changing the Bilingual Education Act (Title VII) to the English Language Acquisition, Language Enhancement, and Academic Achievement Act (Title III; 20 U.S.C. §6861). "This legislation, the 'No Child Left Behind' Act, represents a 180 degree policy turn: the word bilingual has been completely expunged from federal policy. This act portends grim times for our nation's language minority school children" (Santa Ana, 2004, p. 90). The law focused on instructing and assessing non-English-speaking children in English as soon as possible (see also Chapter 4, this volume, for a discussion by Garcia and DeNicolo). Although some educators and policy makers may see the NCLB's press for English as benefiting students, it involves a loss of heritage language and cultural connections for some students, and, as Merwin (1998) states, "the children will not repeat the phrases their parents speak" (p. 67). Coupled with the power and pressure of the dominant culture's influence in schools, this legislation mandating English-only instruction is not new, nor is it removed from what we discuss in this paper. Our purpose here is to introduce research on white monolingual English-speaking teachers' attitudes toward students from linguistically and culturally diverse backgrounds and suggest methods by which teachers can explore their own dispositions in transformative ways in a political environment that seeks to disregard many students' native languages. We intersperse vignettes of teaching throughout our presentation of research and theory to illustrate two teachers' perspectives as they teach linguistically and culturally diverse students. Amy is a monolingual English-speaking white teacher, and Yolanda is a bilingual Latina teacher. All vignettes are based on composite portraits of actual teachers and events in elementary schools. We begin with an overview of the current state of institutional language and literacy expectations in U.S. schools, followed by an exploration of the rationale behind examining individual teacher dispositions. We conclude with two sections illustrating possible ways for educators to explore their own beliefs toward the children they teach.

THE INSTITUTIONAL AND POLITICAL PRESS FOR ENGLISH-ONLY INSTRUCTION

"How can I get them to write an American sentence?" Amy asked three other teachers as they ate lunch. The teachers were discussing their English language learners (ELLs). Amy, a first-grade teacher, was frustrated by what she described as her students' "inability to write a simple sentence in English." As the other teachers nodded in agreement, they all began to discuss their efforts to get their students to pass the mandated standardized test in English. All of the teachers were worried that they had students who could not speak English well but who were required to take the standardized tests in English. This caused the teachers, the school, and the children to be labeled as failures. Amy sighed and added, "The only reason our school is being watched now is because most of our kids speak Spanish. I'm trying to get them up to speed in English, but there is not enough time."

Teachers such as Amy in classrooms today are working within institutions overshadowed by the pressures of the testing required by the NCLB Act, an act that focuses on swift mastery of English. To begin to understand the complexity of the myriad of educational challenges faced by both ELLs and classroom teachers such as Amy, it is important to understand and situate the push for "English-only" mandates in our schools within historical and legal contexts. We are purposefully situating teachers as individuals enacting institutional policy that they did not create on instructional time lines that they have not designed in order to demonstrate the power of policy to silence discourse related to language and culture.

NCLB states the following in relation to English language acquisition: "The purpose ... is to help ensure that students with limited proficiency in English master English and meet the same rigorous standards for academic achievement as all children are expected to meet, including meeting challenging state academic content and student academic achievement standards" (20 U.S.C. §6861, p. 185). As teachers struggle to prepare their students to learn English and pass the required standardized tests, many experience the frustration expressed by Amy. Due to the fact that the teacher population consists largely of white monolingual English-speaking teachers and the student population of U.S. schools continues to become increasingly diverse linguistically and culturally, there is a growing focus on teaching ELLs. Many times teachers are taught how to teach particular populations of children, such as ELLs, with little time to attend to their own attitudes and beliefs about language and culture. Current policy does not address the issue of teachers' attitudes toward their students. In this era of NCLB, teachers are increasingly aware of the need for faster and more proficient English acquisition so their schools are not penalized for low test scores; teachers, however, are not encouraged to explore their own beliefs about mandated English-only instruction. Due to the pressures of the NCLB policy, we feel that teachers are caught up in an environment that has not served them well. Amy is a product of the American education system, a system that has helped shape and that now molds her beliefs and perceptions of how a student in an "American" school should behave, perform, and speak. Yolanda is also a part of the American education system but brings another view into their discussion due to her language background. The following conversation demonstrates their different perspectives:

"My grandparents came from Italy and they learned English and made sure their children learned English, and now they are all successful," said Amy.

Yolanda asks Amy, "Do you or your parents speak Italian, have you kept up the Italian language in your family?"

"No" replies Amy. "Why should we? We speak English. Here that's the language I need to be successful. That's why I so believe that my students need to speak English, too. I want what's best for them. I want them all to be successful!"

Yolanda interjects, "You know, Amy, I'm bilingual. My first language was Spanish, and I was taught in both Spanish and English. Research and history tells us that being bilingual is a measure of success, too, and by law we should be allowing our students access to instruction and assessment in their own language."

"What do you mean, by law?" Amy asks.

Yolanda's understanding and personal experiences of the importance of bilingualism were once recognized by policy. In 1965, under the Johnson administration, the ESEA was established, with an emphasis on educating all children, particularly children of poverty and minority backgrounds and languages (Menchacha-Ochoa, 2006). The year 1968 ushered in the enactment of the Bilingual Education Act (Title VII of the ESEA) and a legal basis for bilingual education. The 1974 Supreme Court decision in Lau v. Nichols focused a new lens on language issues and rights of language-minority students. Using Title VI of the Civil Rights Act, the Supreme Court held that an English-only curriculum excluded public school students who lacked English language skills (Moran, 2005). The Lau Remedies were set in place to guide curricular and instructional practice in U.S. schools regarding language-minority students without excluding the students' home language. Yolanda continues sharing her experiences with Amy:

> "The U.S. has historically required English acquisition. While bilingualism in education did seem to briefly thrive in the U.S., we are back to English-only mandates. I remember teaching English and Spanish to my students. They left our school biliterate, reading and writing in two languages. Now, with NCLB, students have a limited amount of time to take the test in their native language."
>
> Yolanda went on to explain to Amy how the federal policy was set up to ensure that all LEP (*limited English proficient*, a term used by the federal government) and immigrant children would learn English in American schools. "Ah ..." stated Amy, "NCLB requires English learning, so I was right. They should be able to learn to write a sentence in English."
>
> "Yes, of course they will," Yolanda replied. "The historical aspect of language use in this country is actually quite interesting and often tied to politics. After World War I and II there was a big push for English instruction in schools. Laws were established forbidding foreign language instruction, especially German, for students before the eighth grade."
>
> "Wow," exclaimed Amy. "I had no idea there were actual laws restricting language use. I just never thought about it."

As Yolanda stated, bilingual education in the United States has had periods of success in American schools. In the early 1800s states began to authorize and legitimize bilingual education programs in local schools (Ovando, 2003). In addition, curricular instruction was provided in German, Swedish, Dutch, Czech, Norwegian, Danish, French, Polish, and Spanish in public and private schools throughout the United States (Kloss, 1977). Perhaps it was the perception of an increasingly polyglot society or a sense of a growing immigrant nationalism, but by the early 1900s a shift began to occur in the United States toward assimilation and English as the dominant language (Ovando, 2003). The Naturalization Act of 1906 reflects this shift by establishing "that no alien shall hereafter be naturalized or admitted as a citizen of the United States who can not speak the English language" (*www.historycentral.com/documents/Naturalizationact.html*). This act laid the foundation for an educational environment that fosters English as the dominant language in schools. Teachers exist in an educational atmosphere permeated by English-only mandates that influence their views, perceptions, and dispositions regarding the non-native English-speaking children they teach. As Sleeter and Stillman (2005) state, "In reading/language arts, teachers and students are expected to follow the state's prescription. Compliance is enforced mainly through statewide standards testing in English, and through the textbook adoption process" (p. 43). Given the focus on English instruction in schools, it is easy to see how teachers raised in such an environment do not question the expectation that ELLs should conform to English-only instruction. Policy focuses on showing teachers how to teach Standard American English. NCLB advocates "developing programs that strengthen and improve the professional training of educational personnel who work with limited English proficient children" (20 U.S.C. §6861, p. 185). There is no specific mention of requiring teachers to understand their beliefs about their students as well. Therefore, we argue that teachers such as Amy have been left behind historically and in the current political climate. Policy and professional development has focused on how to teach particular groups of children, with little to no attention paid to how teachers' own beliefs about language and culture interact with their teaching practices. In the next section, we explore the definitions of *disposition* and the role it can play in teacher beliefs.

TEACHER DISPOSITIONS

All of us hold personal thoughts about ourselves and the students we teach, but these ideas are often avoided and rarely evaluated critically in the daily work of teaching. For the purposes of this chapter, Hosford's (1980) notion of the silent curriculum will be applied to teacher beliefs toward children from nondominant backgrounds, those who are not native speakers of English, who may be new immigrants to the United States and/or children of color attending schools centered on Standard English acquisition. Our adaptation of Hosford's idea of the silent curriculum refers to the fact that many white monolingual English-speaking teachers, or teachers from the dominant culture, may not feel comfortable directly discussing how they feel about interacting with children and families from cultures different from their own. In Hosford's words, "The Silent Curriculum is created as we teach, and it does affect teaching and learning. It impacts strongly on four major objectives: desire for learning, the three Rs, self-concept, and respect for others" (Hosford, 1980, p. 50). In the following scenario, Amy's disposition toward her students is positive in that she cares about them and wants them to succeed, but there is an underlying subtle belief that they are not going to be successful due to their family environments.

> The following day, as Amy taught her first graders, she was interrupted by her teammate, another first-grade teacher, Kim. Kim stopped by to ask Amy to read one of her student's homework folders. "Look at this," said Kim, handing the student's folder to Amy. As Amy read, she began to nod her head. Amy looked at Kim and said, "This is what I get, too." Kim sighed and added, "I'm worried that these students and their parents just don't get it. I am trying to work on writing in English when they can't even talk in English; how are they going to write in their journals or read at home? Their parents don't emphasize education and some don't try to learn English. I need to just send these kids to the ESL aide." Amy nodded and agreed.

Kim and Amy's disappointment with their students is understandable due to the pressure they know the children will be under in the following grade. Yet their knowledge about the need for home literacy experiences juxtaposed with their desire to just send the students to work with an aide shows how their teaching knowledge is affected by their beliefs. In this case, their knowledge about how to teach and how students' writing develops in a second language did not assist them in problem solving. Amy is caring, but she avoids critically reflecting on the role of language in her students' home lives. Knowing how to teach English learners is crucial for educators such as Amy, but understanding her own beliefs about issues of language and culture plays a role as well. Amy and Kim validate each other's views of the ELL families. White monolingual English-speaking teachers can remain frustrated when it comes to discussing their thoughts about students and families from diverse cultures as they focus on the expectations they have of the families rather than learning more about them.

> In many instances of target language teaching to classes of a multicultural character, it is possible to witness teachers with a world view stopping at their country's border... teachers' lack of knowledge about their students' cultures easily leads to the formation of a protective

shield of ethnocentric approaches based on the only frame of reference they possess—their own culture. (Alptekin, 1981)

As natural as it is for teachers to use their own culture, policy mandates, and the traditional culture of school to evaluate their students, when these ways of thinking are combined with an avoidance of self-reflection, the result can interfere with student and teacher learning. A lack of attention to white monolingual English-speaking teachers' beliefs may create avoidance or negative feelings related to linguistically and culturally diverse students and their families. Dee and Henkin (2002) define cultural diversity as "perceived deviations from White, middle-class, monolingual backgrounds ... perceived differences in skin color, language use, linguistic ability, and socioeconomic status, which may be manifest in the clothes students wear, the words they use, and their attitudes and aspirations related to schooling" (p. 25). Kim's perception that her students' parents do not care about their education is an example of how her beliefs are guiding her instructional decisions. Even though she is aware of how to teach, she focuses on the families' lack of attention to homework. Explorations of teacher beliefs regarding language and race are missing from the systemic changes in education revitalized by NCLB and its tacit call for an English-only emphasis. In this example, Amy and Yolanda discuss one of Amy's ELL students, Carlos:

> Amy sits with students at a reading table; several other students are working at their desks nearby. Yolanda walks in to ask a question and notices Carlos sitting alone at a desk next to a group of students. Carlos is reading a small book from the district-adopted reading series. He sits and attempts to decode the sentence, "The cat and the rat sat." At one point, Amy goes over to Carlos, listens to him read a page, and compliments him on his reading. When she asks him what the story is about, he looks at her and points to the picture of the cat.
>
> Later, the teachers talk about their day, and Amy expresses her frustration at how little the instructional methods she is using have been working with Carlos. "If he could only speak English, I know everything would be so much easier. He is probably in the 'silent period,' so I am just going to leave him alone for a while. I think he is from Mexico."
>
> "Aren't you worried about Carlos falling behind in his reading?" asks Yolanda.
>
> Amy responds, "He has to take the test in English; he is probably going to fail it. I think it would help if his parents would stop speaking Spanish at home."
>
> "But," Yolanda interjects, "what if his parents are reading to him in Spanish and he could read Spanish books? That would help

his literacy development, and that's the goal. I could help you find out more about Carlos's family if you'd like me to."

Although Amy's knowledge of Carlos's second-language development is correct in that he may be in the silent period, it is apparent that her disposition toward his native language, Spanish, and his family is not constructive. Rather than building on what Carlos brings to the classroom, she is looking only at his English proficiency and making assumptions about his family's practices. Amy has knowledge of how students acquire English as a second language, but her beliefs about Carlos are not based on accurate information. When she says that she will leave him alone and then states that his parents should not speak Spanish to him at home, she displays her attitude about the use of Spanish by his family.

Yolanda takes a different stance due to her beliefs and identity as a bilingual person. The importance of beliefs is described by Pajares: "Beliefs subsequently affect perception and strongly influence the processing of new information ... individuals hold on to beliefs based on incorrect or incomplete knowledge even after scientifically correct explanations are presented to them" (Pajares, 1992, p. 317). Amy's beliefs are a part of her disposition toward Carlos, and her frustrations are common. Teacher dispositions are not often discussed in schools today, but they are addressed in the education of future teachers. The National Council for Accreditation of Teacher Education (NCATE) standards related to teacher candidate dispositions cover areas such as race, culture, language, and exceptionalities (NCATE, 2001). Educational research also examines future and practicing teachers' dispositions toward their students and families (Cline & Necochea, 2006; Dee & Henkin, 2002; Gay, 2000; Johnson, 2002). Many professional development programs and teacher support activities focus on how to teach particular student populations, but the spotlight is not always on the teachers themselves (Ball & Lardner, 1997). Universities and researchers use the term *dispositions* in their work with future teachers and in research studies, but teachers usually reserve talk about their own dispositions for close colleagues, friends, and family members.

Negative teacher dispositions can manifest themselves in overt behavior or statements such as "These parents just don't care about education" that reflect negative attitudes about language and cultural issues. Negative teacher dispositions can also be more covert and result in teacher avoidance of students and families or an increased focus on teacher–student differences (Major & Brock, 2003). Some teachers may take a sympathetic stance toward their students, which can lead to the teacher seeing himself or herself as a caretaker or nurturer rather than an educator (Blais, 2006; Pennington, 2007). Other teachers adopt a neutral stance, believing that all students are the same and thus avoiding understanding differences and also strengths. Once teachers leave their teacher preparation programs and begin to work in schools, the topic of dispositions may be included in their evaluations, but most professional development focuses on teaching methods rather than teacher attitudes toward their students. Yet teacher attitudes do exist and are often shared in intimate relationships, as seen in Amy's discussion with her husband, as follows.

> That evening as Amy discusses her day of teaching with her husband over dinner, she asks him what he thinks about her current teaching situation, and her husband states, "So if they come to the United States, why don't they try to learn English? How are you supposed to teach all your classes when they can't understand you? You work so hard and you care so much."
>
> Amy adds, "My kids are so wonderful, but there is no way they can make it in second grade. I have other students whose parents speak English, but they are just uneducated. I don't care what color they are, I care about all of them."

Amy vacillates between negating student differences and criticizing them. Her comments reveal her caring but also a disposition that places blame. Amy's disposition regarding language is tied to race, as stated by Kubota and Lin (2006): "The problem lies in the tendency to equate the native speaker with White and the nonnative speaker with non-White" (p. 481). The clumping of language and racial diversity into one group demonstrates how members of the dominant culture—white, monolingual English speakers such as Amy—can see people outside of their cultural group as different from them yet similar to each other. In school settings white native English-speaking teachers may see immigrant families of color and/or non-native speakers of English as the same. The ways in which we view the identities of others are often not based on anything more than how they look and how they speak (Kubota & Lin, 2006; Mahoney, 1997b). What can make this problematic for white teachers working with diverse student populations is what scholars term the "norms of the dominant culture." Chabram-Dernersesian (1997) defines white dominance in these terms:

> Whiteness is often an overarching sign for the culturally, politically, racially, and economically dominant; whiteness is generally linked to specific agents of domination ... whiteness is often a metaphor for assimilation—here, forced participation in the language, traditions, institutions and beliefs of the economically, racially, and politically dominant group. (pp. 114–115)

The dominant culture in the United States is white, monolingual, and English speaking; therefore, students outside the norms of society are often seen as deficient or outside the norm (Dixson & Rousseau, 2005). Many of these studies reveal that some white teachers do possess negative attitudes toward the cultures, languages, and beliefs of their students if these are different from their own (Marx, 2004). Teachers often do not express their thoughts about these topics because they think these will not be seen as "politically correct." Research has shown that white preservice and inservice teachers can hold onto negative stereotypes and misconceptions regarding students from cultures outside of the white dominant culture (Ference & Bell, 2004; Fishman & McCarthy, 2005; Garmon, 2004; Pennington, 2007) and that many white teachers simply avoid the topic altogether (Case & Hemmings, 2005).

Bridging the gap between being able to teach the use of effective methods with English learners and understanding our dispositions as individuals and how it can affect our instructional practice can be complex and uncomfortable. A teacher can have excellent training and a depth of knowledge about second-language acquisition, literacy methods, and assessment and still have unconstructive attitudes about students and families that can prevent student growth. Teachers can also possess good intentions, be sympathetic with student and family situations, and care deeply about their students and yet retain negative attitudes toward the student's home language that can also impede student growth (Hyland, 2005). One way to discover how we as teachers view students and families who are different from us culturally is to begin to understand and honestly explore our own thoughts, views, and perceptions about ourselves and others. In other words, we need to know ourselves, as well as our students, in order to teach well (see also Chapter 2, this volume, for a discussion by Au). In this case, teaching well is defined as possessing the pedagogical knowledge to teach and understanding the beliefs that affect our teaching attitudes. As Au (1998) states, "Educators' recognition of the inequities possible in a given educational situation depends on an understanding of their own cultural identities as well as the cultural identities of their students" (p. 308). The difficulty many people have with exploring their own identities is expressed in Pajares's statement, "People are often loathe to engage in discussions that touch on what they feel are their most deeply held beliefs (never argue politics or religion), but, when they do, they usually manage to survive the ordeal with preconceptions comfortably intact" (Pajares, 1992, p. 317). Discussing personal beliefs regarding race and language can become a minefield for teachers; we hope to provide a map for teachers to begin to navigate their own deepest held beliefs toward the children and the families they interact with daily.

The following section describes how identity can shape teacher attitudes toward other cultures.

TEACHER IDENTITY

Early one morning before school, Amy walks down the hall and sees Carlos and his father. She stops to talk with them, asking how they are. She is surprised when Carlos's father begins to speak in fluent English; he mentions how much they read with Carlos at home in Spanish and English and how they enjoy making up silly rhymes. Amy later shares her impressions of Carlos's family with Yolanda. "I thought they were new immigrants and did not speak English in their home, since the mother limited her conversations to simple sentences in broken English. After talking with his father, I began to see that my ideas about the family weren't necessarily negative, but I had faulty assumptions. Because I knew his mother spoke Spanish, I just thought that was their only home language."

"It is a common misconception to have a one-dimensional image of immigrant families," said Yolanda. "For example, I have seen teachers talk about a student with a Hispanic surname on their class roster, and they often think the child is from Mexico. They may immediately associate Mexico with poverty, *campesinos* (rural farmers), and a lack of education. In fact, the student may not be Mexican but could be from another Spanish-speaking part of the world—South America (e.g., Argentina, Colombia, Ecuador, Peru), Central America (e.g., El Salvador, Honduras, or Guatemala), or the Caribbean (e.g., Cuba, Dominican Republic), and they may be able to read in their own language. It is important to learn as much as possible about our students and their families before making any assumptions or conclusions about their linguistic or academic abilities. It was great that you had the opportunity to speak to Carlos's father and learn more about his family. If you need help selecting books or planning lesson modifications, I'd be glad to assist you; just let me know."

Amy was relying on mistaken beliefs rather than her knowledge of Carlos and second-language acquisition. Amy is a highly educated and competent teacher, but she has not investigated her own linguistic and cultural identity and the impact it may have on her assumptions about her students. What does it take to put instruction and disposition together as a teacher? We argue that it requires understanding ourselves and our students and how the materials and methods interact not only with our students but also with our beliefs about the students. The goal is for teachers to begin to alter the ratio between reliance on knowledge and beliefs by understanding the role personal beliefs and attitudes play in constructing realities. For this, we borrow from critical white studies. White monolingual English speakers teaching English learners encounter cultural and linguistic differences between teacher and students that can create tension, misunderstandings, or avoidance. Although language is the focus of this book, race is often the additional label tacked onto language (Kubota & Lin, 2006). Policy makers set up NCLB reporting as race-based, as well as using race in addition to language for identifying student populations at risk for school failure. One example of a school's response to this was to target racial groups in the school prior to the mandated testing period. "Administrators ... [held] separate assemblies for black, White and Hispanic students to address low scores on the Texas Assessment of Knowledge and Skills test" (Eriksen, 2007). The field of teaching English to speakers of other languages (TESOL) is beginning to look at race as well. As Kubota and Lin (2006) state, "Rather than being silenced by the discomfort of discussing race, racialization, and racism, the field of TESOL could initiate unique and vibrant inquiries to build on these topics and investigate how they influence identity formation, instructional practices, program development" (p. 473). One way to learn about race as a factor in teaching is to look at research based on racial identity development.

Work on identity can take many directions, but for this chapter we use Helms's (1990) description of white racial identity development and expand it to look at culture and language. Helms's (1990) stages of identity development for whites are listed as follows: (1) the contact stage, (2) the disintegration stage, (3) the reintegration stage, (4) the pseudo-independence stage, (5) the immersion/emersion stage, and (6) the autonomous stage. Many white teachers who teach in culturally diverse schools naturally engage in contact with cultures other than their own. Amy is set into the contact stage by her teaching position. She is a white teacher immersed in a Latino school. In this initial contact stage, Helms (1990) depicts white individuals as not fully recognizing their own whiteness and keeping other groups at a distance. Amy is easily able to teach her Latino/a ELLs everyday without critically thinking about her whiteness or her English dominance in the school. She can choose to interact with other white teachers in most situations. At this stage, many white teachers will state that they do not see themselves as having a culture at all. In contrast, the final stage of Helms's (1990) fully developed white identity is defined by an individual who is aware of his or her white identity and the privilege and power associated with that identity both individually and institutionally and who is now working to eradicate the power differential between whites and other racial groups.

In between these two points, Helms's (1990) stages of contact, disintegration, and reintegration are the phases by which whites begin to recognize and abandon their individual and institutional participation in a society controlled by the dominant culture. White teachers' understanding of the disintegration and reintegration stages is crucial for their growth and can assist them in defining where they exist on the continuum of white identity. The disintegration stage provides a look at how whites begin to acknowledge their white racial identity. This complex process can take two trajectories: Generally, whites may experience a sense of dissonance and choose to question their previous beliefs about their own identities and those of others, or they may try to dramatically avoid contact with other racial groups. White teachers may very easily choose to keep a distance from students and their parents; this can prevent them from learning about students' cultural identities and perspectives.

On the other hand, if the white individual progresses into Helms's reintegration stage, he or she may experience fear and anger toward other cultures. The stance at this stage is that white people have earned their status, whereas other cultures' inferior lifestyles or capabilities contribute to their lower status. This type of language is heard in Amy's earlier conversation with Kim about how the parents were not involved enough with their children. These fearful and negative beliefs may be expressed openly with other whites or tacitly through withdrawal. As Helms states, "Passive expression involves deliberate removal of oneself and/or avoidance of environments in which one might encounter [people of color] ... honest discussion of racial matters is most likely to occur among same-race peers who share or are believed to share a similar view of the world" (p. 60). It is highly likely that whites will remain in the reintegration stage unless a seminal personal event or larger environmental change occurs in the person's life that shatters his or her beliefs. This conclusion is aligned with Pajares's (1992) description of the strength that beliefs have in determining teachers' construction and interpretation of knowledge. Amy's interactions with Yolanda and Carlos's father were opportunities for her to continue her contact with people from other cultures and to learn to examine her own beliefs by contrasting them with new information.

Taking the preceding ideas that Helms (1990) developed and applying them to teacher dispositions toward ELLs can help white teachers see how many of their personal reactions to other cultures are somewhat predictable. For some white teachers, this idea can bring comfort; they see that their feelings of avoidance or frustration are normal and can begin to change them. We hope that white monolingual teachers of children of color who speak languages other than English are able to view their own dispositions honestly and to understand the role their views play in daily classroom instruction. The often uncomfortable and avoided topic of how we view those different from us can become stressful and result in feelings of guilt and hopelessness. Therefore, we as teachers need support and facilitation as we begin to explore our identities and positions. In many ways, Yolanda was a supportive and educative presence for Amy as she reflected about Carlos and his family. Yolanda did not judge Amy's attitudes but provided a strong alternative source of information for her, a factor we discuss in the next section.

BUILDING INDIVIDUAL TEACHER AWARENESS

As Yolanda walks down the hall, she hears students laughing. In the classroom, Amy sits at a table with five students. Two of the students are monolingual English speakers; one student is biliterate in both Vietnamese and English; and two students, including Carlos, are fluent in Spanish. Amy is presenting a new book to the students about lizards. She has a lizard on the table and several books in front of the kids. Each student is touching and talking about the lizard in phrases in English, Vietnamese, and Spanish. There are several books spread out on the table of varying levels, and cards with vocabulary words are scattered among the white boards and journals. A high level of academic language and vocabulary is evident and supported by pictures. Carlos shares his knowledge by adding, "In Mexico we see lizards. They sit in la … in the … sun and eat bugs. They come in many colors … they change colors too! Lizards are reptiles!"

The students were grouped heterogeneously. Amy states, "I decided to group them by interest. Some groups were studying mammals; this group was interested in reptiles. Even though they have varying degrees of English ability, they were able to share their observations and their own background knowledge and to learn a bit of the new academic vocabulary I was presenting."

Once the lesson is over, Amy and Yolanda talk about the students. Amy talks about their language abilities as individuals. "Carlos has really developed an expertise in science and uses his science vocabulary all the time. The other day at lunch he was telling me about how he and his father saw a chameleon." As she continues, she reflected back on her previous thoughts about Carlos, his family, and his abilities. "I thought Carlos was in his silent period and that I could let him work alone until the ESL teacher came to work with him. I assumed his family only spoke Spanish at home and that his parents were not involved in his literacy development. I'm not sure what my ideas were based on other than my own theories, but once I took time to speak with his parents more, observed him interacting in class and on the playground with his peers, and tried to incorporate him into activities, I saw that I was limiting him by my assumptions."

Even though she had spent time studying how to teach ELLs, Amy had not explored the way her own ideas about race and language had tacitly guided her daily teaching decisions and practices. Applying effective pedagogy merged with self-conscious awareness of our own thoughts about the students we teach is vital to leading teachers and students into new areas of academic achievement and increased understanding, respect, and awareness. Cline and Necochea (2006) studied teacher dispositions in a professional development environment and found five themes connected to teacher effectiveness. Three of these themes apply to the larger notions of teacher dispositions related in this chapter: (1) open-mindedness and flexibility, (2) cultural sensitivity, and (3) a pluralistic language orientation. Hosford's (1980) notion of the silent curriculum can be adapted here to present a means for teachers to explore how their dispositions interact with their teaching methods. Hosford focused on self-evaluation as a tool for "improving the Silent Curriculum" (1980, p. 48). Hosford listed three methods for teachers to utilize as they teach: (1) scheduling weekly "think-back time," (2) practicing a new procedure, and (3) seeking out evaluations of our own teaching (1980). Teachers can utilize these ideas and adapt them into tools for exploring our attitudes toward culturally and linguistically diverse students. We suggest that teachers set aside a regular time to reflect and evaluate events from teaching and to (1) honestly examine their personal feelings about students and (2) seek out relationships between culturally and linguistically diverse others in the school and neighborhood in which they teach, in the form of informal conversations and teaching evaluations.

Personal Reflections

One way for teachers to acknowledge their beliefs in the context of the dominant culture's pervasive role in practices and expectations is to learn to self-monitor. Milner (2003) suggests race-reflective journaling led by guiding questions such as the following:

- How will my race influence my work as a teacher with students of color?
- What is the impact of race on my beliefs?

- How do I, as a teacher, situate myself in the education of others, and how do I negotiate the power structures around race in my class to allow students to feel a sense of worth?
- How might racial influences affect my and my students' interest in the classroom?
- How might I connect lessons to those interests? (Milner, 2003, p. 178).

These same questions may be altered to include language by posing questions of ourselves, such as:

- How do my language abilities or limitations affect my work as a teacher of students who speak languages other than English?
- What impact does my English proficiency have on my beliefs about others' English acquisition?
- How do I use English as a help or hindrance as I navigate the power structures of the institution of my school?
- How do I use language in the classroom to provide access to or denial of instruction?
- Am I facilitating communication and respect for all languages among myself, my English learners, and their parents?

Amy's attention to these questions revealed the following in this excerpt from her journal:

"I am a native English speaker and I do not really know any other languages. I grew up hearing Spanish spoken by others but I never had to learn it. It was not important, and as an adult whenever I have traveled to other countries or even the neighborhood where I teach, someone always found a way to communicate with me in English. My language was never an impediment, and I assumed that people would adjust to me, and if they didn't, it did not affect me. I would like to speak Spanish and I have taken lessons, but I don't always have time. This does affect my teaching. I do think that I avoid situations where I know parents do not speak English. I will try to set up a conference, and if they do not respond to the note, I am somewhat relieved. It's hard to have a conference with them. We don't really get anywhere. I'm uncomfortable. I guess it does put me in a powerful position, even though at times when all of the parents outside start talking in Spanish, I feel as though they are doing it on purpose. I wonder if they are talking about me. In my classroom I guess I do not really think about my language as a barrier. I thought that it was good that the students were hearing English every day.

I never thought about how I never asked about their language or tried to learn any words or phrases from them. I know they have to learn English—that is what I focus on—but now I wonder how I can use their language as well. I didn't know Carlos could read and write in Spanish. That knowledge will help his English reading. I just assumed he could not read at all."

Just as Helms (1990) talks about the stages of white identity development, language awareness can be viewed as a process for teachers, beginning with contact and awareness and eventually moving to autonomous and informed relationships and understandings of the role attitudes about language play in teacher dispositions. Amy's journal reveals her move past the reintegration stage and into the pseudo-independent stage. This stage is the beginning of noting one's own role in perpetuating racial division and an overreliance on assumptions. Teachers are consistently put into the role of helping and assisting students. Although this is an admirable stance for a teacher to take, there are potential pitfalls. As Cross (2003) notes, "Even well-intentioned teachers in schools and teacher educators in universities slip into this role of assuming inequality for children of color, frequently under the guise of helping" (p. 209). Many times the good intentions of teachers can prevent them from seeing the strengths of the students and their own shortcomings as teachers (Pennington, 2007). Utilizing critical personal reflections can assist teachers in disrupting their mission of helping with a more balanced and focused eye.

Developing Relationships

Another way for teachers to become more proactive in examining their own dispositions and more informed about their students is to become a part of the larger school community and neighborhood and to involve parents and teachers of color in their teaching decisions. Many scholars advocate taking an active role in the neighborhoods of students (Ladson-Billings, 1994; Moll, Amanti, Neff, & Gonzales, 1992). Amy's relationships with Yolanda and with Carlos's father allowed her to revise her notions of Carlos, which were formed from a distance. Interpreting curriculum and teaching events from the perspective of colleagues and peers from other cultures can assist teachers in seeing views other than their own. Examples might include having home visits with all students and spending time in the community with families rather than holding them to school expectations without understanding their perspectives.

Once teachers begin to understand the importance of knowing their own thoughts about ELLs and their families, the instructional practices and techniques that follow will rest on a more informed foundation. Bringing the notion of teacher dispositions into the routine of literacy teacher education and making it a part of the instructional repertoire is imperative at this time in history as NCLB policy reinforces the need for all students to learn English. Standard English should be taught in schools to all children, but not at the expense of their native language. "Oral proficiency and literacy in the first language can be used to facilitate literacy development in English. Language-minority students are not blank slates" (August & Shanahan, 2006, p. 5). Given the research on teacher dispositions, we know that our personal beliefs influence instructional decisions, and it may be helpful to ask ourselves to reflect critically on our notions about the role that language and race play in the teaching of English. In order to ensure that all of our students receive meaningful education without asking them to abandon their cultural and linguistic identities, teachers will need to examine their feelings about linguistically and culturally diverse students. We concur with Kubota and Lin's (2006) call to TESOL educators:

> We should engage in daily critical reflections of how our ideas of race influence what we teach, how we teach it, and how we understand our students. This should be followed by committed action to confront and eradicate overt and covert racisms with an understanding that they are intricately connected with other injustices and that the commitment for action always requires the awareness of our own racial and other privileges that are both relational and situated. (p. 488)

FINAL THOUGHTS

Our hope for this chapter is to make spaces for monolingual, English-speaking white teachers to view their dispositions toward linguistically and culturally diverse students in transformative ways. First, by understanding that as individuals, teachers work within a larger societal and institutional context that does not support and at times resists such dialogue; and, second, that teachers can create opportunities for our own reflection and growth. We end with a quote from Gloria Anzaldua: "So, if you really want to hurt me, talk badly about my language. Ethnic identity is twin skin to linguistic identity—I am my language" (2004, p. 271). It is our hope that Merwin's (1988) lines will not ring true for linguistically and culturally diverse children in the future. We hope classrooms are filled with the voices of children resounding with the phrases of their parents, along with the phrases of their school, and that they are admired for both.

REFERENCES

Alptekin, C. (1981). Sociopsychological and pedagogic considerations in L2 acquisition. *TESOL Quarterly, 15*(3), 275–284.

Anzaldua, G. (2004). Linguistic terrorism. In O. Santa Ana (Ed.), *Tongue-tied: The lives of multilingual children in public education* (pp. 270–271). New York: Rowman & Littlefield.

Au, K. H. (1998). Social constructivism and the school literacy learning of students of diverse backgrounds. *Journal of Literacy Research, 30*(2), 297–339.

August, D., & Shanahan, T. (2006). *Developing literacy in second-language learners: Report of the National Literacy Panel on Language-Minority Children and Youth.* Mahwah, NJ: Erlbaum.

Ball, A., & Lardner, T. (1997). Dispositions toward language: Teacher constructs of knowledge and the Ann Arbor Black English case. *College Composition and Communication, 48*(4), 469–485.

Blais, D. (2006). Ivory tower. *Teaching Tolerance, 30*, 19–22.

Case, K. A., & Hemmings, A. (2005). Distancing strategies: White women preservice teachers and antiracist curriculum. *Urban Education, 40*(6), 606–626.

Chabram-Dernersesian, A. (1997). On the social construction of whiteness within selected Chicana/o discourses. In R. Frankenburg (Ed.), *Displacing whiteness: Essays in social and cultural criticism* (pp. 107–164). Durham, NC: Duke University Press.

Cline, Z., & Necochea, J. (2006). Teacher dispositions for effective education in the borderlands. *Educational Forum, 70*, 268–282.

Cross, B. E. (2003). Learning or unlearning racism: Transferring teacher education curriculum to classroom practices. *Theory into Practice, 42*(3), 203–209.

Dee, J. R., & Henkin, A. B. (2002). Assessing dispositions toward cultural diversity among preservice teachers. *Urban Education, 37*(1), 22–40.

Dixson, A. D., & Rousseau, C. K. (2005). And we are still not saved: Critical race theory in education ten years later. *Race Ethnicity and Education, 8*(1), 7–27.

Eriksen, H. (2007, March 29). Katy school separates races for TAKS assemblies. *Houston Chronicle.*

Ference, R. A., & Bell, S. (2004). A cross-cultural immersion in the U.S.: Changing preservice teacher attitudes toward Latino ESOL students. *Equity and Excellence in Education, 37*, 343–350.

Fishman, S. M., & McCarthy, L. (2005). Talk about race: When student stories and multicultural curricula are not enough. *Race, Ethnicity and Education, 8*(4), 347–364.

Garmon, M. A. (2004). Changing preservice teachers' attitudes/beliefs about diversity: What are the critical factors? *Journal of Teacher Education, 55*(3), 201–213.

Gay, G. (2000). *Culturally responsive teaching: Theory, research, and practice.* New York: Teachers College Press.

Helms, J. E. (Ed.). (1990). *Black and white racial identity: Theory, research, and practice*. New York: Greenwood Press.

Hosford, P. L. (1980). Improving the silent curriculum. *Theory into Practice, 19*(1), 45–50.

Hyland, N. E. (2005). Being a good teacher of black students? White teachers and unintentional racism. *Curriculum Inquiry, 35*(4), 429–459.

Johnson, L. (2002). "My eyes have been opened": White teachers and racial awareness. *Journal of Teacher Education, 53*(2), 153–167.

Kloss, H. (1977). *The American bilingual tradition*. Rowley, MA: Newbury House Publishers.

Kubota, R., & Lin, A. (2006). Race and TESOL: Introduction to concepts and theories. *TESOL Quarterly, 40*(3), 471–493.

Ladson-Billings, G. (1994). *The dreamkeepers: Successful teachers of African-American children*. San Francisco: Jossey-Bass.

Mahoney, M. (1997b). The social construction of whiteness. In R. Delgado & J. Stefancic (Eds.), *Critical white studies: Looking behind the mirror* (pp. 330–333). Philadelphia: Temple University Press.

Major, E. M., & Brock, C. H. (2003). Fostering positive dispositions toward diversity: Dialogical explorations of a moral dilemma. *Teacher Education Quarterly, 30*(4), 7–26.

Marx, S. (2004). Regarding whiteness: Exploring and intervening in the effects of white racism in teacher education. *Equity and Excellence in Education, 37*, 31–43.

Menchacha-Ochopa, V. (2006). A judicial and legislative perspective of bilingual education. *Catalyst for Change, 34*(2), 49–58.

Merwin, W. S. (1988). *The rain in the trees*. New York: Knopf.

Milner, H. R. (2003). Teacher reflection and race in cultural contexts: History, meanings, and methods in teaching. *Theory into Practice, 42*(3), 173–180.

Moll, L. C., Amanti, C., Neff, D., & Gonzales, N. (1992). Funds of knowledge for teaching: Using a qualitative approach to connect homes and classrooms. *Theory into Practice, 31*, 132–141.

Moran, R. F. (2005). Undone by law: The uncertain legacy of Lau v. Nichols. *16 Berkeley La Raza Law Journal 1*.

National Council for Accreditation of Teacher Education. (2001). *Professional Standards for the Accreditation of Schools, Colleges, and Departments of Education*. Washington, DC: Author.

Ovando, C. J. (2003). Bilingual education in the United States: Historical development and current issues. *Bilingual Research Journal, 27*(1), 1–24.

Pajares, M. F. (1992). Teachers' beliefs and educational research: Cleaning up a messy construct. *Review of Educational Research, 62*(3), 307–332.

Pennington, J. L. (2007). Silence in the classroom/whispers in the halls: Autoethnography as pedagogy in white pre-service teacher education. *Race, Ethnicity and Education, 10*(1), 93–113.

Santa Ana, O. (2004). Chronology of events, court decisions, and legislation affecting language-minority children in American public education. In O. Santa Ana (Ed.), *Tongue-tied: The lives of multilingual children in public education* (pp. 87–106). New York: Rowman & Littlefield.

Sleeter, C., & Stillman, J. (2005). Standardizing knowledge in a multicultural society. *Curriculum Inquiry, 35*(1), 27–46.

CHAPTER 12

Effective Instructional Practices for English Learners

LORI HELMAN

What instructional practices are helpful for ensuring the literacy success of English learners in mainstream classrooms? Is good teaching for English learners the same as good teaching for all students? What should all teachers know about how to implement and tailor their literacy instruction to best serve students who are learning oral English at the same time they are learning to read and write it? This chapter presents an overview of findings in the research literature on effective instructional practices for English learners and highlights many examples of these practices that appear throughout this book.

In Chapter 1 of this volume, I discuss the important role of educational factors in strengthening students' literacy learning. A key ingredient in the quality of instruction that students receive is the teaching practices that are used by individual teachers in their classrooms as they implement literacy lessons. In this chapter I delve more deeply into the specific teaching approaches that facilitate students' learning to read and write in a new language.

RESEARCH BACKGROUND

In their summary of the research on effective literacy teaching for second-language learners, Shanahan and Beck (2006) make several key points:

- The body of research on literacy instruction for students who are English learners is limited, and thus it is difficult to extract generalizations.
- Students' lack of oral proficiency in English may be responsible for the limited gains in literacy learning that were noted in various studies they reviewed.
- Combining effective literacy teaching approaches with oral-language development is recommended.
- The authors suggest that accommodations in instructional routines may be needed to improve effectiveness for English learners, but they do not have the data to describe what these adjustments might look like (Shanahan & Beck, 2006).

In a qualitative review of classroom practices in the same volume, the authors found it difficult to make generalizations about which instructional methods were most effective because of the small sample sizes and the limited scope of data collection. Many examples of scaffolding techniques, such as introducing new vocabulary, connecting students' background experiences, and using comprehension strategy instruction, were noted in the individual studies, however (August & Erickson, 2006).

A recent publication released by the U.S. Department of Education had five key research-based recommendations for effective literacy and language instruction for students who are English learners (Gersten et al., 2007). Although several of the recommendations focused on district- or schoolwide actions, recommendation 2, provide intensive small-group reading interventions; recommendation 3, provide extensive and varied vocabulary instruction; and recommendation 4, develop academic English, are especially important for individual teachers to keep in mind as they plan literacy instruction. As discussed throughout this book, academic vocabulary and language structures must be an integrated component of each literacy lesson for English learners.

Another review of the literature, by Genesee and colleagues, also examined instructional approaches with English learners (Genesee, Lindholm-Leary, Saunders, & Christian, 2005). For the purposes of their review, the authors categorized each research study by its major approach: (1) direct, (2) interactive, and (3) process based. Direct approaches focused on explicit instruction of the skills and strategies of literacy development. Interactive approaches involved working with peers, teachers, and other literacy models. Process-based approaches focused on holistic literacy events and deemphasized skill instruction. Although many interventions consisted of combinations of approaches, the authors found that the most effective instructional practices for English learners involved interactive approaches, or instruction that combined interactive with direct approaches (Genesee et al., 2005). The reasoning for these approaches working best was that interactive approaches allow for adaptation in the context of teaching; that they require students to discuss and apply the content, making it a language-development activity as well; and that direct approaches ensure that specific skills are mastered even within complex literacy tasks. Process approaches without direct or interactive components may be too complex for English learners to deconstruct and interpret.

One particular instructional activity that combined interactive and direct approaches noted in the Genesee et al. (2005) study was instructional conversations (Saunders & Goldenberg, 1999). In an instructional conversation, the teacher has a goal-directed, academic conversation with a small group of students. Research studies have found that instructional conversations, or instructional conversations combined with having students write personal experiences in literature logs, show increased learning results for English learners (Center for Research on Education, Diversity, and Excellence, 2002).

Although the Center for Research on Education, Diversity, and Excellence (CREDE) did not focus solely on effective instruction for English learners, it did highlight techniques that work especially well with this group of students. After a thorough review of the literature on instructional practices for diverse students, CREDE consolidated their findings into five standards for effective pedagogy. These included (1) teachers and students producing together (joint productive activity), (2) developing language and literacy across the curriculum, (3) making meaning, that is, connecting school to students' lives, (4) teaching complex thinking, and (5) teaching through conversation (CREDE, 2002). From the work of CREDE, a model of sheltered instruction emerged that provides a framework for teachers to scaffold instruction for students learning English. This model, the sheltered instruction observation protocol (SIOP), builds on the five standards for effective instruction and fleshes out instructional procedures to guide teachers' planning, implementation, and assessment (Echevarria, Vogt, & Short, 2008).

The SIOP model for sheltered instruction consists of 30 items that are used to make instruction more accessible to English learners, such as clearly defined content and language objectives and the use of hands-on materials (Echevarria, Short, & Powers, 2006). In turn, these items are clustered into eight overarching components to ensure that content is comprehensible for English learners. In a study of sixth- to eighth-grade students, the authors found greater gains in students' academic writing ability when they had received instruction using the sheltered protocol (Echevarria et al., 2006).

Several researchers have proposed constructs for effective instruction for English learners. Gersten and Jiménez (1994) grouped their ideas for literature instruction into eight components: (1) level of challenge, (2) student involvement, (3) support of success, (4) scaffolding/cognitive strategies, (5) mediation/feedback, (6) collaborative learning, (7) sheltered English techniques, and (8) respect for cultural diversity. Baker and colleagues (Baker, Gersten, Haager, & Dingle, 2006) tested an observation instrument for first-grade English learners based on scales of reading instruction designed for native English speakers but added items that addressed sheltered instruction. Observation items were related to modeling, clarifying relationships among concepts, prompting for strategy use, specific feedback, modifying instruction, clear speech and nonverbal support, and the strategic use of students' home language, among others. They found a significant correlation and a relatively strong relation between instructional practices on their measure and English learners' reading growth (Baker et al., 2006). This research builds on established knowledge in the field of second-language learning that guides teachers to connect instruction to students' current level of understanding and to tailor the language in the classroom so that it is comprehensible (Díaz-Rico & Weed, 2002; Peregoy & Boyle, 2001).

De Jong and Harper (2005) describe the complex set of knowledge and skills that mainstream teachers need in order to provide effective instruction for English learners: background knowledge about language and culture and their role in literacy learning; the disposition to facilitate language learning; being cultural facilitators; holding high expectations for English learners; using effective practices to make the content comprehensible; and providing feedback to students (de Jong & Harper, 2005). In a qualitative study of two sixth-grade teachers, Yoon (2007) found greater participation of English learners when the teacher took on the role of cultural facilitator, as described by de Jong and Harper. Rather than focusing on the specific pedagogical approaches of the teachers, Yoon (2007) noted that teachers who included English learners as full participants in class, who modeled an interest and support for students' culture, and who encouraged mainstream students to support English learners' learning in class were able to elicit greater active participation in class. Clearly, being aware of the linguistic and cultural backgrounds of English learners is one aspect of providing effective instruction.

In summary, the research base, although limited, points to the use of instructional strategies in literacy that have been found to be effective with native speakers but acknowledges that teaching for English learners must go beyond "good teaching" to particularly address the linguistic and cultural contexts of second-language students. Care must be taken to provide clear and systematic instruction that students understand, to provide many opportunities for students to engage with teachers and other literacy models, to receive instruction in language development as well as literacy skills, and to be actively involved with the learning material. These key ideas are expanded throughout the rest of this chapter.

STRATEGIES FOR SUPPORTING ENGLISH LEARNERS

During my three decades in education, I have spent about half the time as an elementary school teacher and half the time as a teacher educator. In the many classes, professional development workshops, and in-class coaching I have done, teachers have appreciated learning many of the sheltered techniques that have emerged from the aforementioned research. Because there are numerous ways to support English learners during classroom instruction, teachers have found it helpful to have a schema for organizing the variety of instructional practices found to be effective. In this way, it becomes clear *why* a particular teaching strategy supports student learning, and teachers can use their own ingenuity and professional skills to augment the example strategies in each category. I have called the organizational framework I present "strategies to support English learners," and it categorizes many of the research-based instructional techniques into four larger components: (1) explicit and systematic instruction, (2) engaging in a learning community, (3) highlighting connections, and (4) active construction of knowledge (Bear, Helman, Templeton, Invernizzi, & Johnston, 2007). Figure 12.1 lists the instructional support strategies, clustered into the four overarching components. There is more common sense than scientific formula in my classification schema; at times an instructional strategy may fit easily into more than one category. I offer it as a suggested framework and not as a rigid checklist. The "strategies to support English learners" structure is a guide for teachers in understanding scaffolding approaches and selecting particular strategies that will improve the clarity and effectiveness of their instruction. Teachers have found that it provides a helpful menu for guiding their instruction and have identified additional instructional strategies in their own practice that fit under each of the overarching categories.

One task that I ask teachers to do is to use the list of support strategies to improve on a current literacy lesson that they do with English learners. First, I have teachers observe a lesson and note which, if any, of the support strategies they saw implemented. Next, they consider ways in which the lesson was made more effective by the use of these strategies. Finally, I ask teachers to select two to three of the support

Engaging in a Learning Community		Explicit and Systematic Instruction
• Low-Anxiety Environment • Student-to-Student Interactions • High Expectations • Student-to-Teacher Connections		• Modeling • Visuals and Contextualization • Guided Practice • Metacognition • Instructional-Level Teaching • Focus on Language and Vocabulary • Simple to Complex • Clustering
	Strategies to Support English Learners	
Highlighting Connections		Active Construction of Knowledge
• Whole to Part to Whole • Oral and Written Language • Schema Building • Graphic Organizers • Personal Experiences • Background Knowledge		• Hands-On Activities • Purposeful Activities • Time to Talk • Modified Questioning Strategies • Multiple Intelligences • Music and Rhythm • Total Physical Response

FIGURE 12.1. Strategies to support English learners.

strategies to add to the lesson to enhance its power. Although it is not realistic or desirable to use all of the support strategies in any given lesson, teachers have found that the lessons that include more of these approaches tend to be more engaging and comprehensible for students.

In each chapter of this book, the author/researchers provide the latest research on a particular aspect of literacy instruction with English learners. Authors also describe examples of how to implement their suggested practices in the elementary classroom. The ideas shared throughout the book represent many of the strategies listed in Figure 12.1. In the next sections, I shine a spotlight on the teaching practices mentioned throughout the book and make connections to the support strategies they exemplify. This exercise is a good reminder of the many excellent ideas presented in the book and is also a way to apply the concept of support strategies to various aspects of literacy instruction.

Explicit and Systematic Instruction

Communicating a rich, clear, and precise message is an important aspect of effective instruction for English learners. Students are unlikely to fully understand the content or processes in the literacy classroom simply by hearing a quick stream of words. In the following examples taken from the chapters in this book, the authors demonstrate a variety of ways that teachers can create explicit and systematic instruction.

When teachers demonstrate, or *model*, they provide an example that students can observe in rich detail and follow. Students are able to see and hear how to create a specific product or use the language and literacy behaviors being taught in class. In Chapter 2 of this volume, Au describes how teachers might model oral and written responses to literature for students in order to scaffold their learning of the same behaviors. Montero and Kuhn, in Chapter 8, share an activity called "reading while listening." This activity provides students with a model of fluent reading as they read along so that they will better understand the fluency level they are working toward. In Chapter 9, Brock and colleagues elucidate how comprehension strategies can be modeled so that students can begin to use them on their own.

Visuals and *contextualization* are ways of clarifying instruction with graphic support, real-life objects, simulations, and field experiences so that students have as many clues as possible to gather an understanding of the topic being studied. Many authors in this volume have described examples of visuals, from using illustrated word banks to learn new vocabulary and language patterns (Chapter 3) to providing accessible visual alphabet materials for students (Chapter 6). Throughout the book authors have encouraged the use of pictures, diagrams, realia, and physical actions to motivate students and clarify key vocabulary and new learning.

After a concept or skill has been introduced, it is critical to provide *guided practice* for students in applying the skill with support. The teacher observes and evaluates student learning, gives feedback, and reinforces the students as they practice the new behavior. In Chapter 2, Au explains how teachers can coach students to apply the strategies they have just learned as they read their texts and then can practice these behaviors with a partner. Dutro and Helman (Chapter 3) describe many ways for students to practice oral language structures, and we also set up an "I do, we do, you do" structure so that students first receive modeling, then practice the skill in a guided setting, and finally have an opportunity for independent practice. In Chapter 6, I outline how students chant along during shared reading of texts and how to help students use personal readers to reread familiar texts in a guided setting. In Chapter 8, Montero and Kuhn explain how the repeated reading of text is an effective activity for fluency development. While students participate in guided practice activities, it is critical for teachers to provide explicit feedback on their performance. Garcia and DeNicolo (Chapter 4) describe this process for students who are learning to improve their writing.

Metacognition involves "thinking out loud" about the processes one is using while accomplishing a literacy activity. Authors in this book outline several examples of metacognition: In Chapter 2, Au describes how teachers use a think-aloud procedure to help students arrive at a good title for their stories; in Chapter 4, Garcia and DeNicolo encourage teachers to use metacognition to compare letter–sound correspondences and the meanings of words across languages. Teachers are invited to think out loud with students as they learn new phonics skills (Helman, Chapter 7) and as they apply comprehension strategies (Brock et al., Chapter 9). In Chapter 10, Templeton provides explicit language to use in think-aloud activities for students during a "walking through words" lesson.

Even with the best support and scaffolding techniques, students will not profit from the instruction in the classroom if it is too difficult for them. *Instructional-level teaching* means that teachers assess their students and match classroom tasks and materials to their developmental levels. Chapter 5 by Bear and Smith provides a framework for using students' developmental spelling to assess their literacy levels and form instructional groupings. Instructional-level teaching is also elucidated in many other chapters—from the description of a kindergarten teacher who scaffolds writing instruction to match all of her students' needs (Au, Chapter 2) to taking anecdotal records to match instruction to students' oral and written language levels (Garcia & DeNicolo, Chapter 4). Helman (Chapters 6 and 7) and Montero and Kuhn (Chapter 8) encourage teachers to structure opportunities for students to read books at their instructional and independent levels. Throughout this volume, teachers are asked to continually assess the language and literacy levels of their students in order to tailor instruction to a level of challenge that is "just right"—not too easy and not too hard—for their students.

In order for English learners to comprehend the material they are presented in class, teachers need to *focus on language and vocabulary*. At times this involves modifying the language teachers use in class, such as making sure that the language is comprehensible by monitoring their speed and articulation, facing the listener, emphasizing key words, and avoiding confusing idioms such as "in over her head." Other times a focus on language and vocabulary will mean explicitly teaching key vocabulary words and language structures, such as is modeled in Chapter 3. Other examples of a focus on language and vocabulary throughout this volume include Au's suggestion in Chapter 2 that teachers consider phrasing language in culturally familiar ways for students. In Chapter 6, teachers are encouraged to connect literature and content-area studies so that vocabulary is repeated and interconnected in class. Chapter 7 describes the importance of learning the meaning of words that are studied in the phonics program. Teachers are encouraged to help students learn unknown words in word study activities and to adapt lessons if they contain too many new words.

The focus on language and vocabulary continues throughout later chapters in the book, as well. In Chapter 8, Montero and Kuhn impress on us the need to develop oral language and comprehension while English learners practice their fluency. In Chapter 9, Brock and colleagues describe the importance of checking and clarifying students' understanding of key vocabulary words to facilitate their comprehension of the text. In Chapter 10, Templeton encourages teachers to clarify spelling–meaning relationships for students and to use vocabulary notebooks to record interesting words and spelling–meaning families. Clearly, a focus on language and vocabulary is essential for students to be able to understand and learn from the material they encounter in class.

Another way to make instruction more explicit and systematic is for teachers to move from *simple to complex* topics and procedures. Often, tasks can be broken down into sequential steps, or a scaled-down example can be outlined prior to sharing more complex models. Several examples of this process are highlighted in this volume. First off, in Chapter 2 Au describes the use of minilessons in readers' and writers' workshops. Minilessons are a way to show a simplified version of an activity before students go off to apply it in their own practice. In Chapter 3, Dutro and Helman create varying levels of sentence frames for students at different levels of oral-language proficiency. These sentence frames move from simple to more complex language structures. In Chapter 7, I encourage teachers to follow a systematic sequence of phonics instruction and to start with the simplest contrasts first. In the upper-level word study described in Chapter 10, Templeton communicates the logic of the English spelling system without overwhelming us with its incredible complexity. We are shown how to build increasingly complex words from word roots and affixes, and, as we examine cognates, the focus is first on those that are most clear and direct and later moves to more advanced cognate relationships.

A final suggested strategy for making instruction more systematic and explicit is to *cluster* pieces of information that go together, or organize activities into cohesive sections or chunks. For example, by dividing the strategies to support English learners into four components, I hope the material has become more accessible and understandable to you. In this volume several examples of clustering have been presented. In Chapter 6, thematic studies are suggested as a way to bring related concepts and skills together into manageable bits. Creating charts of simple directions for classroom tasks is described in Chapter 7. Templeton suggests in Chapter 10 that related words should be learned together; when students learn one word in a family, they learn many related words, as well.

Providing systematic and explicit instruction is a key aspect of making classroom instruction accessible to English learners. The multiple strategies presented throughout this volume enhance teachers' repertoires for creating clear and understandable lessons.

Engaging in a Learning Community

Students need to know that they are valued members of a classroom community and that their voices and participation are an essential part of the functioning of the group. All people thrive when they are able to apply what they are learning with others and when they are respected and encouraged to perform at high levels. Throughout this book, chapter authors illustrate strategies that help to create a learning community and to make positive connections among all its participants.

Setting a *low-anxiety environment* allows students to make mistakes and try out new learning. In this atmosphere, students are encouraged to speak up when they don't understand a vocabulary word or a concept or skill they are learning. Deeper thinking and reflection flourish in this learning-focused environment, and all classroom members may be called on to support each other's learning. In Chapter 2, Au describes this as establishing a collaborative tone and inviting students in. In Chapter 4, Garcia and DeNicolo encourage teachers to create predictable routines that establish consistency and a sense of safety. In Chapter 9, Brock and colleagues describe the importance of having students share their confusion and of teachers' supporting all students' literacy attempts. These procedures help establish a low-anxiety environment.

Another way to enhance a literacy learning community is to create opportunities for *student-to-student interactions* within partnerships, cooperative learning teams, and small-group activities. When students are guided to engage in positive interactions in class, they develop relationships, practice skills, and learn from each other. Many student-to-student interaction structures are embedded throughout this book, including cooperative group activities, peer tutoring, book clubs, peer conferences, cross-age reading, and partner activities. Student-to-student connections can also be made in the large group as well; Au describes in Chapter 2 the community sharing of book club discussions. Student-led discussions provide an opportunity for building interpersonal, as well as academic, skills and set the tone for the classroom as a learning community.

For all students to feel engaged and challenged in a learning community, they need to know that teachers hold *high expectations* for them. These expectations are communicated in what teachers say and do with individual students in the classroom. In Chapter 11, Pennington and Salas describe what can happen when a teacher does not hold high expectations for her English-learning students. In other chapters, we hear positive examples of this practice, such as in Chapter 2, when Au describes how teachers set the tone for a classroom "filled with teachers." In Chapter 5, Bear and Smith describe the case of a student who is behind and the teachers who work diligently to move her ahead to the next step in her literacy development. In Chapter 7 and throughout this text, teachers are called on to check for understanding frequently. Authentic assessments help teachers to set appropriately challenging goals for each student. Two professional development techniques that might help teachers set high expectations for students are explored within the chapters as well. In Chapter 9, Brock and colleagues recommend that teachers videotape their teaching and discuss them in small collegial groups. In Chapter 11, Pennington and Salas recommend that teachers seek out evaluations of their own teaching. Both of these activities have the potential to help teachers see whether they are limiting the potential of students by not maintaining high enough expectations.

Another way to enhance interactions in the learning community is through *student-to-teacher connections*. These bonds develop when teachers spend time with students and learn about their home experiences, families, and interests. The bonds grow when teachers work persistently with students even as they experience difficulties or setbacks. In Chapter 2, Au describes how small-group work in class not only increases students' literacy achievement but also helps establish positive relationships between the teacher and students. In addition, both Au and the authors of Chapter 9 suggest that teachers should make themselves available for individual conferences and discussions with students, as some students may feel uncomfortable speaking out in a group when they have a question and as it is not always clear in a big group whether students have clearly understood a lesson.

In Chapter 6 I describe the technique of using students' names in the emergent literacy classroom. Hearing their names used in fun and positive ways in class also helps build a bond between the students and the teacher. In Chapter 11, Pennington and Salas describe how getting to know Carlos and his family helped his teacher have a more positive attitude about his potential and helped her create instruction that better matched his needs and strengths. The authors encourage teachers to become involved in the neighborhoods of their students as one way to strengthen student-to-teacher connections.

Creating a learning community with strong connections among students, teachers, and families is important for motivating students and supporting their success. We see many examples of practical strategies for engaging in a positive learning community throughout this book.

Highlighting Connections

New learning takes hold most easily when students can relate what is being presented in class to the conceptual and academic understandings they already possess. When teachers connect their curricula to the home languages, literacy strengths, personal experiences, and background knowledge of their students, it allows students to build on their current understandings and to see the interrelated nature of academic studies. The authors in this book find many ways to help English learners get the "big picture" by highlighting connections in literacy instruction, as the following examples illustrate.

Whole to part to whole instruction in literacy takes place when skills or subcomponents of reading and writing are introduced and practiced through whole pieces of text, such as books, poems, songs, or articles. Instruction starts with a whole text, then a skill is pulled out for a mini-lesson or practice, and finally the skill is applied in context again. In this way, the purpose of individual literacy skills is always connected to real reading and writing. In Chapters 2, 5, 6, and 7 of this book, we see how students are taught the alphabetical, phonics, and phonological skills appropriate to their level of literacy development with lessons that begin and end by using cohesive pieces of texts so that students make a connection to authentic reading and writing tasks. In Chapter 9, Brock and colleagues describe the helpful process of starting with a whole text, then identifying and studying particular words that are difficult to understand, and finally returning to the text to read the words in context again.

An important connection for students to see is how *oral and written language* match up. This happens when speech is written down and examined, when enlarged print is read together and discussed, or when students read out loud and point to words as they are being read. The authors in this book illustrate several examples of making oral- and written-language connections in literacy instruction. These include providing opportunities for students to use their own developmental writing as they capture personal stories and matching oral to written language by reading memorized poems. Chapter 6 highlights the instructional practice of language experience dictations, in which students tell a story and the teacher writes it down for future rereading. In Chapter 8, Montero and Kuhn describe how to modify the language experience approach by adding photography or bilingual text.

Schema building is a process of connecting new information to other conceptual categories within students' knowledge base. For example, students who are learning about word endings such as *-ment* or *-tion* will profit from connecting these new word parts to other, simpler word endings they may be familiar with, such as *-ed* or *-er*. Then the category of word endings in students' mental file cabinets will be expanded. Many examples of schema building are presented throughout the book. Dutro and Helman (Chapter 3) describe sentence frames that help students build schemata for sentence construction in English. Chapter 6 points out how read-aloud stories can be used to help students create schema for various story structures. Concept sorts are also described in which students of all ages learn vocabulary words and make connections among related objects or ideas. In Chapter 9, Brock and colleagues help students build schemata by providing prereading, during-reading, and after-reading instruction while studying texts. In Chapter 10, Templeton encourages teachers to discuss the relationship among words from a "family," such as *finish, final, finite,* and *infinite*, to develop schemata for individual word roots.

Graphic organizers are visual tools that help students organize their thinking to see conceptual relationships. A Venn diagram, a story map, a double-entry diary, and a chart or table format are all examples of graphic organizers that may be helpful during literacy instruction. In Chapter 9, Brock and colleagues describe the use of a T chart connected to text reading—one example of how to use graphic organizers to help English learners make connections in their literacy curriculum.

Connecting to personal experiences is another powerful way to help students more thoroughly understand a new skill, concept, or idea. Teachers do this when they point out how students' experiences in the classroom or at home relate to the academic content under study in texts. Bridges between the personal and the academic provide an emotional link that supports student learning. In Chapter 2, Au encourages the bridging of personal experiences to academic learning by using the experience–text relationship approach in literature study. In Chapter 3, Dutro and Helman use students' personal experiences to create language-building activities that stretch and engage them in learning English. Pennington and Salas (Chapter 11) make two suggestions for connecting with students' personal experiences: Provide time for students to be in groups based on personal interests and interview family members about the personal experiences of their children.

Connecting to background knowledge is a final example of how teachers might highlight connections for students in the literacy classroom. When teachers build on what students know in their home language, when they make cross-linguistic comparisons, and when they explicitly build on what has already been learned in class, teachers help students relate to and understand new information. In this book several ideas for building on background knowledge are presented. Throughout the book, teachers are encouraged to assess students in their home languages to find out what background literacy knowledge they bring to school. In Chapter 4, Garcia and DeNicolo suggest the use of culturally relevant texts so that assessments are not confounded by a mismatch in cultural background knowledge. Bear and Smith (Chapter 5) advise teachers to compare students' home languages and English so that they can better build on the literate understandings that students bring to class. In Chapter 6, I suggest that emergent readers profit from hearing texts in their home languages before hearing them in English. Templeton (Chapter 10) provides an in-depth outline of how to look for and build on cognates between English and the home language to build on the strength of students' background knowledge.

Highlighting connections for students is crucial so that they truly understand the myriad skills and academic content that are involved in a new language. This book illustrates a variety of ways that teachers can build on what students already know and can present information in a manner that aids their conceptual understanding.

Active Construction of Knowledge

When English learners have an opportunity to actively engage with the academic content in class, such as through hands-on activities and multimodal experiences, there is a better chance that they will understand, remember, and be able to apply what they are learning. Throughout this text, chapter authors present examples of ways to engage students actively with academic learning and through these activities find out whether and where students are experiencing any confusion.

Hands-on activities provide students with opportunities to manipulate learning materials, create projects, go on field trips, and participate in experiments or simulations. Students get to *do* instead of simply *listen*. Some examples of hands-on activities that are presented in this book include my recommendation in Chapter 6 that students participate in hands-on experiences and then write about them and my suggestion in Chapter 7 that students use hands-on sorts and games for word study. In Chapter 10, Templeton encourages students to create their own "dictionary of possible words."

Purposeful activities take place when students can immediately use what they are learning in a real-world task. For example, a student may learn to write in a particular genre and then use that knowledge to create a contribution to a class-made book. In Chapter 2 of this book, Au describes readers' and writers' workshops in linguistically diverse classrooms. This workshop time provides many opportunities for students to read and write for authentic audiences and purposes. In Chapter 3, Dutro and Helman show how language-learning activities can be applied to essential tasks that exist in the real world. In Chapter 6, I illustrate how a thematic unit in a kindergarten class not only teaches literacy skills but is also a vehicle for enhancing social learning within the classroom community. In Chapter 8, Montero and Kuhn highlight the importance of independent reading, a purposeful activity, to help students develop fluent and automatic reading.

When students have *time to talk* in class, they are actively processing the content being studied. Students share their understandings with others, and this helps them link their background experiences to what is being learned. Many of the chapter authors in this volume advocate for opportunities for students to converse in class: In Chapter 2, Au describes the format of talk-story participation and small-group instruction so that students have venues for talking. Dutro and Helman in Chapter 3 suggest a "talking stick" to facilitate students' turn taking. All of the chapters within this volume focus on the need for students to talk to each other and with the teacher to practice and experiment with the content and to show what they know. Authors encourage teachers to set up partner and small-group activities, as well as to ensure that all students' voices are heard in the classroom.

Modified questioning strategies allow teachers to tailor verbal requests to students based on their language proficiency. In this way, all students can be engaged at the appropriate level of linguistic complexity. Students with very limited proficiency in English, as well as those who are refining their academic-language abilities, are able to participate in the classroom discourse when questioning is differentiated. For example, students with limited proficiency may be asked to point or provide a one-word response. As students' language proficiency advances, so do the kinds of questions asked and the level of responses expected. Chapter 3 by Dutro and Helman focuses in great depth on the topic of how to adjust classroom language requirements to students' oral proficiency levels.

Working with *multiple intelligences* is a way to help students master skills and concepts through various learning modes such as discussing, graphing, moving, acting, constructing, illustrating, and writing. Garcia and DeNicolo (Chapter 4) highlight an example of this when they describe using the home language, drawing, and acting out the content of new learning as ways to informally assess students.

Using *music and rhythm* helps students learn and remember the material being studied because they use the beat as an aid to their memory. Students chant, sing, clap along, echo, or tap the beat to poems, stories, and shared readings. In Chapter 6 of this volume, I describe how teachers use songs and rhymes to develop phonological awareness and phonics skills.

Total physical response is a helpful technique for students who are learning English and can profit from nonverbal cues and kinesthetic learning. Students are asked to move, touch, point, copy, follow along, demonstrate, and role-play with their bodies. In Chapters 6 and 7, I describe ways to incorporate movement into phonics activities, such as sorting activities, practicing sight words, or learning the sounds of letters.

The active construction of knowledge helps English learners to better understand, practice, and apply the skills and strategies they are learning. Active learning also keeps English learners from "tuning out" or facing an overload of input in the classroom. When students demonstrate their knowledge of curricular concepts, teachers are able to check for understanding and provide additional support to individuals who are having difficulties.

CONCLUSION

Providing research-based literacy instruction for all students is our first goal as literacy educators. This goal is not sufficient in and of itself, however, to meet the needs of English-learning students. Tailoring literacy instruction for English learners within individual lessons in the classroom is essential to ensure that students understand, are engaged with, and can apply the material they are learning. English learners need explicit and systematic instruction in which teachers model, supplement lessons with visuals and artifacts, make the content comprehensible, focus on vocabulary and language development, and provide opportunities for guided practice. Students must feel involved in the classroom community and know that they are expected to participate and succeed. Students need to connect what they are learning to their background knowledge and personal experiences so that they can build on and expand their academic schemata. When English learners actively construct new knowledge through hands-on and purposeful activities, learn and demonstrate academic content in multiple manners, and have opportunities to talk about what they are learning in academic interactions, scaffolds are constructed to support their success.

Throughout this book, chapter authors make connections between the research base in their field and the instructional practices that flow from this research. Each chapter models many ways to support English learners during classroom instruction using a variety of scaffolding and engagement techniques. I encourage you to try out these instructional activities and to reflect on *why* it is that they are so supportive to the English-learning students you teach. With adjustments to the explicitness, clarity, and engagement requirements of your lessons, you can open doors of understanding to students learning English. By creating structures for interaction and setting high expectations for all students' participation and success in your classroom, you also invite students through the door to join you and your class in an engaging academic learning community.

REFERENCES

August, D., & Erickson, F. (2006). Qualitative studies of classroom and school practices. In D. August & T. Shanahan (Eds.), *Developing literacy in second-language learners: Report of the National Literacy Panel on Language-Minority Children and Youth* (pp. 489–522). Mahwah, NJ: Erlbaum.

Baker, S. K., Gersten, R., Haager, D., & Dingle, M. (2006). Teaching practice and the reading growth of first-grade English learners: Validation of an observation instrument. *Elementary School Journal, 107*(2), 199–219.

Bear, D. R., Helman, L., Templeton, S., Invernizzi, M., & Johnston, F. (2007). *Words their way with English learners: Word study for phonics, vocabulary, and spelling instruction.* Upper Saddle River, NJ: Pearson/Merrill Prentice Hall.

Center for Research on Education, Diversity, and Excellence. (2002). *Research evidence: Five standards for effective pedagogy and student outcomes* (Technical Report No. G1). Santa Cruz: University of California.

de Jong, E. J., & Harper, C. A. (2005). Preparing mainstream teachers for English language learners: Is being a good teacher good enough? *Teacher Education Quarterly, 32*(2), 101–124.

Díaz-Rico, L. T., & Weed, K. Z. (2002). *The crosscultural, language, and academic development handbook: A complete K–12 reference guide.* Boston: Allyn & Bacon.

Echevarria, J., Short, D., & Powers, K. (2006). School reform and standards-based education: A model for English language learners. *Journal of Educational Research, 99*(4), 195–210.

Echevarria, J., Vogt, M. E., & Short, D. J. (2008). *Making content comprehensible for English language learners: The SIOP model* (3rd ed.). Boston: Allyn & Bacon.

Genesee, F., Lindholm-Leary, K., Saunders, W., & Christian, D. (2005). English language learners in U. S. schools: An overview of research findings. *Journal of Education for Students Placed at Risk, 10*(4), 363–385.

Gersten, R., Baker, S. K., Shanahan, T., Linan-Thompson, S., Collins, P., & Scarcella, R. (2007). *Effective literacy and English language instruction for Eng-*

lish learners in the elementary grades: A practice guide (NCEE 2007-4011). Washington, DC: U.S. Department of Education Institute of Education Sciences, National Center for Education Evaluation and Regional Assistance. Retrieved June 15, 2008, from *http://ies.ed.gov/ncee/wwc/publications/practiceguides/#ell_pg*.

Gersten, R., & Jiménez, R. T. (1994). A delicate balance: Enhancing literature instruction for students of English as a second language. *Reading Teacher, 47*(6), 438–449.

Peregoy, S. F., & Boyle, O. F. (2001). *Reading, writing, and learning in ESL: A resource book for K–12 teachers.* New York: Longman.

Saunders, W., & Goldenberg, C. (1999). *The effects of instructional conversations and literature logs on the story comprehension and thematic understanding of English proficient and limited English proficient students.* Santa Cruz: University of California Center for Research on Education, Diversity, and Excellence.

Shanahan, T., & Beck, I. L. (2006). Effective literacy teaching for English language learners. In D. August & T. Shanahan (Eds.), *Developing literacy in second-language learners: Report of the National Literacy Panel on Language-Minority Children and Youth* (pp. 415–488). Mahwah, NJ: Erlbaum.

Yoon, B. (2007). Offering or Limiting Opportunities: Teachers' roles and approaches to English language learners' participation in literacy activities. *Reading Teacher, 61*(3), 216–225.

CHAPTER 13

Literacy Development with English Learners
Concluding Thoughts

LORI HELMAN

> Teachers in multiethnic, multilingual classrooms should adopt the attitude that the room is filled with teachers. Not only other adults, but also each student in the class, is a potential teacher.
> —KATHRYN H. AU (p. 46, this volume)

When visitors enter Lily's third-grade classroom, they notice right away that the students are on task, engaged, and working to do their best. Students are clustered in discussion groups, reading with partners, or working in small-group directed lessons with the teacher. Most of Lily's students are learning English as a new language; her students come from Hmong, English, Somali, and Spanish-speaking backgrounds. Their time in the United States varies, and students range in reading skills from beginning to intermediate readers. Despite this range, Lily has structured ways for the students to read, write, discuss, illustrate, practice, and collaborate on literacy tasks throughout the morning. One reason she is able to do this is that she has created a learning community with high expectations for all. In Lily's class we truly see "that the room is filled with teachers."

Lily's third-grade classroom is set up with many reading and writing materials—some trade books, some commercial textbooks, and some student-created materials. There are also many reference materials around the room: charts outlining classroom procedures and the steps involved in particular literacy activities, such as "Steps for Writer's Workshop," as well as picture dictionaries, reference books, and lists of useful words. Lily teaches reading and writing by assessing her students' development and then working in small groups to differentiate the materials and minilessons she uses for their instruction. A visitor often hears her model her thinking out loud or point out the thinking of a student, such as, "Did you notice something Maleeah did? She has made a connection to a book. So does everyone agree this is where the solution goes?" Lily's questions tend to focus on higher level concepts such as the following examples: "Why? Can you explain?" "What will we do if this comes up in our work group?" "What do you notice about ...?" "What does majority rule mean?" Because her students are developing proficiency in English, Lily also integrates vocabulary work into each small- and large-group lesson that she conducts. She explicitly focuses on the essential words that students must know in order to conceptually understand the topic.

Perhaps you have read this volume to help you, like Lily, become an exemplary teacher of English learners when you join the teaching profession. Or possibly you are an experienced teacher looking to find some new methods or ideas to enhance your teaching skills for linguistically diverse students. It may be that the changing demographics of students in U.S. classrooms and your own school is causing you to rethink the teaching methods and materials you have used for many years in order to better respond to your students' learning possibilities. No matter what your context or background, I hope that this volume has succeeded in three important tasks: (1) highlighting the complex and comprehensive framework needed to effectively develop literacy with English learners, (2) recommending research-based practices in literacy instruction with English learners, and (3) helping you to envision the richness of literacy-learning elementary classrooms with linguistically diverse students. The various chapters in this book explore *what* needs to be taught in second-language literacy instruction, the research base on *why* it is important, and the specific instructional procedures for *how* to do it. Because of the complexity of sociocultural, psychological, linguistic, and educational factors that influence students' literacy learning, the authors of this volume balance multiple theoretical perspectives and seek multileveled practical approaches to accomplishing the goal of literacy success for all students.

Throughout this book one recurrent and troubling theme has been the need for additional research on which instructional methods and contexts best support English learners' literacy learning. Time and again, authors have lamented the fact that although a substantial body of literacy research exists on native English speakers, the research on students who have yet to develop oral proficiency in English is limited. Most literacy-focused research reviews conclude with the call for more efforts to study the effectiveness of instructional practices that are successful in classrooms with English learners. Despite the unquestionable need for more research, chapter authors in this volume have been able to share what *is* known from the qualitative and quantitative research and to present the research base within the comprehensive framework presented in Chapter 1: sociocultural, psychological, linguistic, and educational contexts. Using their deep academic and instructional knowledge, authors have connected the research base to teaching ideas that have shown success in elementary classrooms with English learners. In the next section, I review and highlight some of the key ideas that run through the course of this book.

KEY IDEAS WOVEN THROUGHOUT THE BOOK

As you have read this book, perhaps you found yourself revisiting the same idea or a variation of an idea from one chapter to the next. So, after reading many of the chapters, you notice patterns in the research and instructional advice you are hearing. This is a good thing. Instead of wondering how you will ever learn all of the instructional skills and dispositions needed to be an effective literacy instructor for English learners, you begin to see how several foundational structures and methods can guide your teaching. As I study this volume, I also notice patterns that consistently surface throughout. The six essential ideas I have gleaned include: (1) know your students, their level of language and literacy development, their linguistic backgrounds, and their cultural values; (2) use research-based literacy instruction; (3) create a learning community with high expectations and many opportunities for participation; (4) tailor instruction for English learners; (5) integrate skills and meaning making; and (6) reflect on your teaching practices. These key ideas are manifested in diverse ways throughout the chapters, yet their core principles remain consistent. I now briefly expand on each of these threads.

Know Your Students

To paraphrase Jim Cummins (1998), "If teachers are not learning a lot about their students, students are probably not learning a lot from them." To learn about their students, teachers may use informal measures such as interviews and surveys relating to their cultural backgrounds and interests; authentic assessments to evaluate their background language and literacy knowledge; regular performance assessments to monitor their literacy learning and language development; and more formal measures to identify or screen for reading and writing problems. A consistent message presented throughout this volume is that students' literacy and language development, as well as their cultural backgrounds, *do* matter in designing powerful instruction. Authors point out that English language learner (ELL) is a broad term representing students with a wide range of strengths and learning needs. It is critical for teachers to use assessment data to understand what students know and can do and for these data to be used to teach students at their levels of developmental and language proficiency.

Use Research-Based Literacy Instruction

The goal of this volume is to connect research in second-language literacy instruction with practical teaching strategies. The organizational structure of the book revolves around the key areas outlined by the National Reading Panel—phonemic awareness, phonics, fluency, comprehension, and vocabulary—with additional chapters specifically addressing the sociocultural contexts of teaching English learners (National Institute of Child Health and Human Development, 2000). Each chapter makes a strong case for basing classroom instruction on the research literature in each area of reading development. Throughout, authors share the research base so that readers understand not only *what* and *how* but also *why* this type of instruction is important.

Create a Learning Community with High Expectations and Many Opportunities for Participation

At the beginning of this chapter I quoted Kathryn Au's line from Chapter 2 in this volume about a class that "is filled with teachers." I can't think of a better way to describe a recurrent theme in these pages: that in order for English learners to succeed, they need to have many opportunities to participate in class and share their strengths. To reach their potential, teachers must set high expectations for student success, and students must gain confidence and mastery in the skills and concepts they are learning. This powerful idea emerged over and over again in the variety of instructional grouping arrangements presented in each chapter and in the suggestions for how teachers could use group activities to practice skills with students, such as in the concept of "I do—we do—you do" in Chapter 3. Chapter authors describe ways to design instructional groupings based on students' developmental understandings, to personally confer with students, to guide readers' and writers' workshops, and to use partnerships and cross-age tutors. Classroom structures are set up to encourage collaboration and sharing, and each student's strengths allow him or her to be a teacher in one form or another.

Tailor Instruction for English Learners

An important point that is made in each chapter of this book is that generic "good teaching" is not sufficient for effective instruction with English learners. Because ELLs are learning English, they need extra support to make the content comprehensible for them through clear and explicit instruction and the use of visuals and hands-on materials. Language goals must be a part of every literacy lesson. ELLs bring strengths—a background language and possibly home literacy skills—that may be used as a bridge to literacy in English. ELLs may need adaptations to generic literacy activities, such as explicit vocabulary and academic language study or shortened periods of instructional time when intense concentration is needed. The chapter authors elucidate many ways to provide tailored literacy instruction for English learners—from building on the first language to making cross-linguistic comparisons of the home language and English to building in visual and cultural supports for concept and skill development. Chapter 12 alone provides dozens of ways for instruction to accommodate the background knowledge, experiences, and challenges of English learners learning to read and write in a new language.

Integrate Skills and Meaning Making

There is always a danger that students who are learning a new language will memorize rote skills without having the oral proficiency to understand what they are learning and how these skills apply in real-world tasks. For example, English learners may be able to memorize dozens of high-frequency sight words without knowing what they mean or how they may be used in a sentence. A consistent theme throughout the chapters of this volume is the importance of connecting meaning and purpose to the skills being taught. Chapter authors discuss ways to connect oral language to the printed word, how to move between phonics instruction and reading whole texts, how to use students' developmental writing to guide word study, and the importance of never abandoning a need for comprehension when learning decoding skills. From the earliest readers to those at more advanced levels, a focus on meaning making must be front and center with English learners. For example, chapter authors highlight ways to develop conceptual understanding even before students can read texts on their own. At the other end of the spectrum, cognate studies are an example of combining word analysis skills with exploring meaning within the orthography.

Reflect on Teaching Practices

A final thread that weaves throughout this book is the idea that teachers will improve their work with English learners when they reflect on their own beliefs and dispositions and examine their own teaching practices. From the first chapter through the last, suggestions abound for how teachers can meet regularly with colleagues to share insights, analyze data, view videotapes of teaching, and seek out feedback. Teachers are encouraged to ask students and their families what is working in the classroom instruction and in what ways student learning can best be enhanced. Chapters 2 and 11, in particular, invite teachers to consider how their cultural, linguistic, and socioeconomic values influence the interactions and expectations they have for linguistically diverse students. In the end, teachers are asked to continue to be learners throughout their careers, to learn from the students and communities in their classrooms, to adjust instruction based on assessments of student learning, and to stay updated on the most current professional literature in literacy instruction for diverse students.

QUESTIONS AND NEXT STEPS

At the beginning of this book, you were asked to write down some of the successful literacy teaching experiences you have had with English learners. I hope that you have had a chance to share these thoughts with colleagues as you studied this book. You were also invited to come up with several questions you had about literacy instruction at the elementary grades with English learners. Before you opened this book, you may have wondered, as have many of my graduate students at the university:

- How can we help our teaching be more specific to ELLs?
- How do we know what to teach in language and literacy?
- How do we accommodate multiple levels of language proficiency?
- What does instruction in skills look like for ELLs?
- How do we find resources to meet the needs of English learners?
- How do we learn more about our students' cultures and languages?
- Should ELLs be measured with similar assessments to those for native speakers? How will we know what the root cause of a reading difficulty is?

Take a moment to review the questions you had early on. Which ones have been addressed, and which ones are still unclear to you? Are the questions you had at the beginning of this book still the ones you wonder about now? Why or why not? What might you do as a next step to help you address the questions you still have?

Creating effective literacy instruction for English learners at the elementary grades is a complex task that requires multileveled approaches at the classroom, school, district, and larger governmental levels. It requires the ongoing balance of efforts within sociocultural, psychological, linguistic, and educational frameworks. What resources are available to you and your colleagues as you set the next steps in your professional development? What kinds of ongoing collegial study might you do at your grade level or school? Jot down some ideas for the future learning you might do to continue to study this important area.

In a recent class I taught using the material in this book, I asked students to comment on how what they learned in class affected their professional repertoire and how the new ideas presented would influence their literacy teaching in the coming school year. Their reflections were varied and expressive and reinforced for me that teachers, no matter how long they have been in the field, are forever learning and striving to best meet the needs of their students. Example teachers in my class wrote that they planned to:

> Pursue more connections to families in their classrooms.
> Use students' first languages to assess and help shelter classroom content.
> Set higher expectations for their English learners.
> Assess students' background skills and knowledge.
> Consider alphabetic, as well as cultural, differences when working with students.
> Teach vocabulary more explicitly.
> Seek out materials that represent cultural and linguistic diversity.
> Confront their personal biases.
> Study a new language.
> Pay attention more to students' feelings and motivations.
> Work to include their colleagues in collaborative professional development on this topic.

These are just a sampling of the next steps my students proposed. How do your ideas compare? What is a meaningful way for you to take what you have learned and incorporate it in your classroom?

Think back to Lily, the exemplary teacher from the beginning of this chapter. When I interviewed Lily about her classroom instruction for English learners, she articulated a strong rationale for her classroom program, yet she still had as many questions about her students' learning as she had answers. There are no silver bullets for effective literacy instruction with English learners. Rather, effective instruction is a complex act of balancing technical knowledge about literacy teaching with interpersonal skills that welcome and engage students from diverse backgrounds.

Literacy Development with English Learners: Research-Based Instruction in Grades K–6 provides an overview of the myriad contexts, factors, and teaching approaches that support effective literacy learning for English learners in mainstream classrooms. We started with many questions, and we likely end with many more, only now at a more advanced level. Share what you have discovered with colleagues, try out the sample activities in your classroom, and in the process learn from and collaborate with the families and communities you serve. There is much we know about implementing effective literacy instruction with English learners and much still to learn. Best wishes for cultivating your own "classroom filled with teachers."

REFERENCES

Cummins, J. (1998, Spring) *Linguistic and cognitive issues in learning to read in a second language.* Paper presented at Reading and the English Language Learner Forum, California Reading and Literature Project, Sacramento, CA.

National Institute of Child Health and Human Development. (2000). *Report of the National Reading Panel. Teaching children to read: An evidence-based assessment of the scientific research literature on reading and its implications for reading instruction: Reports of the subgroups* (NIH Publication No. 00-4754). Washington, DC: U.S. Government Printing Office.

Index

Page numbers followed by an *f* or *t* indicate figures or tables.

Academic language, 43
Accents, fluency and, 164
Accommodations
   assessment and, 72–73
   for ELLs, 45–46, 162–163, 235, 256
Achievement. *see also* Low-performing students
   assessment of. *see* Achievement tests; Assessment
   as cultural value, 24, 25
   culturally responsive instruction and, 19
   emergent literacy and, 120–121
   instruction and, 237
   needs for, 61
   oral skill development and, 42
   reading skill and, 45
   small-group instruction and, 30
Achievement tests, 70–72, 82
Active learning strategies, phonics instruction and, 143–145, 147–148
Activities, active construction of knowledge and, 247–248
Adjustments, for ELLs, 12
Administration considerations, of assessments, 69–70
Affective factors, as influence on literacy development, 4*f*, 10–11
Age considerations, fluency and, 159, 165–166
Alphabet knowledge
   assessment of, 129*t*
   emergent literacy and, 119, 120, 125–126, 130, 132–133
   phonics instruction and, 139
   written language and, 96
American Alphabets, 169
Anecdotal records, assessment and, 77–80, 80*f*
Ascendant bilingual learners, 161
Assessment
   California English Language Development Test, 49
   conclusions regarding, 83
   emergent literacy and, 128–129, 129*t*, 130, 131
   high-stakes testing and, 12–13
   home language survey, 67*f*, 68*f*
   IDEA Language Proficiency Test, 70
   informal reading inventory, 99
   instructional groups and, 99–104
   integration of with instruction, 74–81, 83
   introduction to, 64–65
   Iowa Test of Basic Skills, 69
   Language Assessment Scales-Oral, 49
   National Assessment of Educational Progress, 157
   norm-referenced. *see* Norm-referenced assessments
   phonics instruction and, 142–143, 151–153
   Phonological Awareness Literacy Screening, 128
   proficiency and, 41, 49–51
   recommendations for, 81–83
   spelling as, 99

Assessment (*continued*)
  Standards for Educational and Psychological Testing, 70–71
  standards-based. *see* Standards-based assessment
  use of with ELLs, 65–73
  Woodcock–Muñoz Language Survey, 70
  word recognition in isolation, 99
Attitudes, teacher. *see under* Teachers
Authentic assessment, 74–81, 83
Automaticity, reading-while-listening approach and, 171
Autonomous stage, identity development and, 224
Awareness, teacher, 226–230

B

Background, 20–22, 23. *see also* Experience; Knowledge
Beginning reading stage literacy development, 106–108, 119
Behavior, whole-class lessons and, 28
Best Part of Me, The, 169
Bias, assessment and, 71
Bilingual Education Act, 216
Bilingual learners. *see* English language learners
Biliteracy, 9
Blending, phonics instruction and, 139
Book clubs, 28, 31
Brain function, literacy development and, 10
Brick words, 47, 48*f*

C

Cadence, ELLs and, 41
California English Language Development Test, 49
Castañeda v. Pickard, 45
CELDT. *see* California English Language Development Test
Center for Research on Education, Diversity, and Excellence, 236
Challenge, instruction and, 237
Charts. *see* Visual aids
Checklists, assessment and, 79
Citizenship, as purpose of literacy, 19
Clarification, as language function, 48*f*

Clarity, phonics instruction and, 145–147
Classification, as language function, 48*f*
Classroom community. *see* Community
Clustering, explicit instruction and, 242
Cognates
  conclusions regarding, 210
  defining, 7, 197
  English spellings and, 198–200
  "false", 209
  as instructional procedure, 12
  introduction to, 196–197
  phase 1 instruction in, 205–207
  phase 2 instruction in, 207–209
  roots and, 200–205
  vocabulary development and, 7
Cognitive factors, as influence on literacy development, 4*f*, 10
Cognitive strategies, instruction and, 237
Cognitively guided instruction, 12
Collaboration, 21, 31, 237
Committee on the Prevention of Reading Difficulties in Young Children, 120
Communication, globalization and, 19
Communicative competence, 44
Community
  ELLs and, 239*f*, 243–245, 255–256
  empowerment and, 13
  as influence on literacy development, 7–8
  instructional approach for, 12
  retellings and, 76
  social processes of, 20
Community share, Book Club Plus and, 28
Comparisons, as language function, 48*f*
Competence. *see* Communicative competence; Proficiency
Competition, 24, 26, 30, 31
Complexity
  explicit instruction and, 242
  phonics and, 144
  simplification of for assessment, 72
Comprehension skills
  assessment of, 69, 72, 153. *see also* Assessment
  case example of practices regarding, 178–188

conclusions regarding, 191–192
curriculum design for, 188–191
emergent literacy and, 120
fluency and, 158, 159
partnering and, 32
research regarding, 235
retellings and, 77
small-group instruction and, 29–30
upper-level stage and, 110
vocabulary development and, 163
Co-narration, talk story and, 21
Concept knowledge, fluency and, 168t
Concept of word
assessment of, 129t
emergent literacy and, 118, 120, 123, 130, 133
literacy development and, 105–106, 107–108
Concept sorts, emergent literacy and, 127, 130, 131
Concepts of print, fluency and, 159
Conclusions, as language function, 48f
Conferences, peer, 32–33
Connections, 29–30, 239f, 244, 245–247
Construction of knowledge. *see* Knowledge
Contact stage, identity development and, 224
Content instruction
assessment and, 77
cognates and, 205–207, 207–209
emergent literacy and, 130, 133–134
whole-class lessons and, 27
Contextualization, explicit instruction and, 240
Contrasting, as language function, 48f
Control, 24, 28
Conversations, 163, 192, 248
Cooperation, 7, 12, 25, 26, 30, 31
COW. *see* Concept of word
CREDE. *see* Center for Research on Education, Diversity, and Excellence
Cross-age reading, 168t, 171–172
Cross-linguistic bridging, as instructional procedure, 12
Cues, partial, 110

Cultural context. *see* Sociocultural factors of literacy development
Cultural values, 4f, 12, 24, 30. *see also* Culturally responsive instruction; Sociocultural factors of literacy development
Culturally congruent instruction. *see* Culturally responsive instruction
Culturally relevant pedagogy. *see* Culturally responsive instruction
Culturally responsive instruction
assessment and, 75–76, 79, 83
classroom diversity today and, 156
conclusions regarding, 36
fluency and, 168t
group work and, 26–36
introduction to, 18
key issues surrounding, 20–26
research regarding, 237
shared assumptions about, 19–20
teacher dispositions and, 222
Culturally responsive teaching. *see* Culturally responsive instruction

D

David Goes to School, 134
Decoding. *see also* Phonics instruction
emergent literacy and, 120
fluency and, 158, 159–160
instructional approach for, 12
as language tool component, 49
literacy development and, 98–99
Definitional skills, emergent literacy and, 120
Description, as language function, 48f
Determination, as cultural value, 24
Developmental writing, 124. *see also* Writing skill development
Dictation, emergent literacy and, 125
Dictionaries, use of for assessment, 72–73
Differentiated instruction, 99
Digital photography, LEA and, 167–170
Direct instruction, 12, 235–236
Directionality, fluency and, 159
Direction-following, 48f, 164–165
Discourse features, oral-language development and, 163–164
Discourse style, 41

Discussions. *see* Conversations; Discourse style
Disintegration stage, identity development and, 224
Dispositions, teacher. *see under* Teachers
Diverse worldview. *see* Worldview
Diversity. *see* Culturally responsive instruction; Sociocultural factors of literacy development
Documentation, anecdotal records and. *see* Anecdotal records
Dual-language tests, use of for assessment, 73

E

Educational factors of literacy development, 4f, 11–13
Elaboration, as language function, 48f
ELD. *see* Language development
ELLs. *see* English language learners
Emergent literacy
  assessment of, 129t
  conclusions regarding, 134–135
  ELLs and, 117–118, 121–122
  essential activities for, 122–129
  example week of activities for, 130–134
  introduction to, 117–118
  overview of, 118–122, 119f
  as stage, 104–106
Employment, as purpose of literacy, 19
Empowerment, impact of on ELLs, 13
Engagement, 120, 172
English language development. *see* Language development
English language learners
  ascendant bilingual learners and, 161
  assumptions regarding, 192
  characteristics of, 43–44
  demographic information regarding, 156–157, 178–179
  emergent literacy and, 117, 121–122. *see also* Emergent literacy
  ethnic/racial considerations regarding, 221–222
  fluency development and, 162–165
  fully functional bilingual learners, 161–162
  impact of high-stakes testing on, 12–13
  incipient bilingual learners and, 160–161
  literacy instruction for, 2
  research regarding, 235
  teacher dispositions regarding. *see under* Teachers
English-only instruction, 214–217
Environment. *see* Community; Home environment; School environment
Ethnicity, ELLs and, 221–222. *see also* English language learners
ETR approach, 30
Evaluation, teacher-. *see* IRE structure
Exemptions, for ELL assessment, 82
Expectations, 28, 77, 244, 255–256
Experience
  connections with, 246
  ETR approach and, 30
  home–school bridging of, 19–20
  as influence on literacy development, 3
  instructional approach for, 12
  research regarding, 235
Experience-text-relationship approach. *see* ETR approach
Explicit feedback, 80–81
Explicit instruction
  cognates and, 201–205
  comprehension skills and, 191
  conclusions regarding, 60–61
  ELLs and, 12, 42–45, 239f, 240–243
  focused approach to, 46–60
  introduction to, 40–42
  phonics instruction and, 145–147
  structure for, 45–46
Expression, 48f, 110, 159, 168t. *see also* Prosody
Expressive oral language development. *see* Oral skill development

F

False cognates, 209
Families, 14, 19–20, 35, 220–221. *see also* Home environment
Feedback, 80–81, 237, 240
Figurative language, English and, 41
First language
  fluency and, 168t
  influence of on literacy development, 96–97, 113

instruction in, 12
maintenance of competence in, 20
phonics instruction and, 141–143, 153
Flexibility, for ELLs, 12
Fluency, defining, 47
Fluency development
conclusions regarding, 173
considerations regarding, 165–166
ELLs and, 162–165
in English-dominant children, 158–160
explicit instruction and, 43, 61
introduction to, 156–158
literacy development and, 98–99
strategies to promote, 167–172, 168t
Focused approach to explicit language instruction, 46–60, 48f
Formal assessment. *see* Assessment
Forms of language, 47, 61
Freedom, as cultural value, 24, 25
Froggy Goes to School, 134
Fulfillment, as purpose of literacy, 19
Fully functional bilingual learners, 161–162
Functions of language, 46, 48f, 61
Funds of knowledge. *see* Knowledge

G

Generalization, as language function, 48f
Generative vocabulary knowledge, 201
Globalization, employment and, 19
Glossaries, use of for assessment, 72–73
Good teaching, 23–26
Grammar. *see* Syntax
Graphic organizers, 246
Greek roots, 50t, 203–205
Group work
comprehension skills and, 189–190, 190–191, 192
cross-age reading and, 168t, 171–172
culturally responsive instruction and, 25–26, 26–36
emergent literacy and, 122–129
instructional groups and, 99–104
interactions within, 243
Guided practice, explicit instruction and, 240

H

Hands-on activities, active construction of knowledge and, 247
Harry Potter, 162
High-stakes testing, 12–13, 81–82
Home environment, 19–20, 21, 35
Home language. *see* First language
Horrible Harry series books, 108
Hybridity, culturally responsive instruction and, 21

I

I Can Read series books, 108
Idea exchange, small-group instruction and, 31
IDEA Language Proficiency Test, 70
Identity, teacher, 223–226
Idioms, English and, 41
Illustrated Word Banks, 53–56, 54t
Immersion/emersion stage, identity development and, 224
Immigrant population, demographic information regarding, 156–157
Incipient bilingual learners, 160–161
Independence, 24, 32
Independent reading, fluency and, 168t, 172
Independent work time, culturally responsive instruction and, 33–36
Individual time. *see* Independent work time
Individualism, as cultural value, 7, 24, 25
Informal assessment. *see* Assessment
Informal reading inventory, 99
Initiation
talk story and, 21
teacher-. *see* IRE structure
Innovation, instructional, 21
Institutional considerations, English-only instruction and, 214–217
Instruction. *see also* Teaching approaches
conclusions regarding, 249–250
culturally responsive. *see* Culturally responsive instruction
differentiated, 99
effective, 23–26
English-only, 214–217
essentials of, 51–53

Instruction (*continued*)
  explicit. *see* Explicit instruction
  in the first language. *see* First language
  group. *see* Group work
  integration of assessment with, 74–81, 83
  language tools and, 48*f*
  literacy development and, 113
  "one size fits all" analogy for, 73
  part to whole, 245
  of phonics, 140. *see also* Phonics instruction
  quality of, 42
  research regarding, 234–238
  role of, 1
  strategies for, 238–239, 239*f*. *see also specific strategies*
  tailoring for ELLs, 256
  tools for, 53–60
Instructional blueprint for English learners, 46
Instructional groups, 99–104
Instructional-level teaching, 241
Instructions, reading of for assessment, 73
Interactions, peers, 243
Interactive approach to instruction, 12, 235–236
Interdependence, as cultural value, 25
Interest inventories, text selection and, 35
Internet use. *see* Technology
Interviewing, retellings and, 76
Involvement, instruction and, 237
Iowa Test of Basic Skills, 69
IRE structure, 28–29
IRI. *see* Informal reading inventory
ITBS. *see* Iowa Test of Basic Skills

J
Journaling, 189

K
Knowledge
  active construction of, 239*f*, 247–249
  connections with, 246–247
  fluency and, 168*t*
  as influence on literacy development, 4*f*, 9
  retellings and, 76

L
Language arts, assessment of, 70–72
Language Assessment Scales—Oral, 49
Language development, key issues surrounding, 44–45
Language experience approach, 167–170, 168*t*
LAS-O. *see* Language Assessment Scales—Oral
Latin roots, 50*t*, 201–203
Lau v. Nichols, 216
LEA. *see* Language experience approach
Learner English, 97
Learning community. *see* Community
Lecture, 28
LEP. *see* Limited English Proficient
Lesson planning, comprehension skills and, 188–191
Letter name–alphabetic spelling stage development, 106–108, 119
Letter–sound learning, 132–133, 138, 139. *see also* Phonics instruction
Leveling
  fluency and, 159, 165–166
  instructional-level teaching and, 241
  literacy development and, 93–96, 94–95*t*
  phonics instruction and, 140–141
Limited English Proficient, 44, 65
Linguistic control, ELLs and, 163
Linguistic factors of literacy development, 3–7, 4*f*
Listening skill development, 69, 168*t*, 170–171
Literacy development
  assessment and, 99–104
  case example of, 87–90, 89*f*
  conclusions regarding, 113–114
  defining, 78
  developmental model of, 90–93, 91*f*
  factors influencing, 2–13, 4*f*
  importance of, 1
  influence of primary language on, 96–97
  instructional groups and, 99–104
  key issues surrounding, 254–257
  leveling and, 93–96, 94–95*t*
  next steps for, 257–259
  phonics instruction and, 140–141, 153
  stages of, 104–113

Synchrony of, 98–99
Literature studies, emergent literacy and, 130, 133–134
Literature-based instruction, 27
Low-anxiety environment, 243
Low-performing students, 12, 19, 32

M

Maniac Magee, 180, 189
Materialism, as cultural value, 24, 25
Materials, accommodations in, 46
Meaning, 96, 198–200, 256
Mediation, instruction and, 237
Metacognition, 146, 241
Middle-class values. *see* Sociocultural factors of literacy development
Minilessons, 27
Modeling
　explicit instruction and, 240
　fluency and, 47
　phonics instruction and, 145
　small-group instruction and, 31–32
Modified questioning strategies, active construction of knowledge and, 248
Morphology
　defining, 198–199
　as influence on literacy development, 4f, 6, 44
　as language system structure, 97
　oral-language development and, 163–164
　proficiency and, 50t
　spelling–meaning connection and, 198–200
Mortar words, 47, 48f
Motivation, 10–11, 120
Multicultural students. *see* Culturally responsive instruction; English language learners
Multiple intelligences, active construction of knowledge and, 248
Multiple texts, fluency and, 166
Music, active construction of knowledge and, 248–249

N

National Assessment of Educational Progress, 157
National Clearinghouse for English Language Acquisition, 66
National Council for Accreditation of Teacher Education, 220
National Literacy Panel on Language-Minority Children and Youth, 121, 140
National Reading Panel, 120, 139, 172
Natural resources, as cultural value, 24
Naturalization Act of 1906, 217
NCATE. *see* National Council for Accreditation of Teacher Education
NCELA. *see* National Clearinghouse for English Language Acquisition
NCLB. *see* No Child Left Behind
Needs assessment, for ELLs, 12
Nichols, Lau v., 216
No Child Left Behind, 65, 66–70, 73, 81, 213, 215, 216, 224, 230
Norm-referenced assessments, 65–66, 71
NRP. *see* National Reading Panel

O

Objectives, proficiency and, 50t
Observation, 79, 96–97
Omissions, spelling skill development and, 103
Opportunities to learn, 4f, 9, 11, 18
Oral skill development
　achievement and, 42
　assessment of, 69
　ELLs and, 41, 163–165, 235
　emergent literacy and, 120, 125, 128
　fluency and, 159, 166, 168t
　literacy skills and, 5
　proficiency and, 50t
　retellings and, 75–77
　vocabulary development and, 164
　writing skill development and, 245
Orthographic knowledge, 91f, 92, 98, 102, 111, 113
OTL. *see* Opportunities to learn
Overlapping speech, talk story and, 21

P

Pacing, 28, 30
Pairing, culturally responsive instruction and, 32–33
PALS. *see* Phonological Awareness Literacy Screening
Part to whole instruction, 245
Partial cues, 110

Participation, 30, 31, 48f, 255–256
Partnering, culturally responsive instruction and, 32–33
Pattern, written language and, 96
Peers. *see also* Group work
  culturally responsive instruction and, 25–26, 32–33
  interactions with, 243
  teachers and, 113
Performance. *see* Achievement
Perseverance, as cultural value, 24
Personal factors, as influence on literacy development, 4f, 10–11
Personal readers, 124
Personal reflections, of teachers, 227–229
Phonemic awareness
  emergent literacy and, 120
  fluency and, 159
  instructional approach for, 12
  as language system structure, 97
  phonics instruction and, 139
  spelling skill development and, 102
Phonics instruction
  active learning strategies for, 147–148
  assessment and, 142–143, 151–153
  conclusions regarding, 153
  developmental levels and, 140–141
  emergent literacy and, 120
  first language/literacy skills and, 141–143, 153
  importance of clarity/explicitness, 145–147
  introduction to, 138–139
  research regarding, 139–140
  systematic sequence of, 143–145, 153
  text selection and, 149–151, 153
  vocabulary development and, 148–149
Phonological awareness
  assessment of, 129t
  ELLs and, 41
  emergent literacy and, 120–121, 126–127, 130, 132
  as influence on literacy development, 4f, 5, 44
  as language system structure, 97
Phonological Awareness Literacy Screening, 128
Phonology, oral-language development and, 163–164

Photography, LEA and, 167–170
Pickard, Castañeda v., 45
Pluralism, culturally responsive instruction and, 19
Policy considerations
  assessment and, 83
  Bilingual Education Act, 216
  English-only instruction and, 214–217
  Naturalization Act of 1906, 217
  No Child Left Behind, 65, 66–70, 73, 81, 213, 215, 216, 224, 230
  Title III requirements, 45
Practice, explicit instruction and, 240
Pragmatics, 44, 97, 163–164
Prediction, as language function, 48f
Prereading instruction, comprehension skills and, 189–190, 192
Prestige, as influence on literacy development, 4f, 7
Print knowledge, 121, 129t
Process approach to writing, 27
Process based approach to instruction, research regarding, 235–236
Professional development, 4f, 13, 192
Proficiency. *see also* Fluency development
  assessment and, 41, 49–51, 66–70. *see also* Assessment
  characteristics/objectives of, 50t
  ELLs and, 235
  Limited English Proficient as designation of, 44
  oral-language and, 163–165
Programs, as influence on literacy development, 4f
Propositions, as language function, 48f
Prosody
  fluency and, 159, 166, 168t
  literacy development and, 110
  reading-while-listening approach and, 171
Pseudo-independence stage, identity development and, 224
Psychological factors of literacy development, 4f, 9–11
Purposeful activities, active construction of knowledge and, 247–248
Put Reading First, 139

Q

Quality, instructional, 42
Questioning strategies, active construction of knowledge and, 248

R

Race, ELLs and, 221–222. *see also* English language learners
Rates of reading, literacy development and, 110
Read alouds, 28, 32, 122–123, 163, 190–191
Read To, Read With, Write With, Word Study, and Talk With. *see* RRWWT
Readers' workshop. *see* Workshop approach
Reading skill development
  assessment of, 70–72
  concept of word and, 133
  emergent stage of, 104–106
  oral-language development and, 166
  repeated readings and, 168*t*, 170
  spelling skills and, 98–99
  writing skill development and, 98
Reading-while-listening approach, 168*t*, 170–171
Receptive oral language development. *see* Oral skill development
Recognition, small-group instruction and, 29
Records, anecdotal. *see* Anecdotal records
Reflections, of teachers, 227–229, 257
Reinforcement, explicit instruction and, 240
Reintegration stage, identity development and, 224
Relationships, 25, 29, 30, 229–230
Repeated readings, fluency and, 166, 168*t*, 170
Respect, culturally responsive instruction and, 19
Response
  small-group instruction and, 29
  student-. *see* IRE structure
Retellings, assessment and, 75–77
Rhythm, 41, 248–249
Rimes, 138
Root words, 50*t*, 111, 200–205
Routines, 77
RRWWT, 118, 122–129

S

Scaffolding
  comprehension skills and, 189
  explicit instruction and, 241
  independent work time and, 34
  instruction and, 237
  research regarding, 235
  small-group instruction and, 31
  vocabulary development and, 54–55
Schema building, 246
School Bus, 134
School environment
  home–school bridging and, 19–20
  low-anxiety, 243
  reflection of cultural values in, 24
  as social structure, 7–8
Second language literacy development. *see* Literacy development
Segmenting, phonics instruction and, 139
Self-assessment, 80
Self-reliance, as cultural value, 24
Semantics, 44, 97
Sentence construction charts, 56–59, 57*f*, 59*f*
Sequencing, 48*f*, 143–145, 153
Services. *see* Accommodations
SES. *see* Socioeconomic status
Sheltered English instruction, 12, 83, 237
Sheltered instruction observation protocol, 236
Sight-word knowledge, 127–128, 129*t*
SIOP. *see* Sheltered instruction observation protocol
Size considerations, small-group instruction and, 30
Skill instruction, 27, 145, 147–148, 256
Slant of development, 98–99
Small-group instruction, 29–31, 31–32, 190–191, 192
Social ecologies, 96–97
Social processes, 20, 44
Sociocultural factors of literacy development, 4*f*, 7–9, 41, 45
Socioeconomic status, 30
Sound, written language and, 96
Sounding out, ELLs and, 102

Sound–letter learning. *see* Letter–sound learning
Speaking skills. *see* Oral skill development
Spelling skill development
  assessment and, 99–100
  assessment of, 129*t*
  cognates and. *see* Cognates
  ELLs and, 102
  emergent stage of, 104–106
  literacy development and, 91*f*, 92, 113
  reading skill development and, 98–99
  six types of errors and, 99–103
  spelling–meaning connection and, 198–200
  by stage, 101*f*
  stages of, 104–113
Spelling–meaning connection, 198–200
Spirituality, as cultural value, 25
SSR. *see* Sustained silent reading
Stages of literacy development, 104
Standardized testing. *see* Assessment; High-stakes testing
Standards for Educational and Psychological Testing, 70–71
Standards-based assessment, 65–66, 67, 82
Strategy instruction, 27, 235. *see also* Instruction
Structures. *see also* Syntax
  ELLs and, 41
  fluency and, 159
  as influence on literacy development, 4*f*, 11–12
  of language systems, 97
  simplification of for assessment, 72
Student involvement, instruction and, 237
Student-response. *see* IRE structure
Students, knowledge regarding, 254–255
Substitutions, spelling skill development and, 102
Success. *see* Achievement
Summarization, as language function, 48*f*
Surveys, of home language, 67*f*, 68*f*
Sustained silent reading, 34–35
Synchrony of development, 91*f*, 92, 98–99

Syntax
  ELLs and, 41
  fluency and, 159
  as influence on literacy development, 4*f*, 6, 44
  as language system structure, 97
  as language tool component, 47–49
  oral-language development and, 163–164
Systematic ELD lessons, 51–53
Systematic instruction, ELLs and, 239*f*, 240–243

T

Talk story, 20, 21–22
Talking Stick activity, 59–60
Teacher-evaluation. *see* IRE structure
Teacher-initiation. *see* IRE structure
Teachers
  building awareness of, 226–230
  conclusions regarding dispositions of, 230
  connections with, 244
  cultural background of, 23
  cultural values of, 7
  dispositions of, 217–223
  education of. *see* Professional development
  English-only instruction and, 214–217
  identity of, 223–226
  introduction to dispositions of, 213–214
  modeling by. *see* Modeling
  reflection of, 257
  role of, 1
Teaching approaches, 4*f*, 11–12, 23–26. *see also* Culturally responsive instruction
Technology, 12, 19, 97
Testing. *see* Assessment; High-stakes testing
Texts
  ETR approach and, 30
  fluency and, 166
  LEA and, 167–170
  literacy development and, 163
  phonics instruction and, 149–151, 153
  selection of, 35
  small-group instruction and, 31–32
Thematic instruction, 77

Thornwood School, 169
Time considerations, assessment and, 71
Title III requirements, 45
Tools, language, 47, 48*f*
Total physical response, active construction of knowledge and, 249
Transitional reading stage literacy development, 108–110
Translation, as instructional procedure, 12
Tutoring, culturally responsive instruction and, 32–33

U

Upper-level reading/spelling stage literacy development, 110–113, 112*f*
Use of English, as influence on literacy development, 4*f*

V

Validity, of assessments, 71
Values, cultural. *see* Cultural values
Verb tenses, 41, 50*t*
Visual aids
 explicit instruction and, 240
 graphic organizers and, 246
 Illustrated Word Banks, 53–56, 54*t*
 phonics instruction and, 146
 sentence construction charts, 56–59, 57*f*, 59*f*
 Talking Stick activity, 59–60
Vocabulary skills
 anecdotal records and, 77
 assessment of, 129*t*
 cognates and. *see* Cognates
 comprehension and, 163
 comprehension skills and, 192
 ELLs and, 41
 emergent literacy and, 120
 explicit instruction and, 241

 fluency and, 159, 166, 168*t*
 generative knowledge and, 201
 as influence on literacy development, 4*f*, 6–7
 instructional approach for, 12
 as language tool component, 47, 48*f*
 oral-language development and, 164
 phonics instruction and, 139, 143–145, 148–149
 research regarding, 235
 simplification of for assessment, 72
 visuals for, 53–56

W

Wealth, as cultural value, 24, 25
Whole-class instruction, 27–29, 190–191
Within-word pattern spelling stage development, 108–110, 109*f*
Woodcock–Muñoz Language Survey, 70
Word knowledge, 113, 125–128
Word recognition, fluency and, 159, 166, 168*t*
Word recognition in isolation, 99
Workshop approach, culturally responsive instruction and, 26–36
Worldview, culturally responsive instruction and, 21, 25
WRI. *see* Word recognition in isolation
Writers' workshop. *see* Workshop approach
Writing instruction, culturally responsive instruction and, 27
Writing skill development
 assessment of, 69
 concept of word and, 133
 ELLs and, 41
 emergent literacy and, 124–125
 journaling and, 189
 oral-language development and, 245
 proficiency and, 50*t*
 reading skill development and, 98